Shrub Gardening for Flower Arrangement

SHRUB GARDENING
FOR
FLOWER
ARRANGEMENT

SYBIL EMBERTON

FABER AND FABER
LONDON

First published in 1965
New and Revised edition 1973
by Faber and Faber Limited
3 Queen Square London WC1
Printed in Great Britain by
Latimer Trend & Company Ltd Plymouth

ISBN 0 571 10117 8
(Faber Paper Covered Editions)

ISBN 0 571 04778 5
(Hard Bound Editions)

Contents

CONTENTS

7

CONTENTS

Illustrations

All monochrome photographs are by Paul D. Read

9

ILLUSTRATIONS

Preface

This book is intended primarily for flower arrangers who grow, or wish to grow, their own material and I hope very much that they won't find it either presumptuous or didactic. It is not, in any sense, for those who wish to learn about the art of flower arrangement itself. Quite apart from the fact that so many excellent books are available in that particular field, flower arrangers nowadays know so much about the theory and are so highly skilled in the practice of their art that I have no intention of rushing in among the angels here.

However, as my flower arrangement demonstrations have taken me about the country and as I listen to the questions put to the demonstrators at my own flower club, I have become increasingly aware of a very real desire among club members to learn more about the horticultural aspect of the subject. Happily 'I like what I know' is fast becoming too pedestrian for the more adventurous among us.

In my own demonstrations I rarely used any bought flowers and wherever I went among the flower clubs I found the same lively interest in new or unusual flowers, foliage and seed-heads from the shrub garden.

If the latter is one of the happiest of hunting-grounds it is, however, evidently a less familiar one to the average flower club member than the herbaceous border or the greenhouse. Because, as a shrub gardener, I now have twenty-odd years of trial and error behind me, as well as six years of secretarial work for a well-known plantsman and garden designer, perhaps I can bring some unfamiliar material to your notice and at the same time help to spare you some of the growing pains which attend the beginner in the shrub garden.

Twenty-odd years is not long, I know, as shrub gardening goes. But the grounding has been as intensive as I could make it. Apart from reading everything on the subject that I could lay hands on, visiting famous shrub gardens at all seasons and in all kinds of weather, and plodding along on my own in the tough school of personal experience without the help of a gardener, I could hardly fail to absorb a good deal of valuable information through the pores, as it were, in the course of my job at Farall Nurseries, which is a business of a very personal kind, involving much advice by correspondence, even though I was at no time engaged on any practical field work while I was there.

No gardener ever knows it all and I am all too well aware of my own limitations. It is with the greatest diffidence that I put pen to paper at all and I want to make it clear that since the shrub garden I propose to write about is my own—planned, stocked from a standing start and tended from its infancy by myself alone—I can at least claim a first-hand acquaintance with my plants and I am resolved to record nothing here from mere hearsay. If I have reason to refer to some plant that I have never tried to grow for myself I shall say so.

No doubt all sorts of glaring omissions will strike you. Then again, you may well raise your eyebrows at some of the plants that get a mention here. Not all, I admit, are of the stuff that flower arrangers' dreams are made of; but to me they are essential garden decorators and must find a place in my shrub borders, if not in yours.

Perhaps it is not too much to hope that in writing of the trees and shrubs I love so much something of my own enthusiasm for this form of gardening and this immensely rewarding source of material for flower arrangement may rub off on my readers. Fanaticism may be a bit of a bore for those who have to live with it. But, for the fanatic anyway, it is such splendid fun that I should like to think it may be catching.

PART 1

1

Why I am a Shrub Gardener

I am a fanatic by temperament. On looking back it seems that from adolescence onwards I have pursued a constant succession of hares with almost idiotic fervour: from gymnastics and dancing to gardening in a tropical West African climate. This might be diagnosed as a fundamental instability, but I am sure that many a flower arranger will recognize the persistent goading of some sort of creative urge which had never hitherto found its true outlet. The older I get the more exhilarating I find my personal brand of fanaticism. Writing about her own love of gardening, Miss Sackville-West once said, 'The point is not what you get excited about, but the fact that in middle-age you can still get excited at all' and I wholeheartedly share this point of view.

I came to gardening in earnest, as so many of us mothers do, at a time when we are faced with a difficult major readjustment in our lives. Suddenly we realize that the interests which have absorbed our time, energy and devotion for the past eighteen years or so are about to be withdrawn from our immediate reach and that we must now exchange our children for the independent, responsible adults who will continue to occupy much of our thoughts but all too little of our time. For my own part, after experimenting with many alternative obsessions, I find a combination of shrub gardening and flower arrangement to be one of the most rewarding, not only as a means of stopping this psychological gap but also as creative outlets, combining artistry with technical skill, and physical with mental exercise.

I began with a series of mixed borders in which herbaceous perennials predominated, with a few background trees and a scattering of shrubs among them. Then, after five years of gardening along these lines, two books chanced to come my way which started a restless ferment in my mind and set it seething with plans of a different sort. These were *The Flowering Shrub Garden* and *Effective Flowering Shrubs*, by Michael Haworth-Booth.

Nobody, they say, begins as a shrub gardener. And yet I doubt whether anyone who has once fallen under the spell of flowering trees and shrubs ever turns back to herbaceous perennials and other forms of horticulture. One often finds the shrub garden recommended *faute de mieux*, chiefly on the grounds that it is a labour-saver for those not so young as they used to be. And labour-saving it undoubtedly is, provided the shrubs are grown in the way they most enjoy, with a thick mulch of dead leaves or bracken above their roots. If the mulching is done as soon as the fallen leaves are available each autumn—and I admit this is a somewhat laborious, though not unpleasant chore—much of the winter frost is kept out of the ground, moisture is retained in the soil during the periods of drought and, most welcome of all its benefits, little or no weeding will be required. My own young shrubs and trees have grown away so rapidly and healthfully, given these conditions, that before long they will provide their own ground cover and their own leaf mulch without any further help from me.

Tell any middle-aged herbaceous borderer that you are a shrub gardener and the most likely come-back will be, not 'How lovely!', but rather, 'How wise!' I believe that every shrub gardener shares with me the conviction that his own ideal stands head and shoulders above all other forms of horticulture and if I set out to fire your enthusiasm for flowering and otherwise ornamental trees and shrubs it is for reasons more compelling than those of mere expediency. Not only is this the most interesting kind of garden, increasing in beauty year by year, but I believe that it will yield you flower decoration material of greater character, variety and originality than ever you will get from your herbaceous borders.

There are various kinds of non-shrubby material which the majority of flower arrangers regard as indispensable. But

whereas a large proportion of these, whether he
perennial, annual, bulb, rhizome or whatever, tend to g
stiff, straight stalk and to be furnished with rathe
foliage, it is chiefly among the material cut from trees ar
that one finds the naturalistic curves, the arching spray:
the oddly angled or contorted lines, all of which induce
disorder' in flower decoration, which so many of us
achieve.

When I say that I want to whet your appetite for a g
ornamental trees and shrubs my aim is to try to share
the mixture of excitement and deep satisfaction w.
steadily grown in me since my first chance encounter
Haworth-Booth's ideas on the planning and planting o
garden.

2

The Flower Arranger and the Shrub Garden

When first this relentless bee began to buzz inside my gardening bonnet the flower decoration movement was only in its earliest infancy. Although my first interest in the latter subject dates back to my early teens, when I would try to bring some vestige of imagination to the 'doing' of the flowers for the house in the school holidays, I doubt whether I had since made much appreciable headway up to the time of my conversion to shrub gardening. If I thought of trees and shrubs at all as cutting material the range would have been confined to a few hackneyed favourites; and so it was as a gardener rather than as a flower arranger that I was originally converted to the change-over. 'Cut flowers' were still *de rigueur* as the main ingredient for indoor decoration and therefore what seemed best for cutting were spared to form a small picking bed in the kitchen garden when I set about dismantling the large herbaceous borders to make way for my first consignment of shrubs, while the rest were ruthlessly scrapped or given away.

Friends were shocked, and more than somewhat sceptical. Indeed I did sometimes wonder what made me so certain that this time I had the right idea. Looking at those infant trees and shrubs, many of them too young to flower at all for some years yet, I certainly felt some faint misgivings now and then. Should I ever succeed in justifying this apparent foolhardiness, in demonstrating to the scoffers that my kind of garden could provide a spectacle as colourful as their lupins, delphiniums, gaillardias and Michaelmas daisies and one pleasing to the eye at any season, in contrast to the dismal winter stubble of their herbaceous borders—and mine, of previous years?

The credit for such blind faith on my part must go to the two books I have mentioned. A novice in whatever sphere needs, I am sure, to hitch his wagon to some guiding star until he is able to make his own way towards the light. For the gardener this must be someone on whose knowledge and good taste he can implicitly rely while struggling to cultivate these attributes for himself. My own encounter with *The Flowering Shrub Garden* and *Effective Flowering Shrubs* convinced me that their author was the guiding star for me and repeated visits to his demonstration garden at Farall, near Roundhurst, confirmed this. Some years later, when my own shrub garden was still a fairly new venture, in my impatience to learn more, and to learn it faster than first-hand experience at home could teach me, I took a secretarial job at his nurseries.

I am sorry that in his latest book, *The Flowering Shrub Garden Today*, Mr. Haworth-Booth should unwittingly have risked spoiling his own case in a short passage addressed to the flower arranger on page 45. Which of you, I wonder, would be content with flower-heads and foliage cut with no more than five inches of stem, so as to 'ensure that the bushes are not damaged and that the flowers last for a remarkably long time'? Though he assures the flower arranger that her shrub garden will suffice for all her needs I, for one, would require a very large picking border indeed if I could never hope to cut more than a five-inch stub from a matured tree or shrub and I wouldn't now be writing about these as the most satisfying of all material for flower arrangement. And what a load of fun we would miss if we were to abandon the ceaseless hunt for containers in all manner of shapes, sizes, colours, materials, textures and periods, in order to settle for the shallow tray measuring 14 in. × 9 in., the 10-in. cylinder and the row of vases for single specimens which he commends to us as suitable receptacles for the snippets from the shrub garden!

Most of you will be aware that, given the proper conditioning after cutting, the materials he mentions such as camellias, tree peonies, azaleas, rhododendrons, hydrangeas, etc., can be made to last a remarkably long time in water regardless of the length of the stalk. I would stress, however, that one cannot, of course, cut recklessly and at random from such valuable plants, even when they have been growing for a fair number of years. My own advice is: never let your best friend loose among your shrubs with the secateurs and allow yourself any amount of time to stand and stare before deciding *what may be spared without detriment to the plant*. Only when you are clear on this point should you trust yourself to cut at all, and then to cut with the clearest possible idea as to the shape and length of the stems required. Gather material for only one arrangement at a time, so that you know precisely what you are doing and thus avoid wasting precious material by cutting two left-handed sprays when these will be required to flow in opposite directions.

When collecting material from my hillside garden for any occasion involving many different arrangements I have to fight the temptation to cut in a single sortie anything likely to be needed from the bottom end so as to save myself repeatedly plodding up and down the steep slope. By picking for each arrangement separately I find that it is possible to come in with almost exactly the right amount of the right sizes and shapes for whatever it is I have in mind. But I would infinitely rather go back for more if necessary than throw superfluous pieces on the compost heap or, worse still, cram them into an arrangement to avoid waste.

I hope you may take heart when I tell you that, from a garden of only one-third of an acre, in which the plantings are now mostly twenty years old, for the past eight years or so I have been able to pick an assortment of material for demonstrations several times a month;[1] to provide quantities of foliage, in particular, for the use of visiting demonstrators and for practice meetings at my own flower club; to enter a number of arrangements at various exhibitions throughout the year; and even, now and again, to cut big branches, mainly of foliage, for a local florist short of material for wedding pedestals. All this has been possible without the slightest damage to the plants and without noticeably detracting from the garden scene. Indeed, in some cases the plants actually benefit from judicious cutting of this kind.

[1] I no longer do any demonstrating, lecturing or judging.

Aesthetically speaking, the claims of trees and shrubs have in my own case become so compelling that I suppose I'd grit my teeth and persevere with my shrub garden even if this were more troublesome, instead of less so, than any other form of horticulture. And as a flower arranger I'm so much in love with the material it provides that I could almost dispense with a picking border altogether. It was only as a demonstrator that I felt obliged to introduce a few additional choice oddments, and on giving up demonstrating I gladly turned my 'picking bed' over to shrubs. Even for exhibition work and at least as far as the requirements of my own home go I would never feel the need to look beyond the flowers and foliage of my own shrub garden, supplemented only by an occasional forage among the hedgerows, woodlands and waterside.

3

Shrub Gardener versus Flower Arranger

Those who argue that a shrub garden isn't a flower garden are no doubt thinking back to the dark and dismal Victorian shrubberies of their childhood. Although the widely held theory that a shrub garden means a garden without flowers is at least partially founded on fact, in practice this need not be the case. Nevertheless, for some reason flowers are not commonly thought to grow on trees.

One day in May some years ago an old lady visiting the gardens at Leonardslee was resting on a seat when I chanced to pass by. As she surveyed the hillsides ablaze with rhododendrons, azaleas, magnolias and the last of the camellias rising around her on all sides and mirrored in the water beneath I heard her gasp, 'Well! Would you believe it? All that colour and not a single flower!' I find horticultural eavesdropping fascinating and this particular sample struck me as highly comical; and yet I suppose a great many gardeners would consider it neither funny nor even worthy of comment.

So far as flower arrangement goes my taste in colour is markedly *sub fusc*, but in the garden I am old-fashioned enough to require a riot of gay hues and striking contrasts. I could never reconcile myself to a restricted use of living plant material nor confine my craving for bright colour in the garden to a chaste modern-style *décor* of green and silver foliage relieved only by white flowers, where flowers are admitted at all. While some part of me can recognize the dignity and restfulness of the best of these, to me these are not gardeners' gardens. And even less would they be of service to the flower arranger.

If the latter shares with me a predilection for the quiet,

'greyed' hues, for green flowers and for an infinite variety of foliage for cutting she will have to ask herself the question: Is she primarily a gardener or a flower arranger? For, alas, the two are often at variance. One has only to catch a far-off glimpse of *Rhododendron griersonianum* or *Genista lydia* in bloom to be made aware that scarlet and bright yellow are the most telling of all colours at a distance amid the surrounding greenery. To me, as to most of us, a garden would be a dull place without plenty of the cheerful, advancing colours; and yet scarlet is by no means a favourite of mine for indoor use and I rarely work with really bright yellows. Nevertheless, an arrangement of, say, garden roses ranging from coral to deep velvety crimson is a refreshing exercise even for the most ascetic, and surely once in a way we all enjoy a skirmish with clashing reds. As for bright yellow, I believe I am right in saying that life-saving equipment at sea is so coloured because yellow is more easily spotted at a distance than any other colour. It follows, therefore, that the vividly-hued genistas, brooms, halimiums and hypericums must be rated among the most effective of garden shrubs, whereas it is those of cream or primrose yellow colouring which most flower arrangers prefer for cutting.

Too many strong reds, yellows and oranges in the garden may create a hot, restless impression on a summer's day, but I doubt whether the flower arranger-cum-gardener is likely to fall into this error in view of the immense and widespread popularity of white flowers for cutting purposes. Then again, I have found that the darkest reds and deepest purples are not hot at all—indeed they have a positively cooling effect upon the mixture.

Even so, it is none too easy to place some of the delicate tints which can be so lovely indoors but are plain wishy-washy outside, nor all the dull bronzes, dusky maroons, smoky mauves, dusty pinks and other off-beat tones so much beloved of many flower arrangers, without to some extent detracting from the garden spectacle.

For this form of schizophrenia my own remedy is to give the gardener-figure the upper hand, letting the flower arranger string along as best she may. In this way many compromises are possible and the latter will come off better than you might suppose. For instance, the curiously ribbed, dark slaty violet *Clematis × durandii* is one of my top favourites for cutting, but because the colour is too subtly muted to be effective except at close quarters I would hesitate to give up a prominent wall position to it. So it is allowed to climb up into a *Clematis montana rubens* which helps to support its semi-herbaceous growth and finishes its flowering in time to hand over to its dark blue relative. Flowering over a surprisingly long period, *C. × durandii* coincides in bloom with the Hybrid Tea rose 'Pigalle', the climbing rose 'Mermaid' and *Hydrangea* 'Westfalen', in a rather limy little bed at the foot of a house-wall. Now 'Pigalle' is not a rose I'd ever think of putting into a shrub border, but its crimson-purple petals backed with chamois are good with the very dark grey-violet of the clematis and something of the rose's rich colour is reiterated by the hydrangea flowers, which are of a more red-purple in this bed than they would be in the naturally acid soil of the open garden. And all find a pleasing foil in the soft, pale yellow of 'Mermaid' climbing the wall alongside.

One more example may help to illustrate the compromise approach. Almost every flower arranger, I suppose, feels that she must grow *Euphorbia veneta* (ex *wulfenii*) or the equally handsome *E. characias*. And yet these tall, columnar green flower-heads need careful placing if they are to make the grade as garden decorators, which they will do more by virtue of their striking form than by their colour. Their massive pattern can be used by way of contrast to some foliage plant of entirely different form and habit, or perhaps you may care to try the pleasing juxtaposition of *Amelanchier canadensis* with one of these euphorbias, which I hit upon by chance. The pinkish-copper of the young foliage and the airy-fairy white blossom of the amelanchier in early spring make an enchanting setting for the green, maroon-eyed flower-heads of the euphorbias and the combination delights me every time I come upon it.

While it is comparatively easy to find a place in the shrub borders for as much as may be needed for the decoration of one's own home, matters are further complicated for those who go in for demonstration or exhibition work, either of which requires a much wider variety of material than is necessary for one's private enjoyment. I'm sure you will have noticed how difficult it often is, once you have decided what the colour scheme is to be, to find flowers of the right proportions for the dimensions laid down in a competition schedule, or suitable material in scale with an accessory round which a floral design is to be planned.

The actual size of the inflorescence is not necessarily of the first importance in a garden shrub. If we want a mass of prim-rose yellow in the border we may achieve it equally with the multitude of tiny saucers of *Potentilla fruticosa* 'Katherine Dykes' or with the far lesser number of the larger flower trusses of *Rhododendron* 'Gladys'; but the latter would hardly be of service for the 'small arrangement—space allowed 12 in.', although the potentilla may well provide long, sweeping sprays which will not be out of place even in an arrangement of pedestal size; so we should really give some thought to flower sizes and shapes as well as to more usual considerations such as colour, habit, height, spread, and soil requirements.

Medium-sized flowers seem plentiful enough in the garden throughout the main seasons and large flowers or inflorescences are not usually difficult, from the time of the earliest camellias and magnolias to tree peonies, rhododendrons, roses, clematis and hydrangeas, but I do frequently find myself stuck for the smaller ingredients of flower decoration. Given a seeing eye and a little imagination one can contrive miniatures out of all kinds of plant material, particularly wild. But even if I am not much interested in being clever with thimbles, dolls' crockery, lipstick holders, detergent bottle tops, snail shells and the rest of this near-gimmickry, I believe most of us have some charming small relic of old china, metal, or glass, some little rosewood box or piece of alabaster which will serve to hold an arrangement measuring something between nine and fifteen inches to adorn a small table or a narrow shelf.

The size of flower we need for these is to be found in shrubs such as *Spiraea* × *arguta*, amelanchier, the dwarf *Chaenomeles japonica*, the smaller-flowered among the evergreen azaleas and alpine rhododendrons, heaths and heathers, pieris, brooms and genistas, enkianthus, escallonias, deutzias, styrax, zenobia, jasmines, honeysuckles, abelias and the Polyantha Pompon roses, to name just some of the best that come to mind. For lack of the right material exhibitors are too often forced to rely upon tight buds to achieve a miniature effect, only to find that the hot atmosphere of the exhibition hall has expanded these to make a nonsense of their 'small arrangement'.

Of the plants I've just mentioned I would say that even though all are not absolutely first-class garden material the majority are at least worthy of a place in the shrub border on their merits as garden decorators. But I can think of many other flower arrangers' shrubs which are not—such things as the crude pink flowering currant which we can cut and force indoors to such a charming, delicate blush-white; most of the mauve roses and quite a number of Hybrid Teas; the curious, ragged green *Rosa viridiflora*, which hardly looks like a rose at all; *Buddleia × weyerana* 'Golden Glow', whose subtly blended tones are too indeterminate out of doors; and, I venture to suggest, most of the winter-flowering subjects, though this I know to be a controversial statement, which I shall attempt to justify later on. These I hide away in odd corners where I hope they may not be observed and I have to keep a check on myself to ensure that only a very limited number of them are allowed to compete for space with the really effective garden shrubs. Beset by constant temptation, I do my best to remind myself that the gardener-cum-flower arranger with only limited space at her disposal can arrive at a satisfactory compromise only if she exercises the strictest possible eclecticism in her choice.

4

Planning the Shrub Garden

Careful planning is, I suppose, necessary for most kinds of garden, but perhaps more especially for that of the flower arranger, if it is not to sink to the level of a mere nursery for cutting material.

Having been nurtured on Mr. Haworth-Booth's '1, 2, 3, 4 principle' (described in *The Flowering Shrub Garden Today*) I have learned to concentrate what he calls 'flower power' into the period from early spring until autumn—those months in which the garden can be enjoyed at first hand. The more the ground is given over to winter-flowering trees and shrubs the less room there will be for the pageant of colour from March to October. His principle consists, briefly, in dividing up the period into four sections, early spring, late spring, midsummer, and late summer and autumn, and in providing *equally* for each of the four. If you follow this plan, you will rarely need to 'do a Ruth Draper' on your visitors because June or September will have as much to show as April or May. Obviously some periods will please you better than others, but at least you will have an effective spectacle at any time from early spring until the coming of the autumn frosts, after which the evergreens will take over for the winter season. To me the word 'evergreen' has a purely complimentary connotation, indicating a quality much to be desired; but to my neighbour the picture it suggests is depressing, unrelieved dark green masses of *ponticum* and hardy hybrid rhododendrons. In the present context it denotes persisting foliage of very varying colours and these are seen at their best in winter, when the tones are often intensified and there are no flowers to confuse the issue.

27

Advice on the actual lay-out is not for me to give. Certainly you will need to have arrived at some rough idea of the desired size and shape of your borders before you can compile any sizeable order for trees and shrubs; but this seems to me to be a problem to be worked out on the spot rather than dug out of a book without any reference to the lie of the land and the immediate surroundings. I can, however, pass on a few practical tips which I found helpful in tackling the lay-out of my own garden. People usually think it necessary to draw elaborate plans on squared paper when attempting to design a garden and I began with the same idea, but I soon found that everything looked disconcertingly different once it took shape on the ground. What seemed to be a graceful curve on paper was not necessarily so when viewed from terrace, windows or intended vantage points. No amount of working things out to scale was half as practical as indicating visual shapes directly on the ground, using lengths of thickish rope to mark the outline of proposed beds, paths, etc. Rope (or even hosepipe) is much more easily seen than pegs and stones, etc., or other markers which fail to give the effect of a continuous line, particularly where curves and irregular contours are involved. It can also be very easily adjusted until the desired shape is arrived at and pegs can then be added to keep it in position.

Having got the shape of your borders to your liking, canes labelled with the names of the proposed plants may be put in, so that you may form some idea of how much, or how little, is needed. When considering the siting of trees, as distinct from shrubs, you may find it easier to visualize the prospective effect by using large branches stuck into the ground in place of the marker stakes or canes. By working things out on the spot along these lines it can be arranged for trees to provide shade where shade is wanted; the warm, southerly aspects may be reserved for avid sun-lovers; the damp hollows may be set aside for bogside plants and moisture-lovers; and so on. Don't worry if you are none too sure about your placings at this stage. The exercise will at least provide a starting point on which to base your first important order and you may take comfort from the fact that the majority of your initial plantings need not be regarded as irrevocable.

On first consideration you may well feel incompetent to tackle the problem for yourself. Certainly it will save you much trouble to call in an expert to handle the job. But who is this to be? Even those who hand over the making of their garden to a professional should, I think, be clear in their own minds as to the sort of garden they want and give as much thought to his selection as they would to that of an architect for the planning of their home. To hand over to the expert, provided he's the right one for you, will very probably give the best results, but to my mind there's one big snag about it. Whatever his success, all pride of personal achievement would be denied you.

I was one of those who quailed at the prospect of doing my own designing in the first instance, so I picked on the only landscape gardener I could find in the advertisement columns of the local newspaper and invited him to suggest a plan. Today I'm profoundly thankful that not only was his proposed lay-out so pretentious and so boring, but also the estimated cost of the work was so far in excess of my wildest forebodings, that there was nothing for it but to think up this garden on my own. And now, though I would leave this house any day with few regrets, I could never tear up my roots from the garden that I have made and tended over the years and come to love so dearly.

Although I started with herbaceous and mixed borders, rock garden, heath garden and so on, the present plantings are of course largely the outcome of trying to put into practice what I later learned about the making of a shrub garden from *The Flowering Shrub Garden* and *Effective Flowering Shrubs*. Nevertheless, most of the original skeleton design survives intact today, though with a complete change of 'furniture'.

The main part of it consists of a well-kept lawn of irregular shape surrounded on three sides by large shrub borders of curving outline, while beyond this the lower slope is more in the nature of a cultivated wilderness of trees and shrubs, divided into groups of irregular shape by meandering grass walks. In front of the house a good grass lawn again occupies a fair proportion of the space as a foil to the shrub plantings which screen us from the outside world. I tell you this in order to stress what seems to me an important point—that is, the restful effect of green lawns and grass walks to offset the assortment of colour in the borders. Elementary, no doubt. But as my shrub beds become more and more strained at the seams (and they are purposely planted in this way for their own good as well as for their owner's greed) I'm constantly tempted to encroach on the existing lawns. It's only my strong conviction that the general effect would suffer in consequence which keeps the present grassed areas inviolate.

I hope that the comparative success of my own experiment in garden-making will embolden you to try your hand, for it's my belief that any able-bodied tyro who wants to create rather than to caretake can make a passable job of designing his own shrub garden with the help of the books I've mentioned. I make no apology for referring to them so repeatedly because unless I can persuade you of the necessity to read these in order to find out how to do it my own book will be incomplete. Because my gardening education stems so largely from these two sources I have purposely refrained from covering the same ground here. *The Flowering Shrub Garden*, first published in 1938, and *Effective Flowering Shrubs* (1951), were what first set the scene in my imagination, but the years of additional experience and also perhaps the short-listing which have gone to the making of *The Flowering Shrub Garden Today* (1961) would no doubt be of even greater value to present-day garden-makers.

It would be idle to pretend that it will all come right straight away. Inexperience will make endless extra work for you at first, as it did for me—re-planning bits here and there and reshuffling year after year to get the grouping of colours and shapes, the spacing, relative flowering periods or cultural conditions more nearly right among the unfamiliar shrubs which in time we learn to know with the comfortable intimacy that comes of living together.

Far from any general mortality resulting from this treatment among my own shrubs I believe I can claim that I have only once lost a plant from such a cause. Indeed, some may owe their health or their very survival to it. This is not such vandalism as it would appear. To me it seems more reprehensible to leave a plant wrongly placed, a perpetual reproach to the planter, than to risk its removal to a happier site. It is after all a very different business to move a plant from one position to another within one's garden compared with the shock it receives when dispatched from a nursery.

Experience has encouraged me to become increasingly bold about transplanting, for I have found that quite large and difficult moves can often be successfully undertaken provided that the roots are damaged as little as possible when lifting, that a big enough hole is made to accommodate them in their new position without cramping, that the transplanting is performed in a single operation without giving them a chance to dry out and that they are not afterwards allowed to do so. I would even go so far as to say that one cannot make a successful shrub garden without being prepared to do a certain amount of reshuffling, particularly when planning for quick results. For instance, dwarf evergreen azaleas can be planted twice as closely as would be required for permanent grouping and since they are some of the easiest of all shrubs to transplant, there need be no risk in removing alternate plants to form new plantings or to replace other more ephemeral subjects later on.

This is not to say that anything can be switched around indiscriminately. I have successfully transplanted one or two quite large trees and have taken a calculated risk from time to time with a youngish broom, ceanothus or other tap-rooted subject inconveniently placed. But naturally one must use some discretion as to what may or may not be tampered with once it is established. In particular any tree or shrub supplied by the nurseryman as a pot-grown specimen is usually so cultivated for the very reason that it is a bad mover. Magnolia, cistus, romneya, eucalyptus and genista are some examples of plants which resent root disturbance.

5

Soil

Before you decide on the furnishing of your shrub borders you will need to find out two things in particular about your garden. The first is to determine the nature of your soil and the second the nature of your garden climate.

It is surprising that so little is generally understood about the significance of acid, neutral or limy soils to the shrub gardener. Yet this, really, is what matters most to the grower of trees and shrubs. One can get by perfectly well without being able to make head or tail of a thoroughgoing soil analysis, but it is vitally important to be aware of the pH value of one's soil—that is, the degree of acidity or alkalinity. Until this point has been determined it is a waste of time to set about planning an order at all unless you are only interested in lime-tolerating subjects.

It is, of course, possible to have your soil tested professionally, but you can very easily carry out your own soil tests with the help of a simple little outfit which will cost you less than fifty pence and will tell you quite as much as you need to know. I can assure you that the process is very simple. The modest do-it-yourself kit which I use consists of a small spoon-like object divided into two compartments by a low partition; a bottle of chemical fluid; a spatula; a dropper and a sheet of instructions. Having dug up a trowelful of the soil to be tested you mix it thoroughly so as to obtain a representative sample. You then put a little of it into the larger partition, drop some of the fluid on to it and leave it to stand for a few minutes before tilting the spoon to drain it off into the smaller compartment in order to note any change of colour caused by the degree of acidity or liminess present in the soil sample. The directions explain just

Evergreen Azalea 'Palestrina'

PAEONIA suffruticosa 'Ayagoromo'

what each colour variation indicates, from excessive alkalinity at the blue end of the scale to strong acidity at the red end, with neutral represented by a yellowish-green somewhere between the two. I need hardly mention that you should, of course, ignore the recommendations included on the instruction sheet regarding lime-dressings for acid soils, etc., which may be of interest to cabbage-growers but are certainly not for the shrub gardener.

I feel sure it is preferable to do one's own testing if possible, since the soil is likely to vary considerably in different parts of the same garden. For instance, you may have a satisfactorily acid natural soil, as I have, which will suit rhododendrons, azaleas, pieris, kalmias, camellias and other choosy but highly desirable ericaceous subjects, and yet an odd patch here and there may prove to be markedly alkaline—notably the site of a former kitchen garden artificially limed by a previous incumbent, or a bed at the foot of a house-wall in which builders' rubble and mortar have been buried.

In my own case, having two schoolboy sons to consider at the time we came to live here, I felt I must make some part of the steeply sloping site into a reasonably level area of lawn for their benefit and to do this it was necessary to shift large quantities of earth from an ugly artificial terrace behind the house in order to build up a fair-sized level space beyond. As long as the borders flanking the newly-made lawn were stocked with herbaceous perennials I suspected nothing of the trouble in store, knowing so little about soils that I failed even to recognize the great white lumps of lime I was constantly digging up for what they were. Not surprisingly, therefore, when the switch-over from herbaceous plants to shrubs got under way I found myself in serious trouble, realizing belatedly, though luckily not quite too late, that the substance deriving from the terrace was hardly in fact soil at all, but almost entirely builders' rubble and other rubbish.

Day after backaching day I wheeled away barrow-load upon barrow-load of it, to be replaced with a splendid acid compost from the far end of the garden. When the lower slope had been cleared of bracken and coarse grass the debris had all been stacked in huge ramparts round three sides of the lower boundary, for want of anywhere to dispose of it. There, in the course

33

of three or four years it had rotted down to provide me, almost accidentally, with a soil bank of incalculable value. The border in question now contains, amongst other things, such lime-haters as rhododendrons and azaleas, a *Cornus kousa*, an enkian-thus, a camellia and many heaths, heathers and lithospermums, all in the best of health. Nevertheless, in that bed no hydrangea ever comes blue, even 'Vicomtesse de Vibraye' (normally one of the readiest of blueing varieties) remaining constantly pink in these surroundings, though in other parts of the garden its flowers are a vivid butterfly blue.

From this cautionary tale it will be appreciated that even though you may garden in a naturally acid district it's never safe to gamble on the nature of your own soil without a test, wherever it's proposed to lay out a shrub border, plant certain shrubs or trees as lawn specimens, or make shrub beds at the foot of house-walls or in similar positions.

I hesitate to mention Sequestrene. As you probably know, this now makes it possible to grow calcifuge plants in lime or chalk soils: and yet I'm convinced that the only sane and prac-tical way to garden is to work not against your soil but with it. By treating plants intolerant of lime with the iron chelate preparation known as sequestrated iron (sold in this country as Murphy Sequestrene) it is possible to remedy the iron de-ficiency from which these will otherwise suffer when grown on chalk or lime soils. I understand that the treatment needs to be repeated annually in most cases, even though in later years it may sometimes be possible to reduce the dose; and in any event it is by no means cheap. Clearly, therefore, it would be neither practical nor economical to plant ericaceous subjects in a big way in limy conditions; but if one were willing to take the trouble and could be sure of administering the treatment each year at the proper time, it might be worth experimenting with just one or two long-coveted plants hitherto beyond one's scope.

I haven't yet tried out the small tin of Murphy Sequestrene which I bought to experiment with and I have next to no experience of its effects at second-hand, having only twice seen specimen plants after treatment. Although one of these showed good results, I think you will agree that the other was hardly a reliable test when I tell you something of the circumstances. I was shown a *Camellia japonica* hybrid in a naturally limy garden which had been dosed with Sequestrene some months previously and to my eye it still looked so thoroughly sickly and chlorotic that I asked whether the instructions on the tin really had been obeyed to the letter. The owner's answer was that she had given it as much Sequestrene as she could afford!

My own feeling is that the hazards attendant upon this method of growing lime-haters in alkaline soils are much the same as those of attempting to induce a convincing blue colour in hydrangeas grown in similar conditions. In the latter case the prescribed doses of colourant will usually be applied at the proper intervals for a season or two; but sooner or later we forget, or are prevented by circumstances, or we just lose interest—and back goes the colour to red or pink. But at least these hydrangeas won't die of our neglect, whereas failure to keep up the Sequestrene treatment for calcifuge plants in alkaline soils would, I imagine, be fatal.

6

Microclimate

If you are still with me you will by now be in a position to decide for yourself whether your soil is suitable for rhododendrons and other lime-haters; but even given the right type of soil you are not yet home and dry. Although the pH value of your soil may permit the cultivation of rhododendrons, this is no guarantee that the whole vast range of these is necessarily within your scope. Many of the choicest of them may not be for you. This time the limiting factor will be your garden climate and you'll need to find out all you can about this before you order any but the most reliably hardy trees and shrubs.

It won't take you long to find out whether you are gardening in a frost pocket or whether you are blessed with a warm slope from which the frosts can drain away downhill unimpeded. Most favourable of all is a sheltered garden on or near the southern or western seaboards. With the hundreds of garden climates that rank somewhere in between one can only feel one's way gradually.

My own garden falls within this last category. Since it lies on a hillside and consists of a very light, sandy soil (which is warmer than heavy clay) I might be assumed to have got off to a good start. Unfortunately, this is by no means the case, though I find it difficult to understand just why it should be as cold as it is. Hindhead is some eight hundred feet above sea level and this part of the neighbourhood consists of a series of giant corrugations, which perhaps explains why the cold air remains trapped within the ridges instead of making its escape to the lower levels round about. Immediately beyond the bottom of my slope the ground again rises sharply to form another parallel ridge and a further impediment to the escape of the cold air is provided a

36

few yards beyond my boundary by a dense evergreen barrier of pines and huge unclipped laurels. Add to these a north-east aspect and the result is a very cold garden indeed.

Whereas many trees and shrubs are able to endure extreme cold without detriment in the dead of winter when they are in a fully dormant state, they are much more vulnerable if caught by a frost in late spring or early autumn, either when they are putting forth tender new growth or before the sap has receded from the shoots. For some reason I am unable to account for, this garden seems to be more or less immune from early autumn frosts but is never entirely safe from the heart-breaking ravages of a belated frost in May. I never breathe quite freely until my first and favourite display has come and gone undamaged; but in the very poor season of 1962 the whole garden was attacked by frost as late as the night of 31st May–1st June, in the full splendour of its already much belated spring finery.

Waking early that morning, with cold feet in more senses than one, I turned out in dressing-gown and gumboots at 5.30 a.m. to water the frost off whatever might be salvaged before the sun reached it. Though much of the blossom on the earliest of the evergreen azaleas was reduced to a brown pulp, those in bud were saved. Every subsequent night during the first week of June the temperature dropped so low that I felt obliged to repeat the dawn patrol each day, to satisfy myself that there had been no recurrence of frost at the lower end, if not at the top, of the slope.

Living with these geographical conditions, which are entirely beyond my control, has taught me some horse-sense at the cost of many early failures and disappointments. It is significant that if I make a tour of inspection early enough after a cold night the higher parts of the garden may show no signs of frost, while the ground at the lower end may be white from a point about halfway down the hill. And so it follows that certain plants of doubtful hardiness, which have previously perished at the lower end of the garden, will frequently succeed, not only in the snuggest positions at the foot of house-walls, but also in the shrub borders on the higher parts of the slope and in those surrounding the more level area of the lawn behind the house.

Another factor which I have learned to respect as affecting

one's success with the less hardy subjects is that of the mutual aid which they may offer one another. Although for the first few years I had no success at all with hydrangeas, embothriums, choisya, ceanothus, cistuses and some of the more tender of the hebes and rhododendrons except in the shelter of house-walls, I can now grow most of these satisfactorily in the open garden. Their gregarious instincts were evidently frustrated amid the sparsely populated borders of the early years; but now each helps the other to keep the cold at bay, particularly when a liberal proportion of evergreens is included in the plantings. It would, however, be dishonest to claim more than a partial success with the cistuses, many of which suffered badly in the winter of 1961–2. Fortunately, the pretty little *Cistus parviflorus* and the handsome *C.* × *cyprius*, with large white flowers blotched with maroon, are two of the hardiest with me, rarely suffering more than slight damage in a severe winter. On the other hand some of the other good varieties, such as the dwarfs *C.* × *obtusifolius* and *C.* × *lusitanicus* 'Decumbens', take a severe pasting in a bad winter and lose a lot of wood, though they rarely die altogether.

When planting a new garden one may perhaps pick up a clue or two as regards the local climate from friends or neighbours. But if the microclimate—that is, the climate in different parts of a small area—can vary as widely as mine within a meagre one-third of an acre it follows that one needs a first-hand acquaintance with one's own conditions. Since this can only be acquired by means of trial and error the only sensible thing is to go fairly cannily at first, starting with the most dependable subjects and then, as the protective boscage develops, to take a chance on a few of the half-hardy and wait to see what happens.

When in doubt about a plant's constitution it is, *generally speaking*, a wise precaution to 'grow it hard'—that is, don't pamper it with a rich diet and overmuch shelter. Lush, sappy growth is unable to withstand the rigours of a hard winter. Let it fend for itself in a poorish soil in an exposed position and it will be all the hardier for being brought up rough. There are, however, a number of exceptions which are altogether too tender for such treatment.

Do not be scared into permanent over-cautiousness, for it is quite remarkable what one can get away with. You will never know, until you try, just what will, or will not, succeed with you. Personally, I would not even now expect much luck with an embothrium, for instance, and did lose one or two small plants earlier on, but the fine, upstanding specimen I now have in a densely packed border was quite undamaged by the fairly severe winter conditions of 1962, whereas a not specially difficult *Genista tenera* (*virgata*), and a Yulan magnolia which I had not thought of as delicate, were both killed.

Few nurserymen will admit that any but the trustiest old die-hards among the fuchsias are fit for permanent stations out of doors; and yet such varieties as 'Rose of Castile Improved', 'Coachman' and others will come through the hardest winters here with no more protection than a covering of weathered ashes or a live carpeting evergreen over the roots and a sprinkling of slug bait when the new shoots are due to emerge in the spring. In fact the only fuchsia which has so far succumbed to the winter in this garden was a 'Mme Cornelissen', a reputedly hardy outdoor variety, in the winter of 1961–2.

Finally, let me tell you that I now have not only well-established specimens of such 'C' category rhododendrons as 'Lady Chamberlain', 'Dr. Stocker', *concatenans*, 'Arthur Osborn' and others, but even a 'D' rating, 'Redcap', growing vigorously and flowering freely on the upper part of the cold lower slope. For those unfamiliar with the useful method of classification adopted by the *Rhododendron Handbook* I should explain that 'C' indicates 'Hardy along the seaboard and in warm gardens inland' and 'D' is 'Hardy in the south and west but requires shelter even in warm gardens inland'—none of which requirements can be said to be met in the case of my own cold and exposed inland garden. I might justifiably perhaps, after the first few years, have taken a chance on some of the 'B' ratings, which are said to be 'hardy anywhere in the British Isles but require some shade to obtain the best results'. But to play really safe I should almost have to limit my choice to the trusty old hardy hybrids of the 'A' category, which means 'hardy anywhere in the British Isles and may be planted in full exposure if desired'.

7

On the Keeping of Records

I hope you will bear with me if I urge upon you a form of paperwork which I can guarantee as a true short cut to success for beginners. Assuming that we're sufficiently keen on the job to read up all we can about the kinds of things we want to grow, it seems to me essential that we should keep some note of what we learn as we go, if the garden is to reap the full benefit of our reading and other sources of instruction.

Much of what we read will necessarily have been borrowed and will not be at hand for reference later on. And even in such books as we may buy because we cannot get along without them it isn't always easy to track down the information we need in a hurry, particularly if the indexing is none too thorough.

In the long run you'll find it a real time-saver to compile your own garden note-book containing all the cultural and other pertinent information you can collect on every plant you grow. It is in fact quite good fun and can be done in odd moments with very little trouble. Mine takes the form of a foolscap-size loose-leaf binder with stiff covers, and inside I have divided it into alphabetical sections by means of the gummed cardboard letters which are sold by most stationers. Long after you have forgotten where you came across them, you will have the facts you need at your finger-tips—all the details of height and spread, soil requirements, flowering period, whether evergreen or deciduous, preference for sun or shade, degree of hardiness, pruning instructions and so on. I don't find it necessary to be fussy about alphabetical order within the alphabetical divisions themselves. To make each letter section strictly alphabetical would necessitate devoting a separate sheet to each plant and this would make an over-bulky volume and waste paper. Nevertheless, I do find it important to allow generous space under each plant heading to make room for additional information.

I have an idea that most gardeners would be less apprehensive about shrub-growing if their pruning requirements, in particular, were to present less of a problem. Although the majority of trees and shrubs need no regular pruning and will get along far better with too little rather than too much chopping about, the veil of mystery which surrounds pruning technique seems to provide one of the chief deterrents to those without experience of shrub-growing. Consequently, my own garden note-book concentrates in particular on information from all manner of sources on the subject of pruning, including the time of year when any such regular annual operations should be performed.

So far so good. The information is now methodically docketed inside your binder for ready reference. Even when you know it all the busy weeks slip by and the time for some particular operation may well come and go unheeded. I therefore found it necessary to devise a rough pruning calendar compiled from the information in my garden note-book. The calendar deals only with regular annual pruning and I can see at a glance which of my trees and shrubs I should be attending to at any particular season. (See Appendix III.)

One further kind of record seems to me to be equally essential. That is, to keep a meticulous note of every order, including the correct name of the plant, the name of the supplier and the date of the order, subsequently noting whether or not it has been accepted (when ordering by post) and ticking it off on arrival. Apart from the obvious advantage of knowing precisely what to expect, a properly kept order note-book will serve as a check on the name and age of the plant when labels get lost or illegible and will also enable you to tell others where to obtain some article scarce in commerce.

Without such notes quite probably we will have forgotten all about the plants we ordered till they are finally dumped on our doorstep one winter's day. So on with the gumboots and out we go to bundle in our treasures as fast as may be into holes too small for their rootspread, possibly also in waterlogged soil, and so back with all speed to the fireside. The process is probably repeated many times in the course of a planting season and thus, without any preconceived plan to work to, the garden grows up higgledy-piggledy, each new arrival being winkled in here, there, or anywhere, as likely as not ignoring its preference for sun or shade, its fads in the matter of soil, its colour and flowering period in relation to its neighbours' and the amount of space it may be expected to occupy.

8

Shoppers, Beware!

Before we take a look at the trees and shrubs I have chosen for my own garden let me utter a word of warning about ordering unfamiliar plants.

In the first place a few branches or sprays cut from a tree or shrub and shown in a vase on a trade stand will give you little or no idea of the plant's habit of growth. For instance, you would hardly guess, from this type of presentation, that *Viburnum plicatum* 'Mariesii' bears its lacecap flowers on horizontal, tiered branches which give this lovely shrub its whole character.

Then again, you may be misled as to colour and flowering period. For Chelsea, the great horticultural occasion of the year, and no doubt for a number of other big shows, the grower will force some plants into bloom ahead of their natural flowering time and retard others in order to have the widest possible variety on display. Thus, one may select a grouping of rhododendrons for one's garden, all seen in simultaneous bloom in the big marquee, only to find that one habitually flowers in April, one in May or early June and one as late as July—and what's more, the colours don't turn out quite as we'd expected.

Not only does forcing tend to produce a paler hue than normal, but flower colour under the canvas seems to me to take on a somewhat yellower tinge than under the open sky, pinks and reds in particular appearing to have more orange in their make-up than is actually the case. When I once questioned a trade exhibitor about this he confirmed that it was no illusion and that to see a bloom in its true colours one should take it to the outside daylight, much as one does with fabrics in an artificially lighted shop. For obvious reasons this practice is unlikely to be popular with the exhibitor.

I know it's not always possible to examine established, growing specimens of every plant one thinks of buying and of course, to get a look at a sample spray is better than nothing. The very worst sort of pig in a poke is to make up a blind order from a trade catalogue, as I have discovered to my cost in the past. We often take a chance on all manner of unfamiliar things which are made to look desirable enough on paper but will almost certainly cause us disappointment later on. I mention this because even when we are aware of the unwisdom of it the temptation is always there. It's the nurseryman's business to seduce us with superlatives if he can and no doubt he thinks them well deserved, but this is no guarantee that we will.

Assuming that the essential facts regarding soil requirements and degree of hardiness and so on are given in the catalogue, the problem of colour description will remain with us for as long as both we and the nurserymen continue to ignore the existence of the horticultural colour charts. Take *Cistus* 'Silver Pink' for example: you will find this variously described as rose pink, porcelain pink, clear, soft pink, pale pink, flesh pink and silver pink in the lists from some of our leading nurseries. Are you any the wiser? Generally speaking, colour descriptions mean very little unless they conform to some accepted code and I think the greatest ambiguity of all, perhaps, attaches to the pinks and reds.

When Miss Sackville-West likens the colour of *Rosa moyesii* to the dyed leather sheath of an Arab knife I feel we are getting warmer. I know the colour of that leather and could picture the colour of the rose even if I had never seen it. Nevertheless, faithful similes are hard to come by and will not take us very far. Pin down a colour sample on a page and give it an official name and we all know where we are. This is precisely what has been done for us by the compilers of the admirable Horticultural Colour Chart, issued by the British Colour Council in collaboration with the Royal Horticultural Society,[1] about which I shall have more to say later on. A fair number of trade catalogues do now quote their colours from the Chart and we should do our share in spreading its general acceptance.

[1] The R.H.S. has since devised a newer chart with a different system of classification (see page 48).

PART 2

9

Explanatory Notes and Comments

In the second part of this book I propose to describe in detail the trees and shrubs which I've chosen to grow for the dual purpose of garden display and flower decoration.

I've been much exercised in my mind as to how best to set this out for the convenience of the flower arranger who is also by now, we hope, a prospective shrub gardener. If she lacks horticultural experience she's apt to be a little vague about flowering periods and concentrates, understandably, on her preferences in respect of colour and form. Indeed, we flower arrangers all tend to have marked colour prejudices, if only because of what will, or will not, look right with our own curtains, cushions and carpets. This being so, it seems to me that a main framework of colour categories may best suit our purposes. But let us not forget that the flowering time is every bit as important a factor as colour in the planning of a shrub garden.

Obviously neither compartment is watertight—e.g. trees and shrubs that come into flower in April will in many cases carry on well into May, or longer, thus overlapping from the first into the second of our flowering periods. And, similarly, it's almost impossible to decide at what precise point blue becomes violet or orange merges into scarlet, and so on. I shall try as far as possible to classify my plants according to the approximate time at which each *comes into flower* and I shall give the colour as matched against the Horticultural Colour Chart wherever I have been able to do so.

HORTICULTURAL COLOUR CHARTS

Dealing first with the question of colour, I must now explain more fully about the above-mentioned Chart, which I shall refer to from now on as the H.C.C. As I have already said, we habitually bandy about a lot of loose terms where colour is concerned. I doubt whether any two people mean precisely the same thing by lemon yellow, apricot, salmon, orange, peach, etc., to mention just some of the officially charted hues which occur in everyday conversation. In the H.C.C. every one of these commonly used, or misused, terms now has its exact visual definition. The original H.C.C. consists of two loose-leaf volumes together containing two hundred pages, each of which bears four squares of colour. Each page is devoted to a separate hue plus three lighter tints of that basic hue. This amounts, in all, to eight hundred different squares covering so many gradations of colour that it really does seem that the earlier haze of ambiguity need no longer exist, if only the use of the H.C.C. were more generally adopted.

These officially defined hues will appear with capital initial letters in this text, in order to differentiate them from guesswork colour-spotting. Thus *Rhododendron* 'Goldsworth Yellow' may look to me to be a primrose yellow and that is how those two words would then appear in the text; but if I have taken the trouble to match the general presentation of an open flower-truss against the H.C.C. I can state authoritatively that it is one of the lighter tints of Primrose Yellow (601/2), the initial letters of these two words now being printed in capitals to indicate that this is the official H.C.C. hue. The numbers in brackets correspond to one of the four colour samples on each page of the Chart. In this case the number of the basic hue is 601 and the flower colour concerned most nearly matches the second of the lighter tints on the same page, represented by the '/2' following the basic hue number.

In the R.H.S. Chart, which abandons colour naming, a more exact printing process has been used for some eight hundred numbered colour samples bound in four 'fans', including one of greyed hues.

AZALEA mollis 'Queen Emma'

ACER japonicum 'Aureum'

FLOWERING PERIODS

I have already professed my belief that there's no business like show business in this matter of shrub gardening. The show must go on day after day, week after week and month after month. And this continuity, surely, is at least as important to the flower arranger as it is to the gardener, if she is not to find herself with a glut or dearth of material. For this reason, in describing the plants I grow, I propose to subdivide the main colour sections into successive flowering seasons on the lines described on page 27, but with an additional winter-flowering period, making five flowering seasons in all. Finally I shall include what is to me an important section on foliage plants.

I should admit at once that I am not on the whole greatly addicted to winter-flowering trees and shrubs in the garden. Tempting though it may be, in prospect, to plan for blossom under the bleak grey skies of winter, as a spectacle it is not in fact as rewarding as one might think, except perhaps in the most favoured gardens. Take two of the most commonly planted winter-flowering subjects, *Viburnum farreri* (*fragrans*) and *Prunus subhirtella* 'Autumnalis Rosea'. Even if their pallid pink doesn't give you the shivers in mid-winter you must admit that in average conditions their blooming is only intermittent and somewhat reluctant. Furthermore, to do themselves justice many of the winter-flowering subjects need a sheltered nook or the protection of a house-wall, which I would rather allot to something that will pull more weight later on. Alluring though I find the prospect of a home-grown supply of the long, scaly, yellowish-greyish-greenish catkins of *Garrya elliptica* I don't feel inclined to give up the whole of my north wall to it. Wall space is limited and immensely valuable and this one at present accommodates a *Fatsia japonica*, two camellias, a number of hydrangeas and a cool root-run for a clematis which flowers round the corner on a sunnier wall, all of which amounts to a more profitable use of the space available, at least in my view.

Given unlimited space it would be simple enough to find room for a few winter bloomers; and there are quite a number I should like to grow for cutting if my garden were twice the size it is. But we must think in terms of one-third of an acre and I restrict myself to just one or two winter favourites, some of which can be made to work their passage through spring and summer, once their flowers are spent, by acting as host to a clematis or other climbing shrub, for the rest contenting myself with a wide diversity of evergreen shapes and textures contrasting with bare branches for winter interest.

At Hindhead at least, early March is often more akin to winter than to spring and it might well be more prudent to cut out the earliest of the flowers for fear of what the weather may still have in store for the foolhardy. But by this time I am impatient to start the show going once more and over and over again I have proved to myself that it isn't by any means always the *Rhododendron × praecox* in early March, but the later-flowering *R.* 'Elizabeth' or some of the first crop of evergreen azaleas in late April, which get cut off in their prime, or at least partially spoiled, by an untimely frost. And so it seems to me well worth taking a chance on some of the flowers of March, a selection of which are therefore included as precursors to the main display, as distinct from those listed in the more or less close season of winter.

Because I garden in such a cold area it has been particularly difficult to be very precise about flowering periods. If, on a journey to London in the latter part of March I study the passing landscape from the train window, there are times when the countryside around Godalming, for instance, seems to belong to a different world from mine. The lush green fields along the waterside are fringed with a chartreuse curtain of young weeping willow and the gardens along the line bubble over with sugar-pink almond blossom and irrepressible yellow forsythias, while on my bleak hill-top winter still seems to have it all her own way. Spring usually comes to us about a fortnight later than to the plains below. The seasons tend to catch up later on, but my experience as regards the early and late spring flowering periods in particular may be found to differ from that of others in some respects.

Apart from colour and flowering period it may also be useful to indicate whether or not a plant will tolerate limy soil conditions, whether it's evergreen or deciduous and whether its habit is prostrate, dwarf, medium or tall. These details will be shown by code letters as follows:

(a) L-T will appear in the margin immediately below the name of the plant in the case of a lime-tolerator. In the absence of the letters L-T the plant must be assumed to require acid or neutral conditions.

(b) E in the margin beneath the plant name indicates that it is evergreen. Trees or shrubs not so marked are deciduous.

(c) The term 'Prostrate' is self-explanatory. A prostrate habit will be indicated by the letter P in the margin beneath the plant name.

D stands for 'Dwarf' and should be taken to mean up to three feet in height.

M for 'Medium' covers heights between three and eight feet.

T for 'Tall' applies to heights of eight feet and upwards, excluding trees and climbers.

Trees and climbers will be designated as such in the margin.

These divisions must be regarded as approximate only, since the height of a shrub varies a great deal according to the conditions of soil and of sun or shade in which it grows. Generally speaking a plant will be much dwarfer and more compact in relatively poor soil in full sun than in a rich soil in a shady situation. The conduct reports on the plants I am about to describe will necessarily be based on their behaviour in my light, sandy soil (originally very hungry but now considerably enriched by the addition of acid compost and by the rotting down of the leaf mulch over the past two decades); in my cold garden climate; and as far as possible in suitable positions of sun or shade.

10

Conditioning of Cut Material

Since this book is addressed to flower arrangers they may be glad of such tips on the conditioning of plants as I have found effective when using these as cut material, so I have decided to mention the type of preparation I think best in each case where anything other than routine treatment is required. A last explanatory note is therefore necessary in this connection.

ROUTINE TREATMENT

First it's important to take a bucket of water into the garden with you, putting your flowers and foliage straight into the water as they're cut. If they remain out of water for more than about ten minutes after cutting the air tends to seal the stem-ends. These should anyway be re-cut before arranging.

Where no instructions are given at the end of each plant description it may be assumed that the routine process of splitting or crushing the ends of the stems before giving them a long drink in deep water, either cold or tepid, in a cool place is all that is generally required.

Woody stems are all the better for having the bark peeled or scraped off for a few inches from the bottom before treating as above.

For any cut material which is the least bit likely to cause trouble I strongly recommend removing a small portion from the end of the stem *under water*, when giving it the preliminary long drink, or the complete immersion required in certain cases. It will not then be necessary to remove another portion of stem under water when using the material in the actual arrangement.

This is a Japanese trick, and they should know, for they have been handling cut flowers a great deal longer than we have.

BOILING

In case any of my readers are ignorant of the boiling process I should explain that this consists of splitting and scraping the stem-ends and then holding these in a saucepan of boiling water to a depth of about two inches and boiling them for about thirty seconds, taking care to keep the flowers or foliage away from the steam. This can be done by shrouding them in a fine cloth or in tissue paper if necessary, as is sometimes the case with very short stems.

SOAKING

Some material—and much foliage in particular—needs a spell of total immersion in cold or lukewarm water, while other subjects respond best to this soaking treatment if they have already been boiled or singed. The terms 'soak' and 'immerse' are used synonymously throughout.

I think it is true to say that as a general rule immature shoots and tender young leaf-buds, etc., are more liable to flop than mature growth and will therefore need boiling followed by a good soaking if they are to last at all in water, even though ripened shoots cut from the same plants may last well without this extra precaution.

Certain stems need to be carefully slit from top to bottom (the cut should not penetrate deeply) before immersion. The notoriously difficult hellebores, for instance, are entirely dependable and long-lasting in water when so treated.

SINGEING

Some plants, particularly those containing a milky sap, respond best to singeing by holding the tip of the stem in a flame for a few seconds before soaking or plunging into deep water as described above. Examples of plants requiring this treatment are: euphorbias, various kinds of poppy, and clematis. It is not always understood that stems which have been treated in this way may be shortened to the required length, when the time comes to arrange them, without any need for re-singeing.

Having explained in detail the various types of conditioning which I shall be recommending for different plants, for the sake of brevity I shall indicate the required treatment simply by the words 'boil', 'soak' and 'singe'.

MISCELLANEOUS

Various dodges are recommended for individually awkward plants: e.g. large leaves with a tendency to flop may be soaked in a starch solution for several hours or overnight; sometimes slitting of the largest veins, prior to any form of soaking, helps; certain blooms respond to a brief swig of alcohol followed by the customary long drink of water; and boiling for several minutes in vinegar before standing in deep water is worth trying where all else fails. Innumerable tips on special types of conditioning will be found in Sheila Macqueen's *Encyclopaedia of Flower Arranging* (Faber & Faber Ltd.), now available as a paperback.

WARM AND HOT WATER

I should like to add a word here about the miraculous reviving properties of warm and even very hot water. Most flower arrangers will know that it pays to use hot water when 'topping up', but that is not what I am thinking of just now. I remember once leaving some sprays of cream broom lying for hours on a garden path in the midday sun and by the time I missed them they were as good as dead. However, I boiled the stem-tips and left them in very hot water until it cooled, twice changing the cooled water for hot, until finally all was as good as new and lasted just as long as if freshly picked. On a more recent occasion I had promised some sprays of the evergreen azalea, 'Naomi', to a fellow-exhibitor at the Bath and West Show and although I conditioned these carefully they toppled out of their pail of deep water overnight and were a mass of limp corollas when I found them early next morning. I could spare no more of my azalea, so I boiled the stem-ends of the wilted sprays and left them to soak in a bath of water just as warm as the flowers could stand without damage. They quickly revived, travelled some ninety miles by road to Bath and stood up to heat-wave conditions under canvas for four days without further wilting.

PLASTIC BAG TREATMENT

The shock treatment favoured by Mr. George Smith was even more surprising to me when first I heard him describe how he had cut foliage and other material from his garden in Yorkshire, put it straight into a plastic bag and brought it with him to London for use in his demonstrations at the 1962 N.A.F.A.S. Exhibition. And not until it reached the R.H.S. Lecture Hall did this material get one drop of water to drink. When it came out of its plastic bag the stems were put straight into really hot water for an hour or two, after which all emerged miraculously crisp and fresh. This treatment he recommends for roses in particular and for many other flowers, as well as for most kinds of foliage.

I had in fact read of some similar sort of practice in use among some of the commercial rose-growers, but the idea seemed to me too alarming for serious consideration and I put it out of my mind until Mr. Smith demonstrated its efficacy before my eyes. To convince myself, I needed to try it on material that was really important to me instead of merely tinkering about with a few valueless scraps, so I forced myself to try out almost all the material I proposed to use for a demonstration. And while I was about it I determined to push the test to the limit, leaving my foliage and flowers for a full twenty-four hours without water in the tightly closed plastic bag before putting the stems into very hot water. Amongst the foliage so treated the green and white variegated maple, the bronze Japanese maple, *Weigela florida* 'Variegata' and *Physocarpus opulifolius* 'Luteus' all emerged as fresh as paint and lasted well, after about one and a half hours in hot water, only *Philadelphus coronarius* 'Aureus' looking slightly resentful of these brutal attentions. The roses responded splendidly and although the notoriously difficult *Hydrangea paniculata* 'Praecox' turned out in fine condition it only lasted about five days on this occasion, whereas by boiling, soaking and stem-tipping under water I have sometimes kept it twice as long in water. However, the difference might be due to the relative degree of maturity of the flower-heads at the time of picking rather than to one or other type of conditioning.

GROWING CONDITIONS

One last word on the treatment of cutting material. It's my belief that many summer flowers and foliage plants may need conditioning even before they are picked. Few subjects last well in water if they have endured a period of drought before being cut and I find that plants will repay the trouble of keeping them well watered in a dry spell for a week or more before cutting.

11

White Flowers
(a) Early Spring

Camellia japonica Varieties

One of the earliest of spring-flowering shrubs is *Camellia japonica* in its many and varied forms. Though all are thoroughly hardy garden plants those with white or pale pink flowers suffer so much damage to the blooms in rough weather that they are not, generally speaking, a very practical proposition for the open garden, whereas the red or deep pink varieties stand up very much better to the buffeting of wind and rain. All are, of course, outstandingly handsome evergreen foliage plants, regardless of the colour of their flowers. In the absence of any overhead protection, which is what the whites and pale pinks really need in most gardens, in order to prevent browning and bruising of the petals, I grow one of each against my north wall—a position camellias much enjoy and the best I can offer by way of shelter for their delicate flowers.

'Alba Simplex'

E/T   This has perfectly formed single blooms with a cluster of yellow stamens well displayed in the centre of the pure white petals. 'Snow Goose' is a synonym and 'White Swan' is very similar.

Camellias dislike limy soils although, contrary to popular belief, they thrive on clay, so long as this is acid. Given a suitable soil mixture they can be grown successfully in tubs where the alkalinity of the soil makes it impossible to grow them in the open garden, but they will need careful watering to prevent the roots from drying out in such conditions. Camellias should be sited where they will not get the early morning sun, so that the flowers have time to thaw out after a frosty night before the sun's rays reach them. The subject of manure is somewhat controversial, but mine get a forkful above the roots in late summer. All are fine, sturdy plants with healthy-looking, glossy, dark green foliage and the older ones bear tremendous crops of bloom over a long period.

Daphne mezereum 'Alba'

L-T/D The creamy-white *Daphne mezereum* 'Alba', flowering on the naked wood like the better-known purple variety, has a rather leaner and more upright habit, which I have found to benefit from some pinching out of the extreme tips of the young shoots to induce a greater bushiness. Neither form of *Daphne mezereum* should be cut hard though established purple plants will provide plenty of material. Like the purple variety, this one lasts and smells well in water. But both are rather 'miffy' plants, liable to sudden or lingering decline for no accountable reason.

    The flowers are followed by poisonous, bright yellow berries and those left by the birds will provide seedlings readily.

Magnolia denudata (Chinese Yulan)

L-T/ Unfortunately, *Magnolia denudata* is somewhat rare and
Tree correspondingly expensive, for it is one of the loveliest small trees I know, bearing its large, creamy-white goblets in early spring before the leaves appear. Unlike some members of the family, it flowers when quite young, doing best in full sun. It is advisable to give it a sheltered position if possible because of the brittleness of the branches, which are apt to break when exposed to the full force of a gale. I would warn you that the birds

love to peck holes in the flower-buds during the winter, causing them to rot and drop off unopened.

Amelanchier canadensis (Snowy Mespilus)

L-T/
Tree

The Snowy Mespilus is much less of an aristocrat than the magnolia, but it has an exquisite airy daintiness as a cut flower, with its fragile white blossom set off by the light coppery-pink of the young unfurling leaves—provided, that is, that the birds haven't previously stripped it bare of buds, as they do in some years here. It fairly quickly makes a small tree, usually furnished to ground level, from which to cut and come again with impunity, providing material for anything from pedestals to miniatures, and where conditions are to its liking it seeds itself freely, even in the wild. It takes the stage as a rule just a little later than the very earliest of the spring bloomers, but the budded branches can be cut before the flowers open and forced in a warm room. In sheltered gardens it produces vivid autumn leaf colour.

When wanted for immediate use indoors, at its normal flowering time, it is advisable to cut the branches or sprays in bud rather than in full flower, since the petals quickly drop if the flowers are too fully open before they are cut.

Skimmias

L-T/E/
D to M

I'm a little dubious about describing the skimmias as lime-tolerant, for they do in fact have a preference for acid soils, though they consent to grow on slightly limy ones.

Despite the common belief that *Skimmia japonica* 'Foremanii' is self-fertile it's now generally acknowledged as a female, thus requiring a neighbouring male pollinator if grown for its scarlet winter berries. It is, however, the handsomest of its kind as regards foliage, with larger leaves than average. All are first-class plants for shade, but the leaves develop interesting hues in full sun, which are especially effective in the bolder foliage of 'Foremanii' (see page 257). Space permitting, I'd grow three different skimmias, planting the female 'Foremanii' and a male form of *S. japonica* side by side for a bonus of fruits and fine foliage from the former, with the additional benefit of the long-lasting panicles of little cream-white flowers opening from the greenish buds of winter, the males having much showier flowers than the females. The finest variety of the lot, *S. japonica* 'Rubella' (male), would make just as good a husband for my 'Foremanii' as a male *japonica*, but I prefer to keep the beautiful russet-pink-budded 'Rubella' out of sight of berrying females, whose scarlet fruits clash horribly with it throughout the winter. (See page 172.)

Whatever the nurserymen may say, the only true hermaphrodite commonly available is *S. reevesiana (fortunei)* which, please note, insists on an acid soil. It also differs in its longer whitish flower-panicles and darker crimson, oval fruits.

Pieris floribunda and *P. japonica*

E/M
and
E/T
The erect sprays of small, pitcher-shaped, white flowers of *P. floribunda* are rather less attractive than those of the more distinguished-looking *P. japonica*, which are carried in gracefully drooping, fan-shaped sprays tinted brownish-pink in bud and opening to white.

I grow *P. floribunda* because it is considerably hardier than the more desirable *P. japonica*. *P. floribunda* does well in part shade, lasts for weeks in flower and is equally well behaved in water.

Dead-head after flowering.

Prunus 'Tai Haku'

L-T/
Tree
This cherry is a lovely sight in bloom, with its large, single, pure white flowers hung in clusters among the coppery-tinted expanding leaves, but it is usually just too early to complement the main display of early

spring. In late autumn the dying leaves contribute their quota of yellow and flame to the scene.

When cutting from this, or any other cherry, make sure that the cut is made flush with a main branch or good side branch so as not to leave a snaggy end which may damage the tree. *Prunus* 'Tai Haku' is comparatively slow-growing and patience is therefore required for a good many years before it becomes possible to cut the fair-sized lengths which one really needs in order to use this cherry to the best advantage indoors.

Boil, for safety.

Prunus avium (Wild Gean)

L-T/
Tree

Though the best of the Japanese ornamental cherries are more spectacular as garden trees, our native gean has a delicate grace of its own, especially in a semi-wild setting, and is as good as, or better than, many of the larger-flowered garden varieties for indoor decoration if it is cut before the blossom is fully open.

Erica arborea 'Alpina' (Form of Tree Heath)

L-T/E/
M to T

Though the massive, greyish-white flower-spikes of this tree heath are beautiful in themselves I rate it even higher as a foliage plant. If left to itself it makes a tall, often rather untidy shrub, but if trimmed annually in late spring after flowering it will make a densely plumed bush of five feet or so. In this cold garden it has proved reasonably hardy. It will not prosper in a heavily alkaline soil.

(See also Foliage Section, page 260.)

Spiraea × *arguta* (Bride's Bouquet, Bridal Wreath, Bridal Spray, Baby's Breath)

L-T/M

Not prized very highly in horticultural circles, this shrubby spiraea is nevertheless quite well worth garden room and its foam of tiny, chalk-white flowers fanning from the main stem on arching sprays is admirably disposed for the flower arranger. It will stand any amount of cutting, but, unfortunately, it doesn't hang on to its tiny petals quite as tenaciously as one could wish, though it will last well for two or three days in water if cut in good condition.

Regular pruning is desirable to keep it shapely. This consists of removing any old flower-shoots devoid of strong young growth after flowering and of shortening any extra long ones which spoil the shape of the bush.

Evergreen Azaleas

I hope that those of you with alkaline soils will have been pleased to note how many of the trees and shrubs so far dealt with are in fact tolerant of lime. But since I am blessed with an acid soil my garden in springtime is very largely dependent on the early rhododendrons and azaleas and, in particular, on the dwarf evergreen azaleas, which come in almost every colour except yellow and blue and possess many other virtues.

The flowering period of each varies from year to year and consequently some that I shall include in the Early Spring Section might well be classified as late spring subjects and vice versa.

'Palestrina'

E/
D to M 'Palestrina' is one of my favourites among the whites, with greenish-centred, rather large, shapely flowers set off by fresh green foliage. With me it is a first-class garden plant, quite apart from the beauty of the material it provides for cutting. And this is one that can be cut more freely than some, on account of its more upright habit which produces comparatively long flowering shoots, provided it is left to grow unmolested for a number of years.

Even though I now have any amount to cut from I am anxious not to waste any pieces for lack of adequate conditioning and so I usually boil the stem-ends, as described on page 53, for safety, in addition to the routine treatment mentioned in the same chapter.

'White Lady'

E/D   'White Lady' is a more recent introduction which is
       similar to, but no improvement on, 'Palestrina'. The
       green-eyed flower is rather smaller, the foliage less good
       and it is not such a strong grower. Nevertheless it helps to
       provide variety among the not very numerous whites.
           Boil, for safety.

'Kure No Yuki'

E/D   'Kure No Yuki' has much smaller white flowers of the
       hose-in-hose type, profusely borne on a much more
       compact bush. Its very compactness, which commends
       it as a garden plant, makes it less convenient to cut from
       for indoor use.
           Boil, for safety.

Chaenomeles speciosa 'Nivalis' (Form of Japonica)

L-T/M One rarely sees a white form of chaenomeles, but al-
       though it makes less impact as an open-ground shrub
       than the many reds, flames, corals and pinks among
       them 'Nivalis', which is probably the best white one, is
       strikingly effective when trained against a mellow red
       brick wall with its snowy blossom offset by the dark-
       barked shoots. Not having enough wall space to go
       round I don't grow it here, but for limy gardens this and
       the vast assortment of its relations in other hues, heights
       and flower-shapes are especially valuable in the spring
       scene, birds permitting.
           For general comments on Chaenomeles, see page 130.

Prunus laurocerasus (Common Laurel)

L-T/   Boxed in as I am on three sides out of four by other
E/T   people's laurels, I am a little out of love with the noble
       Prunus laurocerasus, known disrespectfully to most of
       us as 'Common Laurel'. And yet, when left to its own
       devices it makes a handsome great shrub which provides
       a variety of material for cutting—not only the glossy

evergreen foliage, but also the spikes of starry-eyed, creamy-white flowers in early spring and the berries which follow in the autumn, first green, then red and finally black.

When the leaves are stripped from the flowering branches the charmingly constructed flower-spikes rarely fail to mystify the uninitiated. They force well if brought into a warm room in fairly tight bud—and this is often a doubly wise precaution, since the fully opened flowers are frequently ruined by frost. The only fault I have to find with them is that the flower-spikes are disposed in rather an awkward, angular manner along a rather too thick branch. As you probably know, the foliage preserves well in glycerine, keeping its gloss and turning to a rich, dark brown.

Iberis sempervirens 'Little Gem' (Form of Shrubby Candytuft)

L-T/
E/P

This shrubby candytuft is not perhaps a plant of great distinction, but in limy gardens it provides quite a useful substitute for the white forms of dwarf evergreen azalea. It makes a low evergreen cushion of dark, rich green which covers itself in spring with the familiar chalk-white candytuft flowers for many weeks and these later provide green seed-heads of interesting form for a small arrangement. The seedlings are usually of inferior quality and less white.

The plants should be cut back quite hard after flowering (unless seed-heads are required) in order to prevent them from becoming straggly.

12

White Flowers
(b) Late Spring

The late spring period is easily the one I love best in my garden, not because the show is rather less full-blooded throughout the summer and autumn but because this is the time when the shrub gardener has the richest and widest range of colour to conjure with, against a setting of tender young unfurling leaves which will mature all too soon to the tougher, dustier, thirsty-looking, darker greens of high summer. This is the time to indulge in a gorgeous riot of colour, to throw in every hue in the spectrum, at any rate in gardens where members of the rhododendron family are at home. My own chief difficulty is to keep my insatiable greed for dwarf evergreen azaleas in check; for one must be firm with oneself if the other flowering periods are to compete on equal terms. Half the fun seems to go out of shrub gardening if we concentrate too much on one crowded month of glorious life in May, to be faced thereafter with a steady decline in the display.

It was Mrs. Sheila Macqueen who first brought it home to me that if you are going in for a really mixed mass arrangement you can make free with all the colours of the rainbow so long as you use no white. And just as white flowers make too startling a hole in an indoor arrangement of widely assorted hues, to a lesser extent this is sometimes also true of white shrubs out of doors. The latter can, if wrongly placed, be too suddenly and too solitarily white in much the same way that an isolated clump of purplish-brown foliage tends to over-advertize itself in certain circumstances. But in the gaudy spring kaleidoscope, where magenta-crimsons, shocking pinks, orange-scarlets and bright

E   65

yellows all find a place, these need to be sobered down by an admixture of blue-violet, lilac, pale pink, cream and white.

Rhododendron mucronatum (or *Azalea ledifolia*)

E/
D to M Speaking as a flower arranger, if I had to choose just one evergreen azalea out of the many kinds I grow that one would be *Rhododendron mucronatum*, which is in fact an evergreen azalea in spite of its name. The flowers are not unlike those of 'Palestrina', pure white with a pronounced green eye, but larger and more solid in outline and in most seasons a little the later of the two. It makes a bigger bush than most, especially when given partial shade.

Boil, for safety.

Rhododendron yunnanense

E/
M to T *Rhododendron yunnanense* is rather a variable species which is difficult to classify as regards colour, being usually white or very pale pinkish-mauve with a spotted red-brown flare. An established plant has a fairy-like grace and charm, but although it's renowned for its freedom of flower I confess to having cherished a plant for the past fifteen years without so far having been rewarded by a single bloom. Its 'A' rating is a token of its hardiness and it's said to put up with a poor position better than most rhododendrons. In spite of my personal experience, which I believe to be exceptional, I still regard this rhododendron as one of the loveliest of garden ornaments and one which should provide enchanting cutting material.

Rhododendron 'Loder's White'

E/T *Rhododendron* 'Loder's White' is a beauty on a much more massive scale. The magnificent great flower-trusses are pink in bud, opening to frilly white blooms of exceptional size. I have found it to be considerably hardier than might be supposed for one of the 'C' category. My own lusty specimen, planted at the same time as *R.*

yunnanense, grows against a north-east wall. Given this slight protection it has never shown the slightest sign of damage and regularly bears a tremendous crop of flowers.

Boil, for safety.

Pieris formosa 'Wakehurst' and *P.* 'Forest Flame'

E/
M to T

I wish I could say the same of the pieris, 'Wakehurst', one of the true aristocrats for a lime-free garden; but, alas, it's a martyr to spring frosts in cold areas. After many years mine has barely added one inch to its stature, the brilliant new leaf growth being regularly frosted back to base and the flower-buds wrecked at the same time. The new season's foliage is such a spectacular scarlet, fading to flame, that the effect is no less vivid than that of a densely flowered azalea for instance, and the clusters of lily-of-the-valley flowers are large and lovely in their own right.

However, the more recent, rather dwarfer variety, 'Forest Flame', is considerably tougher and a little later in putting forth its spring finery, which is only a little less vivid than that of 'Wakehurst'. A small new plant has made good progress in two years here, with the help of some slight frost protection in winter and early spring.

Both enjoy a sheltered position in moist soil and partial shade and both are better dead-headed after flowering.

I believe that the fan-shaped flower-sprays are very reliable in water, but I feel sure that the flamboyant young foliage would need boiling to make it last when cut. This is, however, mere guesswork, as I have not yet cut from either plant.

Halesia monticola (Form of Snowdrop Tree)

Tree

Halesia monticola is the last lime-hater I shall mention in this section. It makes an attractive, much branched tree, but is perhaps on the large side for a small garden. It is hardy and flowers freely at quite an early age, with dangling creamy-white snowdrops closely hung along the spreading branches. These are followed by rows of pendent, pale green seed-pods shaped like tiny flanged pears.

Magnolia wilsonii

L-T/
Tree

I am doubtful whether I should include *Magnolia wilsonii* in this section or the next. Both this and *M. sieboldii* are said to start flowering in late May and in my own garden *M. wilsonii* is always the earlier of the two, so it may just pass as a late spring subject, though the more concentrated display is often delayed until early June in both cases.

M. wilsonii is one of the choicest subjects I know for a limy soil. It fairly quickly makes a sizeable tree and might have done so even more rapidly in my own garden had I realized from the start that magnolias hate being moved.

The large, pendent white flowers with the protruding crimson centre appear to be made of the finest *suède*. They smell delicious and last quite well in water if cut in the advanced bud stage and boiled, but once the cut flower is fully open the petals soon crumple and turn brown. The seed-vessels have a beautiful smoky pinkish casing at the fleshy stage, later bursting open their many compartments to reveal polished orange-scarlet seeds and ultimately drying into curiously curled and sculptured shapes in two tones of brown.

Exbury, Knap Hill and other Hybrid Deciduous Azaleas

M to T

'Milton'—named, let's hope, after the poet, despite the glaring commercial connotation attaching to one of the purest of white azaleas—is unusual in that it has double flowers, a characteristic shared by another true white called 'Whitethroat'. Both, I think, show to better advantage in an arrangement than in the garden, where the singles look more at home. Among the latter 'Alba-

68

core' is pure white, whereas 'Tyrol', 'Mrs. Anthony Waterer' and 'Toucan' open cream before fading to white, and 'Nancy Buchanan' and the very fine variety 'Persil' are white with a yellow blotch.

Pick in opening bud to avoid wilting or dropping and boil.

Viburnum plicatum 'Mariesii'

L-T/M   There are any number of lovely shrubs for the limy garden at this time of year and I would place the various forms of *Viburnum plicatum* very high on the list. The flat white flower-heads of 'Mariesii' are reminiscent of the inflorescence of the lacecap hydrangea and are carried all along the upper side of the horizontal, slightly drooping branches.

Boil and soak.

Viburnum plicatum 'Lanarth'

L-T/M   I have two very beautiful viburnums which bear a close resemblance to 'Mariesii' in flower, but the branches are more rigidly horizontal, with an even more conspicuously tiered habit. They were sent out from a nursery mis-labelled *Viburnum tomentosum* 'Plicatum', the earlier name for the plant I had ordered, but they turned out to be the variety 'Lanarth'.

Boil and soak.

Viburnum plicatum (*tomentosum* 'Plicatum', *tomentosum* 'Sterile') (Japanese Snowball)

L-T/M   *Viburnum plicatum* carries large balls of flower along great arching wands fanning out from ground level. Though the flower-heads themselves bear some resemblance to those of the more familiar Snowball Tree, *plicatum* is an infinitely superior plant, smaller in stature but with much larger flower-balls which are green tinged at first, opening through cream to white and taking on a pinkish flush before they fall.

Boil and soak.

Viburnum opulus 'Sterile' (Snowball Tree, Guelder Rose)

L-T/T   To my mind much less attractive as a garden plant than the Japanese form just described, and yet much more commonly grown, *Viburnum opulus* 'Sterile' makes a bigger, rather muddled shrub or small tree bearing a profusion of smaller snowballs. By virtue of their smaller size and of the fact that this larger tree may be cut almost to the point of vandalism, the flowering branches are, I think, more generally useful to the flower arranger, but if I could only find room for one or other in my garden it would be the Japanese plant rather than the more familiar native.

Boil and soak.

Choisya ternata (Mexican Orange)

L-T/
E/M   The glossy, bright green, fingered leaves of *Choisya ternata* and the clusters of fragrant white flowers suggestive of orange blossom make this an attractive dual-purpose shrub for gardener and flower arranger alike. Of only doubtful hardiness, it doesn't really enjoy my garden climate and yet, in spite of one fatality, I'm still reluctant to abandon my attempts to get this plant established. Although it's said to be equally at home in sun or shade I suspect that a position in full sun would produce a much sturdier bush.

Cytisus multiflorus (White Portugal Broom)

L-T/E/T   *Cytisus multiflorus* is a useful filler among young shrubs which will eventually need the space it temporarily occupies and meanwhile it provides pretty, airy sprays for the flower arranger. It soon becomes a scrawny, unlovely thing unless it is cut hard back annually after flowering (but not into the old wood) and it will benefit from being trimmed several times in the course of a season during its earliest years. Its normal life-span is not a very long one, but it seeds itself so freely that one need never be without it. The seedlings are somewhat variable, some being of a much cleaner white than others, and can be distinguished from those of other brooms before they reach the flowering stage by a pronounced greyish tinge in the green of the stems and leaves.

Clematis

(*N.B.*—The letters N, S, E or W in brackets after the name indicate the most suitable aspect. (O) signifies 'any aspect'.)

L-T/ 'Miss Bateman' (O) is one of the earliest of the large-
Climbers flowered hybrids, bearing white flowers with a slight tinge of mauve and a brownish centre, and with a lovely central band of green on the sepals which is more pronounced on the underside. Though this one flowers just ahead of the first main batch of clematis, in most cases it's difficult to draw the line between late spring and early summer bloomers, many of which, including 'Miss Bateman', may bear a second flower crop in late summer.

Among the species and small-flowered hybrids *Clematis montana* 'Grandiflora' (O) covers itself in white flowers measuring two to three inches across and is one of the earliest. All *montana* types are far more vigorous than the large-flowered hybrids.

All wilt rapidly in water unless singed or boiled.

The large-flowered hybrid clematis have one serious drawback. Without any sort of warning one may suddenly find a fine shoot yards long, or even a whole young plant, with all its leaves dangling limp and lifeless, due to wilt. Affected parts must immediately be cut out and burned, even if this means razing the plant to the ground; but prompt action will usually arrest the damage before the whole plant is affected. The important thing is never to let what's left dry out. Keep the remains, or, at worst, the apparently vacant site, conscientiously watered in dry weather and protect it constantly with slug bait and the chances are that your clematis will shoot again from below ground.

Pruning instructions vary according to the type of clematis and are carefully explained in most good nursery catalogues and elsewhere, so it seems unnecessary to go into a mass of detail on the subject here. In any case opinions vary as to the desirability of pruning some types of clematis at all. I feel sure that it is essential to shorten newly planted clematis to within twelve or eighteen inches from the base, tempting though it may be to leave all those encouraging young green buds, but as far as established plants are concerned, I now side with those who hold that over-enthusiastic pruning may be more harmful than too little, for I once killed a thriving *Clematis* 'Mrs. Cholmondeley' by cutting it back precisely as directed. If your plants are grown on the shady side of trees and shrubs in the borders and allowed to scramble through them towards the sunlight, little or no pruning will be required.

Paeonia suffruticosa hybrids (Tree Peonies)

'Yano Okima' and 'Ren Kaku'

L-T/M   The huge-flowered tree peonies are perhaps the most and magnificent of all plants for limy soils at this, or any
L-T/D   other, season. Two of the finest pure whites are 'Yano Okima' and 'Ren Kaku', both with very large semi-single flowers in which the central cluster of yellow stamens is prominently displayed. The latter name is said to mean 'Flight of Cranes', which is indeed descriptive of the petal formation in this exquisite but slow-growing and rather rare variety.

I am a little diffident about classifying named varieties of the Japanese tree peonies according to colour because they are so often imported with the wrong name labels that it is difficult to be sure of what's what. The best way to make certain of what you're getting is to visit the importer when his stock is in bloom and select the colours and shapes that please you best. The plants can then be reserved for you, for despatch at the proper time. It will repay you to remove the Japanese wooden labels on arrival if these are attached with fine wire which, if left, will cut right into the growing stem as the girth increases. The rusty wire may be difficult to detach, so be careful not to damage or knock off any buds in the process. I think it safer not to attach any kind of name label to the plant itself, at any rate until it is a lot bigger, but to use some kind of labelling device stuck into the ground alongside.

How I wish that these lovely things were not such tricky subjects, particularly in their early years! Not only are they susceptible to botrytis fungus (a brown rot which is crippling but not fatal) but they are also a prey to a galloping consumption known to the Japanese as 'Sudden Death'. Sudden and unaccountable it certainly is, and heartbreaking too, for tree peonies are as costly as they are beautiful. All we can do is to plant them deeply, burying the point of the root graft at least three inches below soil level, protect young plants constantly from slugs, cut back infected parts to healthy wood, remove and burn dead and diseased foliage, dust or spray with a fungicide at intervals from early spring onwards, keep them in good fettle with foliar feeds if necessary, from spring to midsummer and, most important, never despair of a plant when the mysterious killer strikes. I have proved to myself that tree peonies can, and often do, rise from the dead in the sense that even after the last vestige above ground has disappeared for more than a year it may still very probably shoot up again from below ground level. But if you are not constantly on the lookout for the emergence of these new shoots the slugs will mow them down without trace. A setback of this sort when a young plant is struggling back to life will probably be final.

Because of such unaccountable disasters it is often supposed that the tree peony is a tender subject, though nothing could be further from the truth. I would say that this common fallacy is in itself responsible for at least some of the trouble. Anxious gardeners are liable to kill their costly tree peonies with kindness. A friend of mine recently told me that a plant which had made a poor start in her garden was given the protection of a polythene bag throughout the following winter and had prospered exceedingly in consequence. If she only knew it her peony survived in spite of rather than because of the well-meant coddling, since the humid conditions inside a polythene bag provide a

73

perfect breeding ground for the botrytis fungus which is one of the chief enemies of the tree peony. The more airy the position the better it should flourish.

Cut in half-open bud, and boil, for safety.

13

White Flowers
(c) Midsummer

From early June onwards there is a plethora of white-flowered trees and shrubs to choose from, including many of my top favourites for flower decoration and, fortunately, many of them are equally at home in limy gardens.

Hoheria lyallii and *H. glabrata*

L-T/
Tree

These two are so much alike that it's no easy matter for the amateur to tell them apart, except that *H. glabrata* often has rather larger, longer-tipped and less hairy leaves than *H. lyallii*. It pays to plant both if you have room for them, since there is usually about a fortnight's difference between their flowering periods. From the specimens I sent to Wisley for identification it would appear that *H. glabrata* was the earlier in bloom, but the Director considers that 'many plants grown under these two names are hybrids of *H. lyallii* and *H. glabrata* which have arisen in gardens or nurseries as seed raised plants'.

They never fail to appeal to any flower arranger beholding them for the first time. The small, shrubby trees bear a multitude of flowers reminiscent of single white cherry blossom, often with a faint smudge of mauve surrounding the central mass of stamens. They're said to have a sweet, honey scent, which I have never detected. The pretty, heart-shaped, cool-looking green leaves set off the blossom delightfully on the tree, but need a good deal of stripping from the cut branches to show off the flowers to advantage. Although reputed to be slightly tender my two trees get by with little or no winter damage, with the help of dwarf evergreens surrounding the lower parts, and have made rapid growth.

Boil.

Hydrangea paniculata 'Praecox'

L-T/
M to T As its name implies, *Hydrangea paniculata* 'Praecox' is the earliest to flower among the *paniculata* types. It makes a big, sturdy bush with creamy-white flowerheads much less densely constructed than in the more commonly grown *H.p.* 'Grandiflora' and its appearance is that much the more graceful in consequence, particularly as material for the flower arranger.

I do no pruning beyond dead-heading (i.e. back to the first good pair of growth buds) in the spring.

It will repay the most careful conditioning, without which, like most other hydrangeas, it quickly wilts when cut. Some say that hydrangeas must be cut with a bit of the old wood on the stalk, others tell you the opposite. With me it gets everything in the book— splitting and peeling the stem-ends, boiling, immersing in tepid water, removing the stem-tip under water and, finally arranging in warm water. If cut hydrangeas are to be exposed to the hot, arid atmosphere of an exhibition hall it is well worth while to spray the finished arrangement with cold water *in situ* and then cap it with a light tissue paper tent to reduce transpiration, especially if it has to be arranged some time in advance and left overnight before the day of the show. But don't forget to return to remove the tent next morning!

Perhaps only some of these precautions are necessary, but hydrangeas are notoriously tricky material for flower arrangement and I prefer to take no risks. Since the advice I have given here about conditioning applies equally to all kinds of hydrangeas I shall in future refer you back to the details given here.

Hydrangea petiolaris

L-T/
Climber

Hydrangea petiolaris is a climbing variety which makes excellent coverage for a north wall, clinging to the surface with little tentacles like ivy and decorating it with loose creamy-white lacecap inflorescences set off by shiny light green leaves with a very fresh appearance. It will also creep over mounds, banks and tree-stumps or will climb a tree with a tall, bare trunk, such as a pine.

(For conditioning, see under *H. paniculata* 'Praecox', p. 76.)

Philadelphus (Mock Orange, Syringa)

L-T/M

There can be no question about the value of *Philadelphus* 'Belle Étoile' to the flower arranger, quite apart from its outstanding virtues as a garden shrub. Originally I put in the rather clumsy, tall, double 'Virginale' and I gladly scrapped it after a year or two in favour of the much neater and prettier 'Belle Étoile'. This has become such a favourite of mine that I have since made room for five or six plants in different parts of the garden. It is a tidier, dwarfer philadelphus than many, from which it is possible to cut the loveliest great sprays of single, rather square white flowers with a touch of purple at the centre. The rather similar large-flowered 'Beauclerc' and 'Sybille', and × *purpureo-maculatus* with smaller blooms prettily displayed, are all equally garden-worthy and all smell delicious.

These being by nature among the less rampant varieties of philadelphus, they will get by with very little pruning beyond what is cut for indoor use. It does, however, make for a neater and more floriferous bush if the flowered shoots are cut back to strong new growths after flowering and the thin, twiggy tangles removed altogether from time to time.

Some defoliation is necessary to show off the flowers in an arrangement, but I prefer not to strip all the leaves.

Pyracantha atalantioides (or *P. gibbsii*) (Firethorn) and *P.a.* 'Aurea'

L-T/E/T   The pyracanthas not only provide excellent evergreen
or   cover for a north or other wall but also make decorative
Climber   open-ground shrubs when allowed to develop *au naturel*.
If one is not too tidy-minded much of the necessary
pruning even in a wall position may be done by cutting
branches in flower or berry for indoor use. My own,
which are grown as wall shrubs, are not kept very closely
clipped, so that there is always plenty of a useful length
for cutting, but some additional trimming is still necessary. Although the pyracanthas are grown primarily for
their autumn or winter berries (orange-scarlet in the case
of *P. atalantioides* and yellow in the case of *P.a.* 'Aurea')
the clusters of white hawthornlike blossom are equally
useful to the flower arranger.

(For berries see Yellow, Late Summer and Autumn,
page 121, and Apricot to Salmon-Orange, Winter, page
148.)

Large-flowered Clematis Hybrids

L-T/   Among those which flower early in the season (often
Climbers with a second flowering in autumn) several fine whites
include my personal favourite, 'Marie Boisselot' ('Mme
le Coultre') (O), with large velvety sepals and cream
stamens; the rather less solid 'Henryi' (O), with a
maroon-brown centre; 'Mrs. George Jackman' (O),
creamy-white, brown-centred and tending towards semi-
double flowers on the old wood; and 'Duchess of Edin-
burgh' (O), a large, fully double pouffe which is not to
every gardener's taste but has a hypnotic allure for
flower arrangers.

(For general comments, see pages 71-2 and 210-11.)
Singe or boil.

Roses

Before embarking on the subject of roses it may be as well to remind you that the marginal code letters indicating height continue to operate, for roses as for other shrubs, as described on page 51: that is to say, D = up to three feet, M = up to eight feet and T over eight feet. Since the rose is as much a shrub as any it seems to me consistent to adhere to the same yardstick throughout; but in applying uniform criteria for height assessments my own classification of roses will often be at variance with that of the rose catalogues in which height descriptions are purely relative, as between one rose and another. Consequently most of those mentioned except shrub roses and climbers will come into the M range, from three to eight feet, though eight feet is in fact comparatively tall for an H.T. or Floribunda, for example.

Hybrid Teas, Floribundas and Garnettes

L-T/M   In most colours these are bred in bewildering abundance and selection depends so much on personal preference that I propose to limit my remarks on roses generally to shrub types and other oddments, with only an occasional reference to some of the newer or less familiar H.T.s and Floribundas of special value for cutting. New whites are, however, less numerous than coloured innovations, so it may be worth while to mention a few, such as 'Pascali', a beautifully formed ivory-white H.T. deepening to cream at the heart—a fact which is sometimes quoted to its detriment but for me only adds to its charm, unless pure white is *de rigeur*. In that event, the large-flowered, shapely 'White Christmas' should meet the case. The less recent and none-too-free-flowering 'Message', with its touch of green at the centre, provides a lovely bloom for flower arrangement. Among the Floribundas 'Iceberg' still seems to be without a serious rival. And the very long-lasting Garnette types now include one or more whites, though I believe some of these to be more loosely petalled than the original red Garnette. I found a good white at one of the specialists, C. Newberry and Son, of Bulls Green Nursery, Knebworth, Herts. Garnettes are also included in some of the general rose growers' repertoire, among them, at the time of writing, Messrs. Cants of Colchester. But be careful not to confuse the Garnettes with miniature and other dwarf roses in the catalogues, for these aren't at all the same thing.

Climbers

L-T   Among the climbers it pays to look for a repeat flowerer, which at least offers a prospect of a second crop of bloom later in the season, though I've found that not all those described as repeaters fulfil that promise here. If a hint of pink at the centre of the large, elegant flower is acceptable, McGredy's free-flowering 'Swan Lake' is one of the best.

Hybrid Musks

L-T/M   These really earn their space as garden decorators, smothering the bushes in a profusion of bloom at midsummer, with a repeat performance later, in reasonable climates; and they make out better than most roses on light, sandy soils. For cutting they're charming in bud, but the shape of the open flower is less tidy and sophisticated than the sculpted blooms of the best H.T.s and certain Floribundas. The Hybrid Musks include two double whites, 'Pax', which fades from cream to white as it opens upon yellow stamens, and 'Prosperity', in which the white is tinted cream-pink in bud, with fine large flower trusses.

'Frau Karl Druschki' (Hybrid Perpetual)

L-T/   Our old friend 'Frau Karl Druschki' has been with us
M to T   for a very long time, but is hard to beat for vigour and prodigality of bloom, with its huge, slightly blowsy, pure white flowers stained with pink on the outer petals, par-

ticularly in bud. This rose has a tendency to ball up in wet weather, but not as badly as some, and there are always so many new buds waiting to replace the damaged ones. Unlike most roses, 'Frau Karl Druschki' flowers with the utmost abandon right through the summer months, truly earning its title, Hybrid Perpetual.

'Nevada' (Modern Shrub Rose)

L-T/T 'Nevada' makes a fine great bush for the shrub garden, with large, semi-single flowers, sometimes flushed with pale pink in the bud, which open to creamy-white with yellow stamens. The blooms are profusely borne all along the branches in huge, arching wands. 'Nevada' is sometimes said to be continuous-flowering, but I have found this to be an overstatement. In my garden the main display comes in early summer, followed by a second attempt towards the end of August.

Being semi-single the cut flowers do not, of course, hold their petals so well as the more double roses, but if picked in the bud stage they last for at least a couple of days. The huge, curving sprays are wonderful for pedestal arrangements.

'Blanc Double de Coubert' (*Rugosa*)

L-T/M 'Blanc Double de Coubert' is a truly shrubby rose of medium stature with great, wide-open, semi-single flowers of crumpled paper-white, set off by attractively crimped and veined bright green leaves. It fairly bristles with tiny prickles up and down the stem, but for those who have the courage to handle it, it is also delightful indoors.

'Shailer's White Moss' (or 'White Bath') (Moss)

L-T/M In selecting roses for flower arrangement in particular I find myself looking for one of three qualities: either they must have a well-groomed elegant air; or they must suggest an untamed naturalness; or they must possess a chintzy, old-world charm. While the H.T. is the epitome

F

of the *soigné* type and 'Nevada' and 'Blanc Double de Coubert' have the careless abandon of a child of nature, nothing could fill the bill for unsophisticated, old-fashioned charm better than 'Shailer's White Moss' or 'Mme Hardy'.

'Shailer's White Moss' has paper-white flowers, sometimes flushed with pink, which emerge from a casing of thick, dark reddish 'moss' and come on good long stems. Though the flowers are enchanting the shrub is, unfortunately, rather thin and lanky.

'Mme Hardy' (Damask)

L-T/M   The same is true of 'Mme Hardy', whose quartered, rather flat white flower with a green button eye is equally delightful, but I doubt whether it is sufficiently dependable as cut material for exhibition work in any but ideal conditions.

For those who need guidance on the care of the old shrub roses all there is to know about them has been said in various works by Mr. Graham S. Thomas.

All that I propose to say on the cultivation of roses is that not only the true shrub types but most of the Floribundas and some of the Hybrid Teas also look entirely in keeping in the shrub garden when grown as shrubs—which is after all what they really are—among other shrubs. My own garden would be a drab affair indeed from midsummer onwards were it not for the mass of colour the roses bring to the scene from June until October. When grown as shrubs among the shrub borders they mostly need rather lighter pruning than is recommended for plants grown in the more orthodox fashion, in isolated rose-beds.

Deutzia

L-T/   I'm not tremendously enthusiastic about the majority of
M to T   deutzias as effective garden shrubs and grow neither of those I'm about to describe.

Deutzia pulchra has pendulous little single flowers arranged in small panicles and ornamented with yellow stamens. One famous nursery catalogue likens them to 'drooping spikes of lily-of-the-valley', which suggests something of their attraction for cutting purposes. The flowers are sometimes faintly tinged with pink.

Deutzia × *magnifica* is more upright-habited, but less tall than the previous species, barely attaining the minimum eight feet of the other. The densely packed four-inch spikes of large, double stars are in this case carried erect and are markedly chalk-white. They are I think less graceful material for flower arrangement, both on account of the stiffer growth and because of the very exuberance of the flowering, which looks clumsier when cut unless very heavily thinned. Personally, I don't much care for so matt a dead white.

Boil.

Wisteria (Wistaria)

L-T/ White wisteria may be had in Japanese or Chinese forms
Climber, corresponding to the more usual mauves, the Japanese
or shrub *W. floribunda* (*multijuga*) 'Alba' having longer and less
M to T closely flowered racemes than the fragrant Chinese *W. sinensis* 'Alba' and opening rather later. Another Japanese species, *W. venusta*, also sweet-smelling, has exceptionally large flowers packed into dense, short racemes. The chunkier flower pendants probably serve less well for cutting purposes, whereas in the garden all have their separate uses, *W. floribunda* being longer-lasting in flower and more graceful, with its slenderer racemes, for growing over pergolas or through trees, and the others making a better showing on house walls in particular. They may also be trained as free-standing shrubs.

I understand they need a short drink in pure alcoho before following it up with a long 'chaser' of cold water.

Syringa (Lilac)

L-T/T The fairylike species, *Syringa persica*, comes in a white variety not unexpectedly called 'Alba', which has narrow leaves and numerous short, small-flowered panicles meeting on a central flower-stem to form long, arching, foaming fountains of scented bloom—altogether widely differing in make-up from the common run of garden lilacs developed as hybrids of *Syringa vulgaris* (Common Lilac). Of the latter 'Mme Lemoine' is generally acclaimed to be the finest double white, but is rather earlier than the June-flowering 'Souvenir de Alice Harding'. Some good single whites include 'Candeur', 'Maud Notcutt' and 'Vestale'.

Lilac needs to be stripped of its leaves and boiled. Its own foliage may be used, if required, in separate shoots.

Weigela (Sometimes listed as *Diervilla*)

L-T/M The weigelas, though usually thought of as red- or pink-flowered, with even the odd yellow among them, contain some exceptionally beautiful white-flowered kinds which I should love to find room for somewhere. The best include the vigorous 'Bristol Snowflake'; the more compact 'Candida'; 'Mont Blanc', with particularly large, fragrant blooms; and *hortensis* 'Nivea', which also has big, typically foxglove-like flowers of purest white, among pale-backed leaves. All except 'Candida' reach a height of around six feet.

Boil.

Potentilla fruticosa 'Veitchii' (Form of Shrubby Cinquefoil)

L-T/
D to M
The potentillas are very easy to please. *P. fruticosa* 'Veitchii' should succeed anywhere, but its height and compactness will vary from dwarf, when grown in full sun, which it prefers, to rather more than three feet in lush conditions and part shade. It produces long wands of pure white strawberry-flowers over a long period and

although the petals of the potentillas drop fairly quickly there are always so many buds ready to open up on the spray that it makes better cut material than is generally supposed.

Regular pruning is unnecessary, but it is advisable to cut out one or two worn-out stems to ground level occasionally in the autumn, once the plants have reached a fair age.

Pterostyrax hispida

L-T/
Tree
Among the lime-tolerators in my garden at this season I have an interesting little tree, *Pterostyrax hispida*, which is not very commonly seen. It bears fragrant, slender and rather fluffy six-inch flower-panicles of cream-white, followed by showy, spindle-shaped greenish-white seed-vessels. Here it has proved very fast-growing.

Styrax japonica (Form of Snowdrop Tree)

Tree
As a relative of the halesias *Styrax japonica* appropriately shares with them the pseudonym of 'Snowdrop Tree', and it also shares their intolerance of limy soil conditions. It makes a much smaller, very graceful little tree, abundantly decked with dangling, starry snowdrops all along the horizontal boughs when it reaches full flowering size, which it is sometimes rather slow to do. Very young plants establish themselves more quickly than older ones.

It's possible to use these lovely flowering branches for cutting, but they're not very long-lived in water and need careful conditioning, including boiling. The deeper the water they are arranged in the better.

Cornus kousa (Form of Dogwood)

Tree
Cornus kousa is another most desirable little tree for the lime-free garden. This is rather a slow grower, but the mature tree is a wonderful sight when laden with its showy bracts. It colours well in autumn and should also

85

contribute a crop of dimpled fruits like tiny red golf-balls, but on my tree these never come to anything. I have not so far been able to decide whether this is because the birds get them before they mature or whether they need more warmth to ripen them.

The four showy bracts are roughly diamond-shaped, arranged in the form of a cross around the insignificant flower cluster, and are creamy-white when fully open, taking on a pinkish flush before they fall.

Cornus kousa chinensis (Form of Dogwood)

L-T/
Tree
If your soil is unsuitable for *Cornus kousa* you may still grow the Chinese form. *C.k. chinensis* is very similar but although the bracts are larger I think perhaps they lack some of the refinement of the Japanese form.

Mr. Haworth-Booth assures us that to cut, or even unwittingly to graze, a young plant of *C. kousa* results in its certain death. For ten years I have kept my secateurs under restraint: surely my long patience must now be due for its reward.

Magnolia sieboldii (syn. *M. parviflora*)

Tree
The summer-flowering *Magnolia sieboldii* is a little later and a little smaller in stature than *M. wilsonii*, to which it bears a close resemblance in most other respects. The flowers are equally fragrant and very similar in appearance, except that they face sideways rather than downwards. If your soil is alkaline you will have to content yourself with *M. wilsonii*—but if you can also grow the calcifuge *M. sieboldii* you will have a longer succession of bloom. I waited about eight years for my first flower on the latter but since then it has flowered each year with increasing freedom.

Pick in half-open bud stage and boil.

Rhododendron 'Mrs. A. T. de la Mare'

E/T
There are not a great many hardy hybrid rhododen-

drons which can strictly be described as white. One of the loveliest of these is 'Mrs. A. T. de la Mare', with pale pink buds and pure white flowers with a green eye which greatly enhances their attraction. To this may be added particularly good foliage and a sweet scent. Some lists give it a 'B' rating while others quote it as 'C'. Mine has so far made as tough a showing as any, but it seems that it is considered less hardy than the hardiest.

Boil, for safety.

Rhododendron 'Mrs. P. D. Williams'

E/T 'Mrs. P. D. Williams' ('A') has singularly beautiful flowers, which are rather more ivory than white, with a brownish-green blotch, but is not very prolific.

Boil, for safety.

Rhododendron decorum

E/T *Rhododendron decorum* is a lovely species, of 'B' rating, though some forms are said to be hardier than others. The flowers too, are variable, some being of the purest white while others are cream in effect owing to a conspicuous yellow eye. All are reputed to be fragrant. My own plant is, I believe, of a tough constitution, but is only now attaining flowering size, after four years from planting as a layer.

Rhododendron indicum eriocarpum 'Gumpo'

E/D The white form of the evergreen azalea, 'Gumpo', is a delightful dwarf, with large, frilly, green-eyed white flowers, providing an attractive complement to the vivid pink and salmon-orange hues of the other midsummer-flowering varieties. It is so low-growing and compact in habit that I doubt whether it will ever be very useful for cutting.

Daboecia cantabrica 'Alba' (Form of Irish Heath)

E/D *Daboecia cantabrica* 'Alba' is one of the Irish heaths, all of which produce long spikes of bigger flowers than any other heath. I find the large bells of the white form on their slender spikes useful for small arrangements indoors and in the garden the evergreen clumps which remain in flower over a very long period are equally valuable on the edges of the shrub borders.

Early spring is the best time for the annual clipping over which is necessary to prevent legginess and to make for a more concentrated flowering from midsummer onwards.

Zenobia pulverulenta

D to M *Zenobia pulverulenta* comes very near the top of my list of favourite subjects for flower decoration. Too lax and meandering in habit, no doubt, to rank as a first-class garden plant, in detail it is exquisite, fanning out in the most graceful wands of curious, waxy white bells. Their texture is astonishingly resilient, which is, of course, a tremendous asset when transporting cut material about the country. But one must be careful not to snap the rather brittle sprays when doing the partial stripping of the leaves which is necessary for indoor use. This zenobia is surprisingly little known and always scores a *succès fou* in a demonstration. It can, however, only be grown by those with lime-free gardens.

It pays to cut out the flowered wood after flowering.

14

White Flowers and Fruits
(d) Late Summer and Autumn

Eucryphia glutinosa

Tree   To grow *Eucryphia glutinosa* you need not only a lime-free soil but plenty of patience. Slow starter though it is, the ultimate reward is well worth waiting for, when the rather upright, semi-evergreen bush or small tree covers itself with glistening white flowers embellished with a glorious cluster of vivid copper-coloured stamens. The flower is similar in shape to that of a single camellia, only smaller. Unfortunately, the display is fairly soon over, but it is exquisite while it lasts and is followed in late autumn by a fine show of flame and orange-scarlet foliage.

After seven or eight years I tried a position in full sun instead of semi-shade, resolving to throw it out if this didn't produce results. It did, though it would no doubt do even better if it had more moisture at the roots than it gets.

There is also a double form of *E. glutinosa* (often occurring among self-sown seedlings) with rather muddled little flowers in which the beauty of the single variety is entirely lacking; so beware in particular of unflowered seedling gifts from well-intentioned friends and make sure that you get a single-flowered form, than which I know of nothing lovelier, unless it is a really good specimen of *E.* × *intermedia*, which makes a more open-habited small tree of enchanting appearance in a woodland setting.

Eucryphia × *nymansensis*

L-T/
Tree

If your soil prevents you from growing these eucryphias you may care to try the lime-tolerant *E.* × *nymansensis*, which slowly makes a tall, narrow tree of pyramidal form. Although its flowers are very much like those already described I personally find the effect less attractive, because the blooms are too high above one's head for one to look directly into their charming faces. I also believe it is none too hardy.

Magnolia grandiflora 'Goliath', 'Exmouth' and 'Ferruginea'

L-T/E/
Tree

A limy soil is, fortunately, no obstacle to the cultivation of the stately evergreen magnolias, whose enormous, waxy white chalices, set off by the bold and glossy light green leaves, are one of the chief glories of late summer.

I grow only 'Goliath', which is said to be the finest of the *M. grandiflora* varieties as a garden plant. From the point of view of the flower arranger, however, I rather wish that it had been the very similar 'Exmouth', which has the added attraction of a ginger-brown felting, or indumentum, on the underside of the evergreen leaves or, rustiest of all, 'Ferruginea'.

These magnolias flower at quite an early age. They are hardy enough to be grown in the open except in the north, but they make faster progress and flower more freely when grown against a high south wall, so long as the soil is rich and moist. As wall-cover they can do with a fair amount of incidental pruning, such as they will get at the hands of the flower arranger. The truly magnificent foliage lasts for a very long time in water and is one of the best of subjects for preservation by the glycerine treatment.

Romneya trichocalyx (Form of Californian Tree Poppy)

L-T/M

Romneya is another plant whose central works, like those of the eucryphias, make an important contribution

90

to its beauty. It has huge, wide-open, paper-white poppy-flowers with attractively crumpled petals surrounding a fine pompon of yellow stamens.

The romneyas need to be cut back to the base each April. In my own garden they regularly get killed to ground level each winter but, being semi-herbaceous in character, they are none the worse for this and lose no time in throwing up tall shoots clothed with attractively divided grey-green leaves and a profusion of the huge poppies in late summer. Earwigs often burrow into the centre and cause the petals to fall prematurely unless the ground round the plants is liberally dusted in good time with BHC or some other form of deterrent. All the romneyas enjoy the sunniest possible position.

They provide lovely material for flower arrangement but need to be cut when the buds are only half open if they are to last well in water.

Singe.

Escallonia × iveyi

L-T/E/ The white *Escallonia × iveyi* gives me the greatest satis-
M to T faction, both indoors and out. It is less lax in habit than many of the escallonias, bearing rather upright panicles of comparatively large, fragrant white flowers. The flowers are delightful, but even if they were not I believe this escallonia would almost be worth growing for its round, glossy dark green foliage. Reputedly somewhat tender, my own plant has weathered many a hard winter with comparatively little damage and where breakages are caused by the weight of snow it puts forth new growth very freely.

Escallonias are said to require dead-heading after flowering.

Buddleia davidii 'White Bouquet'

L-T/T As a flower arranger I find the long, densely flowered spikes of the buddleias a valuable contrast in form. As garden plants the white buddleias are much less spectacular than some of the vivid modern purple hybrids. I chose 'White Bouquet' because I prefer its faintly cream tinge to the dead white of others such as 'Peace', for instance.

Pruning should wait until April or thereabouts, when the previous year's growth should be cut back almost to its base.

Hydrangea paniculata 'Floribunda' and *H.p.* 'Tardiva'

L-T/T and L-T/ M to T Two of the late-flowering varieties of *Hydrangea paniculata* also help to vary the preponderance of circular flower shapes with their loose, airy panicles of exceptionally graceful form. These are the rather rare *H.p.* 'Floribunda' and the even scarcer and still later-flowering *H.p.* 'Tardiva', both of which bear pure white flower-heads which become tinged with pink before passing into desiccation. They are made up of sterile and fertile florets formed into a loose cone-shape. The former fairly quickly becomes a tall, spreading shrub and although my experience of the latter is limited to comparatively young plants I would say that *H.p.* 'Tardiva' makes less exuberant growth.

All I do by way of pruning the *paniculata* varieties is to remove the dead heads in the spring.

For conditioning instructions see under *H.p.* 'Praecox', page 76.

Hydrangea × *macrophylla* 'Mme Émile Mouillère' and *H. cinerea* 'Sterilis'

L-T/M Of the 'bun-shapes', *Hydrangea* 'Mme Émile Mouillère' is a first-class white with an inconspicuous blue or pink eye, depending on the *p*H value of the soil. The inflorescence passes through a particularly attractive greenish-cream stage before turning to pure white when fully open, later taking on a pink tinge before the drying petals fade to palest green.

Opinions differ about the pruning of the *H.* × *macrophylla* varieties. All I do is to cut out one or two of the oldest stems to ground level in winter and, if some shoots should lose the terminal bud in a hard winter, I shorten these to a pair of flower-buds (recognizable by their fatness) in early spring.

Hydrangea cinerea 'Sterilis' is also bun-shaped, but the flower-head is composed of quantities of much smaller sterile florets than the other and is of a generally greener complexion. Less showy, no doubt, as a garden decorator, it is nevertheless of outstanding beauty as a cut bloom and is much prized by discerning flower arrangers. Prune as above.

All types of hydrangea need careful preparation when used in flower arrangement and I find it worth while to go through all the motions described on page 76, for safety's sake, if more than a very short-stemmed flower-head is required.

Sorbaria arborea

L-T/
M to T

Sorbaria arborea, which used to be included among the shrubby spiraeas, bears huge, drooping plumes of creamy-white flowers in late summer. These graceful, feathery panicles are lovely for cutting, but I don't rate the general effect very highly in the garden.

S. arborea will grow to a lanky fifteen feet or so unless it is cut back to the ground annually in spring; it will then make a much more compact shrub of five feet, with flowers at the tips of the new growth.

Boil.

Deutzia setchuenensis corymbiflora

L-T/M

Until recently I have avoided the deutzias altogether in this garden. This was because I was unfamiliar with the delicate white foam of *Deutzia setchuenensis corymbiflora*. The flat corymbs of innumerable tiny white stars are as dainty as gypsophila and a great deal more interesting. I think these should provide enchanting cutting material when my tiny bush will allow of this. It may take some little time, however, for it is a slow-growing

93

deutzia. It is also none too hardy, though so far it has held its own well enough through two bad winters.

Old flowering wood should be removed in autumn.

I have only tried one tiny piece in water and my impression was that it may not last too well when cut. It may be necessary to do some experimenting as regards conditioning methods.

Yucca flaccida

L-T/E/M *Yucca flaccida* flowers when quite young, throwing up ivory-white flower-spikes on a heroic scale from a rosette of semi-rigid, evergreen blades which have their own decorative merit both in and out of doors. For all its exotic air this yucca seems surprisingly tough in a sunny position and unlike some of its kin, it is not so ultra-tropical in appearance as to look out of place, if rightly sited.

Large-flowered Clematis Hybrids and Clematis Species

L-T/ Climbers As mentioned on page 78, the majority of the large-flowered hybrids listed in late spring and early summer can almost always be relied upon for a second show in late summer or autumn. I have found 'Henryi' (O) and 'Marie Boisselot' ('Mme le Coultre') (O) especially dependable in this respect. As far as I'm aware 'Huldine' is the only white-flowered hybrid to be added in the present context. It has rather smaller than average blooms with a sheen suggestive of mother-of-pearl resulting from a white upper surface backed with a band of lilac-mauve fading paler at the edges of the rounded, rather reflexed sepals. The stamens are pale green.

'Huldine' is the only one of the above which may be hard pruned.

Among the species *Clematis flammula* (ESW) is a vigorous almond-scented white, with small flowers borne in great abundance from August to October.

For general comments on clematis see pages 71-2 and 210-11.

Singe or boil.

Fatsia japonica (Aralia *sieboldii*) (*not* Castor Oil Plant)

L-T/E/   *Fatsia japonica* is one of the most handsome of ever-
M to T   green foliage shrubs, immensely valuable both to the gardener and to the flower arranger. The latter in particular will also be delighted with the large, milky-white flower-heads which may or may not appear in late autumn, depending, I think, on one's garden climate. In formation the globular clusters of little flowers composing the panicles resemble those of the ivy.

For general comments, see Foliage Section, page 258.

Symphoricarpos rivularis 'Constance Spry' (Form of Snowberry)

L-T/M   The superlative variety sold by the Sunningdale Nurseries and named after Mrs. Spry, from whom they originally obtained this opulent-looking, free-berrying form, is so far superior to the old familiar snowberry as to deserve a place somewhere in the shrub garden. Even so, I doubt whether one would wish to give it too prominent a position, since it is undeniably dull to look at at all times of the year except in the autumn when heavily laden with the unusually large, pure white fruits.

Cut out a few old stems to ground level and remove any overcrowded weak ones annually in early spring.

Although the leaves quickly wither in water the berries last for weeks when cut and it therefore seems preferable to strip the foliage entirely. Some defoliation is in any case necessary in order to make the most of the clusters of fat berries in an arrangement.

Pernettya mucronata 'Alba'

E/D to M This is another good white-berried shrub, but this time only for lime-free gardens. If you want a real profusion of berries you must plant a male among your females. Although I find *P.m.* 'Alba' rather less invasive than others all pernettyas form dense, spreading thickets in time and consequently need placing with care. Their height depends largely on whether they grow in sun or shade.

Erica vagans (Cornish Heath)

E/D   Although the *Erica carnea* varieties are included on the grounds that one is happy to gather whatever makings of a tiny posy may be found in flower in winter, generally speaking the other dwarfer types of heath will be found in Appendix II, as valuable verge plants for the borders but not of much use for cutting. However, *Erica vagans* has quite tall, dense plumes of tight-packed flowers. The variety 'Alba' has brown and 'Lyonesse' yellow anthers protruding from each floret. This species thrives in quite heavy soil and will even put up with very slightly limy conditions, which is unusual except among the winter-flowering *carneas*.

Calluna vulgaris 'Searlei Aurea' (Form of Heather)

E/D   *Calluna vulgaris* 'Searlei Aurea' is one of the larger white heathers, which makes a bold, decorative clump with solid spikes of flower, but is chiefly remarkable for its splendid lime-yellow foliage. (See Foliage Section, page 257.)

All these heaths and heathers need clipping over annually in the spring, just before they start into new growth.

Sorbus (Mountain Ash, Rowan) cashmiriana and S. hupehensis

L-T/   Most of us are familiar with the orange, scarlet or
Tree   yellow-berried rowans, but the beautiful white-fruited forms are much more rarely planted. *S. cashmiriana* has exceptionally large, glistening white fruits (half an inch in diameter) which persist well into the winter, after the attractive fern-like foliage is gone; and the white berries of *S. hupehensis*, though only half the size of the fore-going, are delightfully tinged with palest pink, combin-

VIBURNUM plicatum

PAEONIA suffruticosa 'Hira-no-yuki'

ing with fine autumn leaf colour. It's surprising that flower arrangers aren't more generally alive to the merits of these two rowans for autumn and winter decoration.

15

White Flowers
(e) Winter

Erica carnea 'Springwood' (Form of Winter-flowering Heath)

L-T/E/P *Erica carnea* 'Springwood' comes in both a pink and a white form and either is a first-class evergreen carpeter, particularly useful in limy gardens where the summer-flowering types will not succeed. The white 'Springwood' bears long, rather loose spikes of little white bells with protruding brown anthers against a background of unusually vivid, light green foliage and lasts in flower for very many weeks, carrying on well into early spring.

Some clipping back is advisable after flowering, but the very prostrate varieties need less regular attention in this respect than those of more upright habit.

Prunus subhirtella 'Autumnalis' (Winter-flowering Cherry)

L-T/ In cold areas I don't much care for fragile-looking
Tree blooms timed to endure the rigours of winter. But in an average climate one can expect an intermittent display from this cherry, with its clustered, semi-double blooms three-quarters of an inch wide. At best its flowering is spasmodic and at worst it makes a frail ghost in the winter scene, happy only when brought indoors, and playing a timid game of peep-bo in the garden during alternating spells of frost and milder weather. (See also page 172.)

Boil.

16

Cream to Yellow Flowers
(a) Early Spring

I think it depends very much on your bullfinch population as to whether some of the early spring bloomers are worth growing at all. In my own garden the depredations of bullfinches, sparrows and tits at this season drive me to near despair. A cocoon of sewing cotton wound in and out among the bushes has hitherto been the only really effective deterrent I have known, but the tangle is maddening when trying to cut pieces for the house and there is, in any case, a limit to the amount of cotton-winding one can undertake and often it is not practical. More recently I have had considerable success with the repellent spray, Curb.

Forsythia × intermedia 'Spectabilis'

L-T/   Year after year in early winter the ground beneath my
M to T *Forsythia × intermedia* 'Spectabilis' was green with
        flower-bud shucks, discarded by the birds, before any
        really severe cold could have made them want for food.
        Since the shrub has no virtue beyond the generous burst
        of brave Aureolin Yellow (3/1) to which we are entitled
        in early spring it fails to earn its keep when its flowering
        is too sparse to make its mark. I confess that sheer
        weight of numbers tends to make me just a little bored
        with it and mine has gone unlamented.

Forsythia 'Lynwood'

L-T/   If you are more of a forsythia addict than I, you may
M to T want to try the much-boosted newer variety 'Lynwood',
        with larger individual flowers, very freely borne. This is

said to be an improvement on 'Spectabilis'. No doubt the bullfinches and tits find it every bit as delectable as the other.

It is generally recommended that the old flowering wood should be removed after blooming.

Forsythia suspensa

L-T/ M to T One that I much prefer for flower arrangement is *Forsythia suspensa*, with sparser flowers of a much softer sulphur yellow borne on long, drooping wands from which it gets its specific name. Obviously the attributes which commend it to the flower arranger are precisely those that detract from its merits as a garden shrub. To be at all effective in the garden this forsythia must be severely cut back after flowering to within a bud or two of the old wood; otherwise a flowerless tangle results. Since the birds saw to it that mine was flowerless anyway, this one, too, has now been discarded in my garden.

Corylopsis spicata

L-T/T I hope that the moral of what follows will not be lost on any who are prone to the temptation of catalogue-shopping. Although I was familiar with the general appearance of the genus *Corylopsis* I didn't know one variety from another when I selected *Corylopsis spicata* after narrowing the choice down to this or *C. pauciflora*. It is a tall, spreading shrub requiring quite a lot of space, bearing drooping racemes of cowslip-scented Dresden Yellow (64/1) flowers on rather stiffly angled branches. The flower-clusters themselves are attractive enough, but they are rather widely spaced on shoots which are singularly awkward for cutting purposes.

Corylopsis pauciflora

L-T?/M I have since regretted that I picked on *Corylopsis spicata* rather than the more miniature *C. pauciflora*, which is not by any means few-flowered and bears these in graceful, drooping sprays of primrose-yellow emerging from creamy-green bracts. Hilliers state it to be calcifuge, but the R.H.S. *Dictionary of Gardening* makes no mention of this. It does, however, suggest a rather tender constitution.

Mahonia aquifolium (Holly-Leaved Barberry)

L-T/E/ D to M *Mahonia aquifolium* will be dealt with separately as a foliage plant, in which its chief merit lies, but it also deserves a mention among the earliest of the yellow-flowered spring shrubs. The fragrant little yellow bells are carried in dense, upright clusters which are ready to take over just as the long, drooping racemes of the more aristocratic *M. japonica* are finishing their winter show. *M. aquifolium* is particularly unfussy and since it also produces fat bunches of inky-blue fruits in summer in addition to its attractive evergreen foliage it certainly deserves one of those odd corners which are to be found in every garden. (See also page 259.)

Kerria japonica

L-T/M *Kerria japonica* is the single-flowered form of the much less deservedly popular *K.j.* 'Pleniflora', whose coarse, double, orange-yellow balls we all know so well. This can only be an instance of liking what we know, for certainly those who know both are almost unanimous in their preference for the more refined single form, which has bright yellow flowers not unlike those of the potentilla. Although the plant is deciduous the bare, bright green wands fanning out from ground level in dense clusters add a pleasant touch of colour to the winter landscape.

I find both the foliage and the bare stems quite effective as cut material, but have not tried using the flowers indoors, largely because of my personal prejudice against bright yellow for this purpose.

Prunus serrulata 'Gioiko'

L-T/
Tree

When I say that I grow a yellow-flowered cherry this is immediately assumed to be 'Yukon', which is indeed similar but, I think, less attractive. I first discovered 'Gioiko' by a lucky accident and have never encountered it elsewhere since the spring day in 1950 when I wandered by chance through the central display hall of a London store, where large branches of this cherry in bloom were being shown by Messrs. Hillier in a trade display of spring-flowering subjects. Though much less of a fanatic about flower arrangement at that time than I am today I found 'Gioiko' irresistible and placed an order on the spot and I now have a well-established tree. Fat, shiny, copper-coloured buds unfold into clusters of large, semi-single, greenish-sulphur flowers with slightly frilled petals which fade through palest yellow to a pinkish tinge before they fall, and this against the dark, blue-green background of a neighbour's pine trees is an enchanting garden spectacle.

This was one of the first trees to be planted in my garden and so far the birds have only once reduced its whole-hearted flowering to a mean spattering of bloom. Being a half-standard, it branches out only a few feet above ground level and years ago attained a spread of some thirty feet, providing plenty of exquisite material for flower arrangement so long as one cuts judiciously, with due regard to the shape of the tree. (See also pages 60–61.)

Here's a tip you may care to try with any ornamental cherry. A year or two ago my husband had complained that some of the lower branches of 'Gioiko' overhanging the lawn got in his way when mowing, so I tied some of the more pliable side-branches in a backward curve away from the lawn and left them to grow in that way. By the time the perishable raffia tie had rotted these branches had assumed the graceful and naturalistic permanent curves which are so precious to the flower arranger but rarely to be found in the rather stiff growth of an ornamental cherry.

Boil, for safety.

Rhododendron 'Unique'

E/M Of all rhododendrons I think some of the loveliest are those of pale yellow colouring which flower in early spring. For the lucky gardener with a lime-free soil *Rhododendron* 'Unique' can usually be relied upon to coincide in bloom with *Prunus* 'Gioiko', forming a compact bush with flowers of rather similar colouring. The two combine exquisitely when used together in a flower arrangement, particularly when associated with flame-coloured azaleas and maroon parrot tulips. The flower-trusses are peach-pink in bud, opening to a pale yellow edged at first with pink and fading to cream.

I know of no more dependable rhododendron both for freedom of flower and for repeating the process with unfailing regularity from year to year. It is in fact so generous of its flowers that it is possible to cut several trusses from the crowded centre of quite a youngish specimen without their being missed—and two or three of these are enough to add distinction to a really large arrangement.

Being of the 'B' category it does best in part shade, where it quickly develops into a compact bush.

Boiling is advisable, but not essential.

Rhododendron 'Goldsworth Yellow'

E/M *Rhododendron* 'Goldsworth Yellow' is a much less tidy grower than 'Unique', but the flower-trusses are no less lovely, opening from apricot-coloured buds to a clear Primrose Yellow (601/2), rather deeper in colour, that is, than 'Unique'. It flowers, conveniently, somewhat later than the latter and its distinctly straggling habit makes it possible to cut the trusses with long stems, with actual advantage to the plant.

In spite of its 'B' rating I grow 'Goldsworth Yellow' in a fairly sunny position in order to counteract its regrettable tendency to sprawl.

Boil, for safety.

Rhododendron 'Gladys' (sometimes known as 'Letty Edwards')

E/
M to T
This has flowers of palest primrose, flushed with pale apricot-pink on the outside, at about the same time as 'Goldsworth Yellow'. It requires part shade ('B' rating) and, in my experience, takes longer than many to settle down and flower with real freedom—five years in the case of my bush.

Boil, for safety.

Rhododendron campylocarpum elatum ('B')

E/M
The clear yellow, bell-shaped flowers, red-spotted on the inside, form loose trusses opening from reddish-apricot buds among pleasing, spoon-shaped foliage. This is said to be a rapid grower, though I have not found it so.

Boil.

Rhododendron 'Dr. Stocker'

E/T
The exquisite, large, ivory-cream flowers of 'Dr. Stocker' are borne in loose trusses which my fingers itch to cut. Although not considered very hardy ('C' rating), the layer which came to me from more favourable climate and woodland conditions has suffered no damage in a sheltered position here.

Rhododendron ambiguum

E/M
This is a rhododendron for the flower arranger more than for the gardener. When first I saw it two years ago, as a compact, medium-sized, small-leaved shrub, it was massed with neat little flower-trusses of a fascinating pale yellowish-green, or greenish-yellow; but when I returned the following season one single sprig was in fact all that we could find in flower. It has, however, a

reputation for freedom of flower, though it has rightly been described as rather dull-looking when young. Its 'A' rating testifies to its hardiness.

Rhododendron concatenans

E/M This is a very lovely species, ('B'), rarely more than about four feet high, with bell-shaped flowers of an unusual orange-yellow (Yellow Ochre, 07/1) and outstandingly beautiful glaucous foliage. (See also Foliage Section, page 241.)

Boil, for safety.

Rhododendron 'Yellow Hammer'

E/
D to M *Rhododendron* 'Yellow Hammer' has a taller, lankier habit than most of the other alpine varieties. In spite of its 'B' rating it does well in full sun. Its attractive little tubular bells are of a slightly deeper yellow than most (light Sulphur Yellow, 1/3). This is probably the most useful of the dwarfs for the flower arranger, since its naturally lanky character makes it possible to cut pieces of serviceable length from an established specimen, especially when grown in the shade.

Boil, for safety.

Rhododendron chryseum

E/D *Rhododendron chryseum* is a true dwarf of 'A' category hardiness. It makes a neat, low mound of bronze-green foliage studded in early spring with minute pale yellow flowers (Primrose Yellow, 601/2).

Rhododendron hanceanum 'Nanum'

E/D I doubt whether one would ever be able to cut anything except for a very small arrangement either from *R. chryseum* or from the even dwarfer *Rhododendron hanceanum* 'Nanum', which has rather larger flowers of a very pale creamy-yellow with conspicuous brown anthers on a compact little bush. Though rated 'B' it does splendidly in my garden on a rocky bank in full exposure, making a densely rounded cushion no more than a foot high.

Azalea mollis

M to T Some of the early *Azalea mollis* varieties are often in flower before the end of April, including a wide assortment of yellows which are more valuable for cutting than for garden decoration. I have a few unnamed *A. mollis* seedlings from which I cut delightful flowering branches but the later-flowering types of modern deciduous azalea are, however, much superior as garden shrubs.

Boil, for safety.

Cytisus × praecox (Form of Broom)

L-T/M *Cytisus × praecox* is one of the early-flowering brooms of medium size which bears a profusion of small, pale Empire Yellow (603/1) pea-flowers on gracefully arching sprays. It is comparatively cheap to buy, fast-growing and evergreen in appearance. It is unfortunately thought by some to smell of cat.

It needs to be clipped over fairly hard after flowering, even more than once a year in its first few seasons, to encourage compactness. Don't cut into the old wood.

Stachyurus praecox

L-T/T So early is the flowering of *Stachyurus praecox* that it might almost rank as a winter bloomer, being usually in full spate from February to March. Slender tails up to four inches long consist of from twelve to twenty little cowslip-like pale yellow flowers loosely strung along a central pendent stem attached to reddish-purple shoots. The autumn colour in the leaves is good and this singularly attractive and unfussy shrub flowers at a very early age. It readily lends itself to training as a wall plant and my own has made rapid growth, including a surprising number of flower tassels, in its first season against a bleak north-east wall. I first saw this stachyurus used in

Mrs. Spry's establishment at Winkfield and I marvel that anything so delightful and at the same time so exceptionally early should be so little known to the flower-arranging fraternity.

Jasminum primulinum (Primrose Jasmine)

L-T/E?/ Climber In flower from March until late spring this jasmine has unusually large, semi-double flowers measuring up to one and a half inches across. It is more or less evergreen and although commonly recommended only for a warm wall position in specially mild areas, or even for a cool greenhouse, I know of a thriving specimen climbing a sunny wall in a very average garden climate in an inland district of Suffolk. It would probably need some winter protection and it certainly requires a good deal of careful training and tying in. The nickname Primrose Jasmine isn't especially appropriate, since the lovely flowers are in fact coloured vivid yellow.

I haven't tried it for cutting, but expect it would need boiling.

17

Cream to Yellow Flowers
(b) Late Spring

Rosa spinosissima 'Frühlingsgold'

L-T/T   There are one or two splendid shrub roses which flower
in late spring. Perhaps the best known of these is the
Rosa spinosissima hybrid, 'Frühlingsgold', whose tall,
arching branches are laden with large, semi-single,
creamy-yellow flowers centred with more richly coloured
stamens. Like all single or semi-single roses, its petals
drop more quickly in water than those of the more
double types; but so long as it is not required to last
more than a couple of days it is a real beauty for the
flower arranger.

Little or no pruning is required (see under *R.* ×
cantabrigiensis).

Rosa × *cantabrigiensis*

L-T/T   Though comparatively little known, this tall-growing,
graceful species is one of my favourite garden shrubs at
this season, bearing long sprays of single flowers of
about two inches in diameter. The flowers are similar to
those of the more commonly planted *R. hugonis*, except
that they are of a paler yellow.

Once again, this is not very long-lived as cut material,
though new buds continuously open up to maintain a
succession of bloom on the long, graceful wands. It is
refreshingly disease-free and altogether one of the least
troublesome of roses, requiring little or no pruning

beyond the occasional removal of some of the oldest wood at ground level.

Syringa (Lilac)

If I had a lot more room than I have I should probably grow one or two of the familiar white and purple lilacs for cutting purposes, but I am not much enamoured of the *Syringa vulgaris* hybrids as garden shrubs and even as a flower arranger I am not at all conscious of the lack of them.

Canadian Hybrids

L-T/T Much more attractive, to my eye, is the airy tracery of the Canadian hybrids, in which the graceful panicles are made up of countless smaller flowers more loosely arranged than in the more popular heavy-headed types. But because no lilac is much worth looking at for fifty weeks out of fifty-two I grudge them space.

Syringa vulgaris 'Primrose'

L-T/T The one I do grow is *Syringa vulgaris* 'Primrose', the pale yellow newcomer among the *vulgaris* hybrids; and it is still very much on probation with me. Up to now the few flower-panicles it has borne have been of a drab, off-white and were so undersized and poorly furnished that I am still wondering whether I have been sold a pup. I have read, however, that such behaviour is characteristic of this particular variety in its earliest years, so possibly it needs still more time to show itself in its true colours. The cut blooms on display at Chelsea Flower Shows are undeniably attractive to the flower arranger.

Dead heads should be removed from the bushes after flowering and intercrossing branches and thin, muddled twigs cut out at the same time.

With regard to conditioning it is necessary to strip most of the leaves and if it is required to include its own foliage in an arrangement this should be used in separate sprays, otherwise the leaves will deprive the flower-heads of water. Boiling revives lilac if it tends to flop when cut.

Laburnum × vossii

L-T/
Tree
The fact that *Laburnum × vossii* is less densely laden with flower-heads than other varieties seems to me a recommendation rather than a criticism, making it my favourite of its kind. There may be fewer of its drooping Canary Yellow (2) racemes, but they are so exceptionally long that the tree in flower takes on a delicate kind of Japanese grace, particularly when seen, as mine is, against the coppery foliage of *Acer palmatum* 'Atropur-pureum'. At other seasons it is useful in providing support for a clematis and light shade for the group of orange-red, yellow and cream azaleas which are grown alongside to coincide with the laburnum in bloom. Since laburnums, like other leguminous subjects, take no nitrogen from the soil other shrubs can be planted close against them without having to fight for their share of nourishment.

Deciduous Azaleas

'Silver Slipper' (Exbury)

M
'Silver Slipper' is apricot-pink in bud, opening to ex-quisite cream-coloured flower trusses flared with yellow which make a cool-looking contrast to the hot, orange-red *A*. 'Devon' in the group beneath the laburnum. I regard this as one of the most beautiful of all deciduous azaleas.

Boil, for safety.

Rhododendron occidentale

M
Most of this group flower in late spring and include a number with yellow flares on a white ground, giving an overall effect of pale yellow.

110

Azalea 'Daviesii'

M I believe this is now classed among the Ghents. The buds are of pale pinkish-apricot and the opened flowers creamy-yellow flushed with pink and deeper yellow. This is one of the most charming of the old varieties, lovely in flower, sweetly scented and reliable with autumn colour.

  Boil, for safety.

Azalea 'Narcissiflora Plena'

M to T I find the starry, doubled, pale Lemon Yellow (4/2) flowers rather artificial in appearance, though this very fragrant old Ghent variety has undeniable charm. I am glad, however, to have it to cut from, especially as the rather formal flower is a great deal prettier indoors than out.

  Boil, for safety.

Rhododendron luteum

M There are now so many varieties which smell just as good and look so much lovelier than the familiar wild species that I hardly think *Rhododendron luteum* (also known as *Azalea pontica*) deserves a place in the small garden today.

  Boil, for safety.

Potentilla fruticosa 'Katherine Dykes' (Form of Shrubby Cinquefoil)

L-T/M *Potentilla fruticosa* 'Katherine Dykes' is not commonly used by the flower arranger, possibly because the pretty little pale Sulphur Yellow (1/2) strawberry-flowers so quickly shed their petals. However, if care is taken to pick well-budded sprays so as to ensure a succession of flower this cannot fairly be held against it as cut material. The bush throws up such a dense mass of arching stems and twiggy shoots from ground level that plenty of well-shaped pieces are usually to be found for any kind of arrangement. One of the earliest potentillas in flower, it carries on a non-stop show throughout the summer into autumn. The bare, light brown twigs and little round seed-heads of the same hue provide useful line and subdued colour in late season arrangements of foliage and fruits.

Be on your guard about accepting a nurseryman's substitute for 'Katherine Dykes'. His 'nearest' will almost certainly be 'Friedrichsenii' and its flower is just about identical in colour, size and shape; but it seems to be much less free-flowering.

No regular pruning is necessary, but I find it advisable to cut out one or two of the oldest stems occasionally to ground level.

Cytisus (*Sarothamnus*) *scoparius* 'Sulphureus' (Moonlight Broom)

L-T/M   I believe that *Cytisus scoparius* 'Sulphureus' is less tolerant of lime than the brooms described in the Early Spring Section, but that it will do well enough on a very slightly alkaline soil. The flowers are a good deal larger than those of *C.* × *praecox*, but of much the same pale Empire Yellow colouring.

It, too, needs regular cutting back to keep it compact and prolong its life.

Cornus (*Benthamidia*) *nuttallii*

L-T/   Handsomest of all the flowering cornuses, this makes a
Tree   delightful small tree ornamented with up to six-inch-wide, scented 'flowers' formed of cream bracts which flush pinkish with age, surrounding a greenish central pompon into which the minute true flowers are clustered. The flowering is rather earlier than for those described on pages 85-6.

I think this might need boiling.

ENKIANTHUS campanulatus

RHODODENDRON 'Loder's White'

Clematis 'Yellow Queen'

L-T/
Climber
'Yellow Queen', raised by Treasures and also available from Great Dixter Nurseries, is a distinct new colour break among large-flowered hybrids. The pleasing, pale primrose blooms with cream stamens persist well into midsummer. To me it looks just a fraction flimsy, but I've not had occasion to examine it more closely than on the raiser's stand at Chelsea. It needs semi-shade to prevent fading.

For general comments on clematis see pages 71–2 and 210–11.

Singe or boil.

Paeonia suffruticosa 'Hira-no-yuki'

L T/M
And now we come to another of the lovely moutans, or tree peonies, 'Hira-no-yuki', whose flower is to my mind among the very loveliest of all. It is a large, beautifully shaped semi-single of palest cream, with two rows of petals, the outer row being slightly pointed at the tips. (For general comments see pages 72–4.)

Paeonia lutea ludlowii

L-T/M
Paeonia lutea ludlowii is not only a splendid foliage plant clothed with decorative bright green leaves throughout the summer, making a handsome shrub of six feet or so, but it also bears clusters of cup-shaped yellow flowers, smaller than those of the moutans, which open rather in advance of the leaves.

For general comments see pages 72–4.

18

Cream to Yellow Flowers
(c) Midsummer

The shrub gardener becomes more than somewhat dependent on yellows, reds and whites at this time of year, when the colour range available is much less varied than that of the springtime palette. Since some of the yellows are not specially useful for cutting I'll deal briefly with those that may possibly be used, relegating the rest to Appendix II, with the emphatic stipulation that all are indispensable garden shrubs.

Genista cinerea and *G. tenera* (*virgata*)

L-T/T
and
L-T/T

I treasure *Genista cinerea* and the slightly later-flowering and *G. tenera* only for garden decoration, but I have known demonstrators who professed a great admiration for the long sprays of tiny, bright yellow pea-flowers and feathery, greyish-green foliage. Both make almost tree-like shrubs of evergreen appearance which are transformed into a dense cloud of vivid yellow when in flower.

All genistas need trimming over after flowering.

Liriodendron tulipifera (Tulip Tree of N. America)

L-T/
Tree

We all cast envious eyes at the strange yallery-greenery of the somewhat tulip-like flower with the orange markings borne on large trees which appear to have been growing for centuries. But *Liriodendron tulipifera* is in fact surprisingly fast-growing and has the further virtue of fine yellow autumn leaf colour.

A friend who experimented with her cut flowers for me found that those put straight into cold water remained better-looking than those whose stems were boiled.

Potentilla fruticosa 'Vilmoriniana' (Form of Shrubby Cinquefoil)

L-T/
D to M

I think *Potentilla fruticosa* 'Vilmoriniana' may have possibilities for the flower arranger, because the growth is comparatively long and very upright, with attractive, silky-textured, silvery-green leaves. The charming ivory-cream flowers are not, however, produced with quite the abundance that characterizes 'Katherine Dykes' and as a garden shrub this variety is less effective.

Cytisus battandieri (Form of Broom)

L-T/T
or Tree

This July-flowering broom not only does so much later than the majority of its relations but it would in fact scarcely be recognized as one of them by those unfamiliar with its great corn-cob-like heads of pineapple-scented yellow pea-flowers offset by the silky, silvery down covering its three-lobed, laburnum-like leaves. It's hardy enough to be grown as a bush or small tree in the open border in all but the coldest gardens, where it will need the protection of a high, sunny wall, against which it may be trained flat. It benefits from some shortening of the shoots in spring or, if left awhile, it will quickly afford great lengths of fine foliage for flower arrangement; but it should not be cut after midsummer.
Boil.

Tilia (Lime, Linden)

L-T/
Tree

I think the most graceful of any is *Tilia petiolaris*, the Weeping Silver Lime, a large tree with silver-backed leaves; but because it seems to have proved in some way harmful to bees its planting is now frowned upon. We may, however, console ourselves that several other species are much more generously adorned with the small cream flowers borne in clusters protruding beyond a long, pale green bract. Some are also less susceptible than others to the unsightly sooty mould deriving from honeydew secreted by aphids. Among the latter are *T. miqueliana*, equipped with clusters of up to twenty flowers in June, and the July-flowering *T. mongolica*, which may number as many as thirty to a cluster. Both remain manageable-sized trees.

Flower arrangers won't need to be reminded that sprays need to be stripped of their foliage to display the flowers indoors.

Lonicera (Honeysuckle)

Honeysuckles embrace a surprising variety of types, from self-supporting shrubs—some of them winter-flowering—to evergreen foliage plants and summer-flowering climbers. Our present concern is with the latter.

Lonicera etrusca 'Superba'

L-T/
Climber
This Mediterranean honeysuckle isn't one of the hardiest but it has the advantage of being semi-evergreen. Young plants take their time about flowering, eventually bearing clusters of fragrant trumpets opening from cream to deeper yellow.

Lonicera japonica halliana

L-T/E/
Climber
Lonicera japonica halliana is more convincingly evergreen, with exceptionally strong-scented flowers, opening from white to palish yellow—perhaps slightly wishy-washy, but one of the most popular and particularly hardy.

Lonicera × tellmanniana

L/T/
Climber
This is a fine candidate for a heavily shaded site of the kind not usually in great demand in the shrub garden. The scentless flowers are a vivid yellow touched with red

at the tips in bud, and the large, untypical oval leaves are a further asset.

Lonicera tragophylla

L-T/
Climber

As one of the parents of the foregoing, *L. tragophylla* shares certain of its characteristics, including a preference for almost total shade, a lack of scent and a somewhat similar leaf pattern. The bright yellow flowers are as much as three or four inches in length, which puts this honeysuckle among the most spectacular of the yellow-flowered kinds.

All honeysuckles are poor lasters unless they're boiled before giving a *short* soaking or a long, cool drink, removing the stem-tip under water.

Roses

In terms of shrub garden decoration quantities of single or only semi-double roses will usually constitute more effective blocks of colour than the fewer though larger blobs of the many-petalled sorts dotted about on a bush at any one time. But if one's first consideration is a supply of long-lasting blooms for cutting it's advisable to concentrate on fully double varieties, which will remain intact much longer than the singles or semi-doubles, since the latter kinds drop their petals quickly once their very accessible stamens have been pollinated.

Hybrid Teas, Floribundas and Garnettes

L-T/
M

For this reason I think the captivating but not very full-petalled H.T. 'McGredy's Yellow' and the subtly tinted Floribundas 'Chanelle' and 'Ivory Fashion' fall short of cutting requirements, whereas our full-flowered old friend, 'Peace', still ranks high for large arrangements because of its durability as a cut flower. Among the newer, more average-sized, adequately petalled yellow H.T.s 'Peer Gynt' (from Cant or Mattock) rather resembles a smaller, round-faced, deeper hued 'Peace'; 'King's Ransom' is another rich yellow, high-centred

117

and said to be particularly disease-resistant; and 'Grandpa Dickson' opens through greenish-ivory to large, shapely pale yellow blooms. An older favourite of mine, 'Golden Melody', a very lovely large pale yellow of classic form, is described as vigorous and a good doer in cold areas but, alas, neither claim has proved itself in my garden, where it has almost died out.

The best of the newer Floribundas include McGredy's first-class and much planted 'Arthur Bell', a good, large, round-faced bloom of Chrome Yellow (605) which pales with age; LeGrice's 'Goldgleam', which he considers an improvement on his immensely popular 'Allgold', with quantities of larger blooms over a long period and Mattock's moonlit ivory yellow 'Moon Maiden' (pale Mimosa Yellow, with deeper-hued buds).

The little, rosette-type Garnettes, with their multifarious petals and unequalled lasting qualities, are sometimes thought unsuitable for the garden; but despite the fact that they're so extensively grown under glass for the floristry trade they are of course entirely hardy and I find their rather smaller scale most convenient for siting among front-row plants in the shrub borders. These roses now cover quite a wide range of colours, including yellow. Newberry's 'Yellow Garnette', like their white, is less solidly petalled than the original red, but I've found it a good laster, in a pleasing medium yellow.

Climbers

L-T   For the reasons given earlier the popular single yellow 'Mermaid', with its contrasting boss of deeper hued stamens, is much less useful for cutting than a gorgeous, blowsy great bloom such as the old cream-sulphur 'Paul's Lemon Pillar'. But the latter only has one season of flower, whereas the warm yellow 'Casino', opening from elegant, deeper-toned buds, and the soft lemon yellow 'Elegance' (now over thirty years old, but as shapely as the best of recent introductions), which is indeed elegant at every stage, are both reputedly repeat-

118

flowering—though my 'Elegance' has never yet vouch-safed a second flowering in a single season here.

For general comments on roses see pages 79 and 82.

Deciduous Azaleas

There is no need to pay the much higher price commanded by the named varieties if you want an attractive assortment of the deciduous azaleas. Visit the growers when the plants are in flower and select colours from among the unnamed seedlings, have them labelled with your name and with their own flower colour and wait for delivery sometime after leaf fall, when the plants are dormant.

Ghent Azalea 'Nancy Waterer'

M 'Nancy Waterer' (Amber Yellow, 505), makes a pleasing group with *Rhododendron* 'Purple Splendour' and *R.* 'Mrs. T. H. Lowinsky' though I doubt whether I would go out of my way to acquire it today, and yet the flower is sturdy and pleasantly coloured and the bush puts up a very satisfactory performance every year.

Boil, for safety.

'Harvest Moon' (Knap Hill)

M The pale Straw Yellow 'Harvest Moon' seems to me a much more choice azalea. Whenever possible I like to plant a group of three colours to flower simultaneously and in this case 'Harvest Moon' is associated with the dark purple of another *Rhododendron* 'Purple Splendour' (to my mind a great garden decorator) and with the soft orange-pink of an unnamed azalea seedling of the Farall strain personally selected in bloom. I think that a three-colour group is much more interesting than the two-coloured contrast or harmony commonly recommended by garden planners and plantsmen. Violet, pale yellow and flame; pink, purple and lime; scarlet, yellow and white; white, lemon and apricot; light yellow, candy pink and silver: all these, and any number of other permutations and combinations in the shrub border seem to me so much more exciting than just pairing colours.

Boil azaleas, for safety.

Eucalyptus gunnii

L-T/E/
Tree

Eucalyptus gunnii is more usually thought of as a fast-growing, hardy, glaucous evergreen tree (see page 240). It is perhaps not generally known that a mature tree will produce a foam of little creamy flowers at midsummer which would commend themselves to any flower arranger.

Laburnum alpinum

L-T/
Tree

Laburnum alpinum has a rather denser habit than *L.* × *vossii* and is often considered the more desirable on this account and it takes over more or less where the rather earlier *L.* × *vossii* leaves off. For flower arrangement it's less good than *L.* × *vossii* by reason of its very density, which makes for less graceful cutting material.

19

Cream to Yellow Flowers and Fruits
(d) Late Summer and Autumn

Apart from the roses, which have already been dealt with in the previous section, but which will continue to flower until the onset of winter, there are few yellow-flowered subjects of much value for flower arrangement to be added here.

Pyracantha atalantioides 'Aurea' (Form of Firethorn)

L-T/E/T *Pyracantha atalantioides* 'Aurea' has also been mentioned earlier as a white-flowered shrub for midsummer, but it is much more important to me for its yellow berries in the autumn. Growing on a north-east wall, it has quickly shot up to the top of the house, successfully hiding an ugly collection of drainpipes with its evergreen foliage.

In this particular garden this is as far as its value goes as an ornamental shrub as a rule; for although it is laden each year with a most exuberant crop of berries, the birds relish these better than anything else in the garden and strip the plant like lightning the moment the fruits ripen, if not before. Fortunately, I love to use branches of these berries in the yellowish-green stage, when they are still sufficiently unripe to be unpalatable bird fodder and so I am able to cut all I want before the plunder starts. However, in the Arctic winter of 1963, the berries inexplicably remained virtually untouched for the very first time.

For general comments, see page 78.

121

Cotoneaster 'Exburiensis' and *C.* 'Rothschildianus'

L-T/E/T Born of identical parents these two similar cotoneasters differ chiefly in that *C.* 'Rothschildianus' is taller and more spreading than the other. Their fine, large clusters of deep yellow berries are birdproof (locally, as yet) and so last well into the New Year. Both may be grown as open-ground specimens or as wall shrubs.

Coriaria terminalis xanthocarpa and *Viburnum opulus* 'Xanthocarpum'

L-T/D Flower arrangers are mostly familiar with the flattish
and clusters of large, glistening apricot-yellow berries of this
L-T/M viburnum, but fewer seem to have come across the fine sprays of translucent, deep yellow fruits borne by *Coriaria terminalis xanthocarpa*, a Sikkimese shrub with a low-growing, spreading and suckering habit. The bigger, upstanding virburnum is sometimes only sparsely fruited unless several are grown together, as is often advisable, even among the self-sufficient pollinators, for abundance of berry, but the coriaria manages a fine crop single-handed. If so outstanding a plant is so rarely seen it can only be that it's so rarely listed. In about a dozen of the more comprehensive or discriminating shrub catalogues I've only found it in those of Messrs. Hillier, Marchant of Wimborne and Treasure of Tenbury. If ordering, it's important to give the name of this coriaria in full. *Xanthocarpa* means yellow-fruited and distinguishes it from other forms of the same shrub bearing black or red fruits.

Boil the coriaria only if the leaves are left on.

Clematis orientalis (ESW) and *C. tangutica* (ESW)—small flowered species.

L-T/ The first has nodding, deep orange-yellow flowers two
Climbers inches wide, with such thick sepals as to have earned it the nickname of 'Orange Peel Clematis'. In *C. tangutica* the bright yellow sepals are of about the same size, but

are much more incurved, giving a Chinese lantern shape to the flower. Both are decorated with brown stamens and the scented *C. tangutica* has especially fine seed-heads. In my opinion the latter is the more worth while of two fairly similar species.

Singe or boil.

Hypericum patulum 'Hidcote' (Form of Shrubby St. John's Wort)

L-T/E/M The vivid yellow saucers of the hypericums are indispensable at this time of year and *Hypericum patulum* 'Hidcote' is one of the finest. It has large, firm flowers, about two inches across, of bright Buttercup Yellow (5/1), on rather a big bush, may be grown in sun or shade and, unlike H. 'Rowallane', is hardy enough for almost any garden.

The flowers remain larger and the bush neater if cut back fairly hard in the spring.

Hypericum kouytchense (Form of Shrubby St. John's Wort)

L-T/M The older *Hypericum kouytchense* is generally considered inferior to 'Hidcote'. But it has the advantage of gracefully arching sprays of green and copper-coloured seed-heads, which make a most attractive contribution to certain autumn arrangements. It should properly be cut hard back in the spring.

Hypericum × moseranum (Form of Shrubby St. John's Wort)

L-T/D *Hypericum × moseranum* has surprisingly large flowers for such a dwarf plant. They are about the same size as those of 'Hidcote' and are strikingly ornamented with a ring of vivid orange stamens. It is inclined, however, to be a tender variety, but after most winters it will break again in the spring. The dead wood should be cut out as soon as the young growth begins. (I'm assured on the highest authority that the omission of the customary *i* in *moseranum* is correct, though very rarely practised.)

20

Cream to Yellow Flowers
(e) Winter

Hamamelis mollis (Witch Hazel)

Barely
L-T/
Tree
In contrast to most winter-flowering subjects, there is nothing half-hearted or pinched-looking about *Hamamelis mollis*, provided the soil is to its liking. In describing it as barely lime-tolerant I mean to say that although slightly alkaline conditions would not be fatal it is unlikely to give of its best in such circumstances.

From December to February the bare branches are abundantly starred with the quaint, sweet-smelling, spidery flowers (Aureolin Yellow, 3), which emerge unscathed from frost and snow as fresh and gay as paint.

True, *H. mollis* is a dull shrub throughout spring and summer, but in this garden it then works its passage as a host to *Clematis* 'Lasurstern', to provide colour in May and June and sometimes again in September. In autumn the hazel leaves turn to a vivid and uniform Chrome Yellow (605) by way of contrast to the reds of the surrounding cherries and azaleas.

Hamamelis mollis lasts well in water and with its curiously angled habit of growth provides interesting lines for indoor decoration. It is, however, rather slow-growing and the branches rarely seem to make new growth from the point at which they are cut. So use your secateurs with care. My own witch hazel is conveniently placed just a little too close to a path, so my conscience doesn't trouble me when I cut pieces from it to keep it within bounds.

Mahonia japonica (Form of Barberry)

L-T/E/
M to T

There is a rare old muddle in the nursery catalogues over *Mahonia japonica* and *M. bealei*. More often than not the splendid *M. japonica* is listed as *M. bealei*, which is in fact much inferior both in foliage and in flower. Whereas the true *M. japonica* bears immense sculptured whorls of prickly, pinnate evergreen leaves radiating from a central cluster of long, drooping sprays of light Canary Yellow (2/2) lily-of-the-valley flowers, *M. bealei* has shorter and more upright flower-stems which are much less attractive both in and out of doors. When ordering, you need to be explicit.

Much as I value the graceful, fragrant flower-sprays of *M. japonica* throughout the winter months, I rate it even more highly as an evergreen foliage plant. (See page 259.)

The flowers shed their petals rather quickly in water, but are utterly charming in small winter arrangements for the three or four days that they will last. The very tough stem-ends need hammering to enable them to take up water.

Cornus mas (Cornelian Cherry)

L-T/
Tree

No great ornament to the garden for most of the year, *Cornus mas* produces fluffy little primrose-yellow flower-clusters on the naked branches in February and March and these are such fascinating material for flower arrangement that I acquired a plant a year or two ago in defiance of my sworn principles as a gardener.

Commonly known as the Cornelian Cherry by reason of its scarlet fruits, it may be expected to make some further contribution towards its keep in this respect.

Jasminum nudiflorum

L-T/
Climber

The familiar winter jasmine (Aureolin Yellow, 3/1) can easily be squeezed in somewhere in the garden, since it thrusts happily through other shrubs in any soil or

125

aspect. I have one plant at the top and another at the bottom of a five-foot, north-facing, dry wall covered with *Cotoneaster horizontalis*. It will flower right through the winter when weather permits, but any open flowers caught by frost will, of course, be spoiled.

Cut this for the house as freely as you like. And cut the sprays in tight bud if frosty weather threatens so that the flowers may be saved to unfold indoors.

21

Apricot to Salmon-Orange Flowers
(a) Early Spring

If I leave all the fascinating off-beat colourings out of my reckoning and consider only the clean, straightforward hues available to the flower arranger this is far and away my favourite colour group, and one that is at least as effective in the garden as it is indoors.

I received the most generous help and encouragement at the start of my shrub gardening efforts, as well as many more tangible contributions, from an old lady whose tastes ran very much to blue-pinks and magenta-crimsons rather than to orange-pinks and scarlets and I became secretly ashamed of my own natural *penchant* for flame and coral hues. And so I set myself to cultivate a forced liking for a lot of muddy, purplish-pinks, which I have since been busy off-loading over the years with a sense of enormous relief. Self-confidence only comes with knowledge of one's subject and I had so much to learn.

Azalea mollis

M   In early spring the apricot to salmon-orange colouring comes mainly from the azaleas and the chaenomeles. The latter will be available for limy gardens, but for those who have a lime-free soil there is a lovely range of flame hues among the *mollis* azaleas, which are the earliest of the deciduous types. Believing that I get better value from some of the rather later-flowering deciduous azaleas, I grow only a few unnamed *A. mollis* seedlings, chiefly for early bloom for the house.

127

Azalea mollis 'Queen Emma'

M I have, however, one named variety which is among the loveliest of the deciduous azaleas in my garden. This is 'Queen Emma', with large flowers of the soft orange-apricot that charts at Chinese Coral (614)—as exquisite a colour as any I know. It is grouped with the early rhododendrons 'Goldsworth Yellow' and the light violet-coloured 'Susan' and the effect is really delightful. *R*. 'Susan' has what seems to me a totally undeserved reputation as shy-flowering.

Boil, for safety.

Azalea kaempferi

M to T The semi-evergreen species, *Azalea kaempferi*, is very variable in colour, habit and flowering time. The four or five different specimens I have range from one of the palest tints of Porcelain Rose (520/2) to Delft Rose (020/1), which is quite considerably deeper, and some remain dwarf and bushy while others grow tall and open-habited, providing long lengths for cutting.

Boil, for safety.

Evergreen Azalea 'Orange Beauty'

E/D 'Orange Beauty' is one of the most attractive *kaempferi* hybrids. This is a slightly darker shade of Delft Rose (020 as against 020/1) and is my favourite of all the orange-hued evergreen hybrids for colour. It does, however, scorch badly if exposed to hot sunshine. When grown in part shade it becomes looser in habit, and then affords better pieces for cutting.

(See page 62.)

Boil, for safety.

Chaenomeles × *superba* 'Knap Hill Scarlet' (Form of Japonica)

L-T/M So long as the birds leave it alone *Chaenomeles* 'Knap Hill Scarlet' is a splendid garden variety with exceptionally large, single flowers of Mandarin Red (17) and big green quince-fruits in the autumn, but for cutting I prefer some of the dwarfer varieties which carry their blossoms on slenderer stems.

Chaenomeles japonica, C. maulei and *C.* 'Dwarf Poppy Red'

All
L-T/D

Among these are the species, *Chaenomeles japonica* and *C. maulei*, whose smaller flowers are about one hue more orange than those of 'Knap Hill Scarlet', charting at Poppy Red (16/1); and a rather larger-flowered variety which, though named 'Dwarf Poppy Red', works out in fact as light Fire Red (15/1).

Chaenomeles 'Boule de Feu' and others

L-T/
D to M

'Boule de Feu' eventually makes a rather larger bush than the foregoing. The semi-double flowers are Fire Red. Other good hybrids in a similar colour range are 'Aurore' and 'Renée Mossell' ('Fascination'), both of which often flower again in the autumn, 'Elly Mossell', 'Spitfire', 'Brilliant', 'Vermilion' and 'Minerva'.

Chaenomeles 'Cameo' and *C.* 'Yaegaki'

L-T/M

Some of the rare, soft coral hues are beginning to be a little less hard to come by. One of these is 'Cameo', described by Messrs. Jackman as having a beautifully formed double coral flower and of broad and bushy growth. Possibly 'Yaegaki' may be Chinese for cameo, since 'Yaegaki' is also a double coral, available from M. Haworth-Booth, of Farall Nurseries. I've seen neither of these.

Chaenomeles 'Coral Sea' and *C.* 'Chosan'

L-T/M

The single-flowered, less recent 'Coral Sea' has in the past been equally scarce but I had the good luck to be allowed to layer a piece for myself on a plant in a friend's garden years ago and now have a fine specimen of my own. 'Coral Sea' is a single soft coral, at present listed by M. Haworth-Booth and by John Scott of Merriott. Sherrard's Nurseries do 'Chosan', which they

I

describe as 'a lovely spreading shrub with apricot-peach flowers'. Its habit appears to differ from that of 'Coral Sea', though similar in colour.

I have to wind yards of cotton among the branches of the chaenomeles to protect the buds from the ravages of the birds; but this is well worth while.

In the case of the hybrid varieties suckers should be removed from the base and the bushes should be thinned out after flowering and I believe that a greater crop of flowers results from hard spurring back.

All the chaenomeles are good for forcing as cut material, but as might be expected the flowers will then be much paler than normal.

In autumn they produce interesting, quince-like fruits in a variety of sizes, shapes and colourings.

(See also Green Section, Late Summer and Autumn, page 229.)

22

Apricot to Salmon-Orange Flowers
(b) Late Spring

For gardeners on limy soils there is not a great deal of choice in this colour range during May, when azaleas and rhododendrons lead the field for beauty and wealth of choice in more favoured areas, though, of course, the chaenomeles will carry on throughout this period.

Paeonia lutea Hybrids (Tree Peonies)

> Perhaps the only plants of really superlative merit for limy gardens in this colour range are the *Paeonia lutea* hybrids and these are mostly scarce and costly. I have only two of the less expensive of these.

'Mme Louis Henry'

L-T/M One is 'Mme Louis Henry', an indescribable copperish, yellowish-reddish, only slightly double beauty with yellow stamens, which looks like shot silk and seems to be a particularly healthy doer.

'Satin Rouge'

L-T/M The other is 'Satin Rouge', whose flowers are rather similar in colour, but much more double than those of 'Mme Louis Henry'. It was one of the victims of 'Sudden Death' in my garden, but thanks to timely attentions with the slug bait after giving it up for lost I now have quite a large and healthy-looking flowering plant.

> For general comments on tree peonies, see pages 72–4.

131

Rose 'Mme Édouard Herriot' (*Daily Mail* Rose)

L-T/
Climber

Now forty years old or more, the climbing rose 'Mme Édouard Herriot' can still hold her own with most of her new rivals for colour, form, freedom of flower and length of flowering period. I first became aware of the quality of this rose at Sissinghurst Castle, where a whole house-wall of mellow ancient brick was fairly aglow with its large, warm salmon-orange (Begonia, 619) H.T. blooms in late spring. Growing against my warmest house-wall, this is one of the earliest in flower, happily coinciding in bloom with the powder-blue *Ceanothus impressus* which grows alongside and with the pale lemon-yellow climbing rose 'Elegance' beyond. It produces several bursts of flower in a single season and apart from an occasional touch of mildew 'Mme Édouard Herriot' is one of the most disease-free roses in my garden.

For general comments on roses, see pages 79 and 82.

Cytisus 'Lord Lambourne' (Form of Broom)

L-T/M

'Lord Lambourne' is one of those brooms which are said to put up with a small degree of liminess in the soil. It is a mahogany-crimson and pale yellow bicolour, combining pleasingly with a blue ceanothus and the lime-yellow foliage of *Physocarpus opulifolius* 'Luteus'; but on the whole I prefer a uniform flower colour to the confused effect of the bicolours, for cutting and for garden decoration.

Like all brooms, *Cytisus* 'Lord Lambourne' needs regular trimming, particularly in its early years (see page 70).

Enkianthus campanulatus

T

I suppose it must be admitted that as a flowering shrub for garden decoration *Enkianthus campanulatus* is not one of the most effective, though its dainty little clusters of striped coral and cream bells are enchanting at close quarters. The foliage is delightful in springtime, when it makes an airy pattern of delicate apple-green, and in late autumn, when it turns to brilliant flame, yellow, scarlet and bronze. Also the little coral bells are succeeded by clusters of tip-tilted, beadlike, buff seed-pods.

As a flower arranger I love every part of this shrub in every stage—and not least the dainty little seed-heads. When cut, the flowering branches need a good deal of careful defoliation to reveal the pendent flower-clusters.

Rhododendrons

Rhododendron 'Lady Chamberlain'

E/M to T Among the rhododendrons in this colour group the *cinnabarinum* × 'Royal Flush' hybrid, 'Lady Chamberlain', is one of the real aristocrats. The waxy, tubular flowers of light Vermilion (18/1) lined with pale tangerine (Chinese Coral, 614) hang in loose trusses among the markedly glaucous young leaves, making a perfect natural colour harmony. In spite of its 'C' rating and its exotic appearance this exquisite rhododendron has proved remarkably hardy in a sheltered and partly shaded position in my cold garden, which originally proved too inclement for the parent, 'Royal Flush'.

Boil, for safety.

Rhododendron 'Mrs. W. C. Slocock'

E/M   *Rhododendron* 'Mrs. W. C. Slocock' ('B') has, over ten years, been outstandingly generous with its glorious trusses of apricot-pink shading to yellow, despite a reputation to the contrary.

Boil, for safety.

Deciduous Azaleas

Farall Strain

M   In this colour category I have a number of unnamed seedlings of the Farall strain raised by Mr. Haworth-

Booth, which I was able to select from the nurseries when in flower. This strain has produced some first-class azaleas with bold, squarish flowers of strong construction which are much more weather-proof than those of the flimsier *mollis* types. From a wide colour range I was able to choose several attractive hues of coral and flame.

Boil, for safety.

Azalea 'Coccinea Speciosa' (Ghent)

M   'Coccinea Speciosa' is of a startlingly brilliant reddish-orange. In the garden it needs rather careful placing, associating fittingly with some of the cream *occidentalis* types and providing a striking foil to silver and grey foliages.

Boil, for safety.

Evergreen Azaleas

'Princess Juliana' and 'Hollandia'

Both   A lovely range of flame hues is to be found among the
E/D   evergreen azaleas from early spring until well into the summer. Among those that usually bloom a little later than the earliest are 'Princess Juliana' and 'Hollandia', both with rather large flowers of a deep pinkish-orange, similar in colour to 'Orange Beauty'. (See also page 62.)

'Louise' and 'Leo'

Both   A little later still, but flowering before those that belong
E/D to M to the Midsummer Section, are 'Louise' and 'Leo', each of which makes a comparatively tall, loosely branched bush with large flowers of a fine, glistening orange-pink (Delft Rose, 020). Their habit of growth makes it possible to cut some branches at an earlier stage of their life than is feasible with the more compact types.

Boil evergreen azaleas, for safety.

23

Apricot to Salmon-Orange Flowers
(c) Midsummer

Shrub gardeners on limy soils will be largely dependent on roses—and perhaps on lilies—to contribute colour in this range in June and early July. In my acid soil I am able to add to these some fine late-flowering rhododendrons and azaleas.

Rhododendrons

Rhododendron 'Fabia'

E/M   *Rhododendron* 'Fabia' looks so choice that one automatically assumes it to be more difficult than its 'B' rating suggests, but this is not so. It makes a comparatively small, compact bush of about four feet high by five feet wide and bears loosely clustered, drooping bells varying in colour from light Mandarin Red (17/2) to Begonia (619/1).

   Unlike most of the hardy hybrids this woodland type does not readily make fresh growth from the point at which it has been cut; so let the bush grow to a good size before cutting and then ponder well before you take action.

   Boil, for safety.

Rhododendron 'Goldsworth Orange'

E/M   *R.* 'Goldsworth Orange' is another exotic-looking beauty which has a reasonably tough constitution ('B'). Pink in bud, it opens to a genuine, though unusual, pale orange (in effect, Maize Yellow, 607/1). It makes a

135

compact, rather slow-growing, low bush. One can of course cut more freely from this than from 'Fabia', but I'm disappointed to find that this exquisitely hued bloom stands less well in water than the majority of rhododendrons. It must be cut in the opening bud stage to last at all well and needs careful conditioning.

'Goldsworth Orange' *must* be boiled to make it last satisfactorily in water.

Evergreen Azaleas

Rhododendron indicum macranthum, R.i. 'Midsummer' and *R.i.* 'Balsaminaeflorum'

All E/D The flowering season of the dwarf evergreen azaleas is prolonged well into midsummer by *Rhododendron indicum macranthum* and its varieties 'Midsummer' and 'Balsaminaeflorum', all of which are of a more or less uniform light orange-pink. *R.i. macranthum* is a first-class garden plant; at its best 'Midsummer' is equally good, though variable; and 'Balsaminaeflorum', slightly pinker than *R.i. macranthum* (officially charted at Porcelain Rose, 620/1), has unreal-looking, double flowers of charming design suggestive of little gardenias, on a comparatively prostrate bush. These are delightful material for cutting, when the plant can spare them.

Boil, for safety.

Azalea kaempferi 'Daimio' and *A.k.* 'Mikado'

Both M Of the taller-growing *kaempferi* hybrids the semi-evergreen azaleas, 'Mikado' and 'Daimio', are probably more useful to the flower arranger than the *Rhododendron indicum* varieties on account of their more upright, open habit. 'Mikado' is slightly earlier than 'Daimio' and both have flowers of light Vermilion (18/2). In its lighter tints vermilion is happily not the screaming pillar-box red that one might expect from experience with paints.

Boil, for safety.

Ghent Azaleas

'Flamingo'

M   One of the most valuable azaleas is the extra-late Ghent variety, 'Flamingo'. It is rather scarce and correspondingly expensive and I have only just acquired a plant. Too small to cut from as yet, it will one day provide lovely, pale orange-apricot flowers (light Marigold Orange, 11/2) as late as July.

      I would boil, for safety.

'Bouquet de Flore' and 'General Trauff'

Both M Both these are attractive and 'Bouquet de Flore' I think especially so, in a mixture of pink and white and orange-yellow. There are now many other Ghent varieties which are even more useful and attractive.

      Boil, for safety.

Roses

Hybrid Teas, Floribundas and Garnettes

This must surely be the hybridizer's favourite colour range, in which H.T.s and Floribundas in particular keep rolling off the production lines so fast and in such numbers that the choice as to what to grow must, I think, be an individual one. For those who own the R.H.S. Colour Chart at least one grower, LeGrice, makes selection feasible, sight unseen, by carefully matching his colour grouping against the Chart numbers. After a reminder about the provisos mentioned on page 117 governing one's choice of bloom I might add here that one needs also to look for a healthy constitution, steering clear of any specially addicted to black spot, mildew, balling up in wet weather and other crippling tendencies. The most dependable specialist rose catalogues will usually point out the faults as well as the special virtues of individual varieties. (Here again I have LeGrice's admirable catalogue chiefly in mind.) So, without venturing here into the maze of apricots and salmon-orange hues in the precise sense, I propose only to take a look at some of the strangely off-beat brownish hues which, while not fitting very neatly into any of our general colour compartments, belong more nearly in this category than elsewhere.

L-T/M 'Fantan' is, as far as I know, the only H.T. to which this applies, with rather flat, open blooms in a highly subtle combination of coppery-bronze, apricot and brown; and although the buds tend to spoil in prolonged rain the flowers last particularly well in water if weather conditions have been to their liking before cutting. Mine came originally from Gandy, but I can now find it listed only by LeGrice.

There is nowadays quite an assortment of Floribundas in these brownish tints, some of them bred specially for or even at the request of the flower arranging community—sure proof, if proof were needed, of the ever-growing influence of the movement on, and of its benefits from, horticulture in our time. Among these, I believe, is LeGrice's 'Tom Brown', in two tones of brown, said to produce its double flowers in profusion, both singly and in very large clusters. With the flower arranger in mind, the same firm have now introduced a reddish-mahogany Floribunda, starting at Oxblood Red, opening to Erythrite Red and fading to purple-brown. This was specially selected by Mrs. Steward to be named 'Jocelyn' in her honour. To receive the accolade of this most distinguished of flower arrangers and first chairman of the National Association of Flower Arrangement Societies this one really has to be good!

'Brownie' was one of the first ventures into this kind of colouring, as far as I remember at about the same time as 'Café', but for my taste bearing no comparison with the superlative coloration of the latter. Whereas I find 'Brownie' downright ugly, with its ill-accorded hotchpotch of pink, yellow and brown all too clearly demarcated, in 'Café' the colour changes uniformly from the glowing copper of the bud stage, opening through fairly strong coffee colour to an overall *café au lait* when fully expanded, before fading to a faintly mauvish tinge at the last. It is floriferous to the point of embarrassment, causing a heart-rending wastage of bud when cutting one of the huge clusters with a sufficient number of blooms at the right stage of development. But this can't be held against it as a fault—indeed, it makes for a tremendous display in the garden—whereas the weakness of the stalk supporting individual flower-heads is a genuine flaw in its make-up, but even this can be overcome by discreet wiring of individual heads when used for cutting. It also becomes a useless mess in prolonged spells of wet weather. It did, I believe, go out of production for a time, before a sufficiently large number of admirers came to know of it and clamour for it. My own plants came from McGredy and from the Dundee firm of Croll years ago, but among the few current rose catalogues in my possession I find both 'Café' and 'Brownie' listed ('stock limited') by LeGrice. Several 'Café' owners have also assured me that it may be had from Gandy, but I have my doubts.

'Amberlight', bred by LeGrice, and much less widely known, is one which I got originally more for cutting purposes than as a garden decorator, but this beautifully shaded rose has really a somewhat inadequate number of petals to last as well as one might hope as a cut bloom, except in its exquisite opening bud stage. However, the warm copper-bronze buds expand to a rather yellower, light brownish-apricot (the Egyptian Buff of the old Chart) than the rest, providing unique colour and lighting up well in the shrub borders. It's very free-flowering and rather dwarfer than average.

Finally among the Floribundas in this colour range, but getting still further away from the true browns are two more LeGrice introductions, 'Vesper', which has much more soft orange-apricot in its complexion, with only the slightest overtone of brown, and 'Artistic', described by the raisers as 'golden brown fading salmon scented flowers on strong, wiry stems', but to my eye the hint of brown is less apparent here than in any of the foregoing. Both make a vivid splash of very lovely colour in the garden and, as in the case of 'Amberlight', are still within the right colour range to combine harmoniously with the browner-toned roses for floral decoration.

If I may seem to have given disproportionate space to roses of tanned complexion it is that I know of no discriminating flower arranger who isn't besotted about them, though without always knowing where to find them. As mentioned on page 139 I've named suppliers only from the limited number of up-to-date lists in my possession (1971–2); but it must be evident that Messrs. E. B. LeGrice, of N. Walsham, Norfolk, are more directly in sympathy with the flower arranger's needs than most, and I should guess that Messrs. Gandy, of N. Kilworth, Rugby, are probably the next best bet for the unusual, provided we lose no time in creating a demand for it. It's certainly in our own interests to search out any off-beat hues of special interest to us just as fast as we can, because rose growers generally can't afford to wait too long for the public demand necessary to make a stock of any one item worth their while, so that some valuable find may well turn out to have been 'discontinued' by the time we get to know of it and start asking for it.

L-T/
D to M As for the Garnettes, it may not be generally known that these now also include one or two apricot or salmon-orange hues. LeGrice lists 'Garnet Apricot' ('yellow shaded pink'), though he's not in favour of what he calls Garnet Roses for garden use; and 'Sonora' (apricot) and 'Zorina' (salmon-orange) are both stocked by Newberry, who say these are among the American introductions which differ somewhat from the true Garnette both in shape and in the slightly larger flower. These two looked to me more like miniature H.T.s, both delightfully coloured, and the white and yellow sample blooms deriving from the same American group and

obligingly sent to me by Messrs. Newberry were sufficiently similar to the prototype to make excellent little full-petalled blooms for cutting. The samples survived a postal journey in a rather squashed parcel and perked up sufficiently, after boiling, to last several days in indoor arrangements in full bloom. I thought them good enough to order some plants for myself.

Climbers

L-T Among repeat-flowering climbing roses the orange-salmon H.T.-shaped 'Schoolgirl' is I think more deservedly popular than any. She is lovely to look at, of graceful form, thoroughly well-behaved and fully earns her excellent reports. In quite a long list of recurrent flowering climbers Cants of Colchester include several unknown to me and Gandy, Mattock and others indicate repeaters, which now come in almost all colours, in their general lists of climbing roses.

Hybrid Musk

L-T/M My favourite Hybrid Musk in this section is 'Buff Beauty', with fully double two- to three-inch blooms of good shape and delicious fragrance, borne in large sprays. The colour is that of tawny apricots and cream, staged against a fitting background of purplish-bronze-tinted leaves.

For general comments on roses see pages 79, 82 and 117.

Buddleia globosa (Chilean Orange Ball Tree)

L-T/T This buddleia is perhaps too ubiquitous to win much esteem from the connoisseur. Vulgar it may be, but its colour is useful to me for indoor decoration and its vivid yellow-orange ball-shaped clusters up to eight inches long light up a shrub border so well in early summer, when the majority of the *davidii* hybrids are as yet unconscious of their responsibilities for late summer colour, that I've recently added one to my own garden, in which it won't be despised as a poor relation. Its flower pattern bears no resemblance to the familiar elongated wedge shape which most of us associate with the name, buddleia, this one having a much closer affinity with the ball-flowered clusters of the buff-hued later summer hybrid, *B.* × *weyerana*, of which it's one of the parents. *Buddleia globosa* is semi-evergreen, with agreeable grey-green foliage to consort with its orange flowers, and it's a very rapid grower, making a tall shrub within two years of planting. It may be kept smaller by cutting the flowered shoots hard back almost to their base after flowering in mild localities otherwise shorten them only slightly.

Boil.

Lonicera (Honeysuckle)

There are times when a flower arranger entrusted with an arrangement say in flame or in crimson to fit in with its surroundings for some great occasion may be dismayed by a total inability to track down any flowers of the prescribed colour. But the experienced will lose no sleep over the dilemma, being well aware that much the same effect may be arrived at by combining a soft-toned yellow with an over-emphatic orange-red in the one case, or deep scarlet with purple in the other, much as one uses paints, without necessarily mixing them very thoroughly, to arrive at the compromise hue. The same principle must be applied here in classifying the climbing honeysuckles as regards colour, since they are almost invariably parti-coloured and therefore need to be assessed on their overall effect when viewed from a short distance.

L-T/ some E/ Climbers According to my reckoning, the following qualify for inclusion in this colour section: *Lonicera* × *brownii* 'Fuchsoides', which amounts to deep coral, is semi-evergreen and flowers from spring to August. *L. giraldii*, in a combination of purplish-red and cream-yellow, is extraordinarily hairy all over, both on the evergreen leaves and on the outside of the flowers, which open during June and July. *L.* × *heckrottii* is a deciduous

142

honeysuckle, flowering with great freedom from June to September. It is immensely fragrant and the combination of orange-yellow and pinkish crimson is vivid in effect. *L. periclymenum* 'Belgica' (Early Dutch Honeysuckle) has a cream-yellow base flushed with deep pinkish-flame to crimson. This is another fragrant one, flowering from spring through June, when it may be followed by *L. periclymenum* 'Serotina', which will take over more or less where the other left off, carrying on right into the autumn. The colour is deeper than that of the earlier 'Belgica'.

For conditioning see page 117.

Phormium tenax (New Zealand Flax)

L-T/E/T *Phormium tenax* is grown chiefly for its arresting sword-shaped foliage, but it is also a striking plant in flower, with immensely tall, stiff panicles of deep mahogany-orange flowers at midsummer. These bold spikes may successfully be dried in the seed-head stage.

(See also Foliage Section, pages 236, 250 and 258.)

24

Apricot to Salmon-Orange Flowers and Fruits
(d) Late Summer and Autumn

Polyantha Pompon Roses

'Coral Cluster', 'Paul Crampel', 'Conchita', 'Little Dorrit', 'Orange King', 'Gloria Mundi'

All
L-T/D   From July onwards the Polyantha Pompon roses are a most valuable stand-by, both for the gardener and for the flower arranger, opening to take up the display just as the earlier types are pausing to gather energy for a second burst of flower later on. And they come in a number of most attractive colours. Since my own taste runs to salmon and coral hues those I grow range mainly from the lightest Azalea Pink (618/2–3) of 'Coral Cluster' at the pale end to the vivid orange-scarlet (Orient Red, 819) of 'Paul Crampel' at the other. In between come 'Conchita' and 'Little Dorrit' in light tints of Porcelain Rose (620/1–2); 'Orange King', with extra-small, tight button-blooms in various tints of Azalea Pink (618); and 'Gloria Mundi', whose Delft Rose (020) flowers are oddly streaked with a hint of purple.

'Golden Salmon Supérieure'

L-T/M   I have not included 'Golden Salmon Supérieure' in the above group, all of which are well below three feet in height, because I find this a much more vigorous grower, attaining not less than four feet. The orange-pink colour is one of the best, charting at one of the lighter tints of Scarlet (19/1).

LEUCOTHOE fontanesiana and *HEBE pinguifolia* 'Pagei'

MAGNOLIA wilsonii

All make excellent shrubs and as cut flowers the contrasting miniature-flowered sprays are most welcome in association with the large, circular shapes of most other types of rose. They do seem, however, particularly prone to mildew, both in wet weather and in dry. Unless this is either prevented by timely spraying, or at least checked, the flowers are useless.

For general comments on roses, see pages 79 and 82.

Campsis × *tagliabuana* 'Mme Galen' (American Trumpet Vine)

L-T/
Climber The climbing *Campsis* 'Mme Galen' has truly gorgeous trumpet-flowers of deep orange-flame with a backing of fine chamois leather, but it needs a really warm wall and mild weather. My plant now regularly develops flower-buds, but these have either formed so late in the season that they fail to open before the onset of winter or have dropped unopened in more propitious circumstances because I carelessly allowed the roots to dry out.

No flower arranger who has once set eyes on its elongated, fleshy trumpets of glowing coppery-orange backed with buff can wait to grow her own.

When at length it has covered the required wall-space this campsis should be spurred back like a vine to induce freedom of flower. Don't be alarmed by a certain amount of die-back at the tips of the shoots in winter. This is to be expected in the best regulated gardens.

Fuchsia 'Mrs. Rundle' and *F.* 'Coachman'

L-T/P Two of my most engaging fuchsias come into this
and colour category. The trailing 'Mrs. Rundle' is carmine
L-T/D and orange and the more upright dwarf variety, 'Coachman', is of a similar orange-salmon in effect. Although neither is listed among the hardy garden varieties both have survived many years in this cold garden with no more protection than a shovelful of weathered ashes above their roots in winter, or the natural blanket afforded by a nearby evergreen carpeter. They die down to ground level in winter, but they have never failed to

K 145

reappear in late spring, when the newly emerging shoots should be carefully protected from slugs. The dead wood should be removed in spring.

I boil the stems and strip them of most of their leaves.

Buddleia × *weyerana* 'Golden Glow'

L-T/T   In *Buddleia* × *weyerana* 'Golden Glow' the florets come in rather globular clusters along the spike and are a curious combination of pale orange and cream with a hint of mauve, amounting to a soft creamy-buff. The shrub is not very effective in the garden, but the cut flower is subtle in colour and useful in shape. It is an admirable companion to the Floribunda rose, 'Café'.

For general comments on buddleias, see page 92.

Malus 'John Downie' (Form of Flowering Crab)

L-T/   Whereas many varieties of crab are planted for their
Tree   delightful spring blossom, others are even more decorative in autumn when loaded with their gaily coloured fruits. 'John Downie' is perhaps more spectacular than any, with rather large, oval crab apples combining bright yellow with scarlet and flame.

Phygelius capensis

L-T/E/   *Phygelius capensis* requires a sunny position if it is to
D to M produce the elegant wands of tubular orange-scarlet flowers which widen at the tip of the tube to reveal a yellow mouth. Like the fuchsias it may die down in winter but is rarely killed outright. When grown in the open it remains at about three feet, but it makes quite a tall wall plant.

The long-stemmed, airy panicles may be used with charming effect in both large and small arrangements.

Berberis wilsoniae (Form of Barberry)

L-T/D   The closely clustered, translucent coral berries of *Berberis wilsoniae* are favourite flower arrangement material with most of us. In particular I love to use the sprays when they are wreathed in half-ripe fruits of ghostly alabaster hues. It takes courage to handle it at all, for it is armed with murderous spines. It is almost essential to strip most of the leaves when using the berried sprays indoors.

Zauschneria microphylla (Californian Fuchsia)

L-T/D   In my garden *Zauschneria microphylla* dies down to the ground in winter, but it never fails to reappear. It is a pretty, spreading little sub-shrub with grey-green leaves and spikes of small, tubular flowers of a beautiful flame colour. It flowers rather late in the autumn here, forming an attractive group with the white-flowered *Erica vagans* 'Lyonesse' and the dark violet *Hebe* 'Autumn Glory'.

25

Apricot to Salmon-Orange Fruits
(e) Winter

Pyracantha atalantioides (syn. *P. gibbsii*) (Firethorn)

L-T/E/T
or
Climber
The orange-red berries of *Pyracantha atalantioides* ripen much later than those of the yellow-berried form and there are usually plenty left by the birds in late December, when they make a change from holly berries in Christmas arrangements and will take the place of the latter when these are scarce. But the birds won't leave them alone indefinitely. One Christmas I used the orange-berried clusters in a door-knocker decoration and every one of the berries had been stripped by Twelfth Night!

For flowers and general comments, see page 78.

Hippophae rhamnoides (Sea Buckthorn)

L-T/T
A group of these large, silver-grey, willow-leaved shrubs will reward the grower with quantities of yellow-orange berries borne on the female plants from September to February. (One lusty male is adequate among eight females.) This is a specially suitable choice for seaside or other windswept gardens and also for bird-plagued areas, the fruits being so sour that birds are reputed never to touch them, allowing one to enjoy this unusually long-lived display right through the winter.

26

Pink Flowers
(a) Early Spring

Camellia × *williamsii* 'J. C. Williams' and 'Donation'

E/T   Having learnt to regard the reds as the most satisfactory garden decorators (because the flowers withstand weather damage better than the pale pinks and whites) it is only comparatively recently that I have added any pink ones to the garden. I had hankered after *C.* × *williamsii* 'J. C. Williams' for many years before I finally fell for its exquisite single Rose Pink (427) blooms with the central cluster of yellow stamens, which so greatly enhances the charm of the single or semi-single types. The more recent 'Donation', a deeper pink and more double, is considered one of the best of all *williamsii* hybrids. These are every bit as hardy as the *C. japonica* varieties, are in fact remarkably weatherproof in flower despite their delicate hue and bloom with abandon over a long period on reaching a reasonable size, which they do comparatively quickly.

Camellia japonica Varieties:

'Magnoliaeflora'

E/T   I find the semi-double, pale blush-pink blooms of *Camellia* 'Magnoliaeflora' irresistible. It is officially charted as the lightest tint of Dawn Pink (523/3) but the colour is in fact somewhat variable. I have seen plants with flowers so pale as to be almost white, thus losing much of their appeal. I was careful to ask for a good

149

pink colour when ordering mine and have not been disappointed. I have done the best I can to avoid weather damage by planting it, together with my one white variety, against the north-west wall of the house. I should feel still happier if I were able to give them some overhead protection to ward off the buffeting of wind and rain.

'Furoan' and 'Hanafuki'

E/M to T 'Furoan' and 'Hanafuki' are considered to be two of the finest pink *Camellia japonica* hybrids. 'Furoan' is an apple blossom pink, somewhat flatly cupped single with an immense decorative boss of yellow stamens and 'Hanafuki' a deeper pink, attractively cup-shaped semi-double. 'Hanafuki' is described as of medium growth, which possibly means that it will not exceed eight feet.

For general comments on camellias, see pages 57–8.

Ribes sanguineum (Flowering Currant)

L-T/T As a gardener I grudge this plant standing room and yet this despised currant is a real asset to the flower arranger when the flower-tassels are subdued to blush-pink or white by forcing for indoor use, instead of being left to open to a harsh crimson-pink in the garden. Unfortunately, it has a tendency to smell of cats.

Pale Pink Form

L-T/T I have a second very much paler pink form (probably *R. sanguineum* 'Carneum'), grown from nameless cuttings. This makes delightful cutting material in its natural state, but is not of special distinction as a garden shrub.

Prunus cerasifera 'Nigra'

L-T/ Tree In the last few years I have become convinced that the purplish-brown foliage of *Prunus cerasifera* 'Nigra' is worse than useless as cut material, but when I first planted the garden I had a fond idea that it was indispensable for flower arrangement. Leafy branches of this prunus never fail to appear in competition niches and equally surely they never fail to lose marks for the exhibitor. Flower arrangers who want this purplish-brown colouring will be much safer with the more caterpillar-proof purple-leaved forms of *Cotinus coggygria*, *Berberis thunbergii* or *Acer palmatum*, provided these are properly conditioned. In many gardens the birds strip the tree almost bare of flowers.

Prunus × *blireiana*

L-T/
Tree

Prunus × *blireiana*, with foliage of rather similar colouring which is equally popular with caterpillars, has delightfully frivolous-looking bright candy-pink rosettes which I am really sorry to forgo. But the birds left me no choice and since a large, flowerless mass of nibbled purple-brown foliage was not worth its keep it was thrown out. However, for anyone not troubled with bullfinches the gay little double pompon flowers are well worth having.

Prunus serrulata spontanea (or *P. mutabilis*)

L-T/
Tree

This cherry fairly quickly makes quite a large tree, laden with pink-budded blossom which opens to comparatively small white flowers in spite of the birds. The coppery young foliage, which is typical of so many of the most attractive Japanese cherries, turns to green throughout the summer, ending in a blaze of flame, scarlet and crimson in the fall. Branches cut in bud have a delicate grace as material for flower arrangement, but the little flowers shed their petals rather quickly once they are fully open.

For general comments on prunus, see page 61.

Chaenomeles 'Moerloosii' and 'Pink Lady' (Japonicas)

L-T/T
and M

Two of the few chaenomeles to qualify for this colour section are 'Moerloosii', pink-cheeked like apple blossom on the outside and white within, and the smaller-flowered, more compact 'Pink Lady', both of which show up to better advantage than the more orange-reds against red brick.

When grown as a wall-shrub the side shoots need to be spurred back and cotton is necessary to keep the bullfinches at bay.

For general comments on chaenomeles, see page 130.

Evergreen Azaleas

The timing of the spring-flowering evergreen azaleas varies somewhat from year to year. Consequently most of those listed here are more or less interchangeable with those in the Late Spring Section. 'Kirin' and 'Myacino' are particularly early-flowering exceptions.

'Kirin'

E/D   'Kirin' has pretty little hose-in-hose flowers of light Neyron Rose (623/1). It seems to be less hardy than many so I grow it at the foot of one of the house-walls.

'Myacino'

E/D   'Myacino' charts at a light Rose Madder (23/2), which is a clear pink with some blue in its make-up. It makes a pleasing and timely foil to the dwarf violet-flowered *Rhododendron* 'Bluebird', of equally early-flowering habit.

'Hinomayo' and 'Esmeralda'

Both   'Hinomayo' and 'Esmeralda' are both light Phlox Pink
E/D   (625/2) and somewhat similar in appearance, but 'Hino-mayo' flowers more freely and for the longer period. It makes a dense, low bush closely packed with flowers. In part shade it develops a looser habit and will conveniently throw out a long arm here and there which can be cut without detriment to the plant.

'Kurume Pink', 'Takasago' and 'Azuma Kagami'

All Other good pink varieties in my garden are:

E/D   'Kurume Pink', which I chart at Empire Rose (0621)
—the same colour as *Cornus florida rubra*;

'Takasago', in which the colour of the flower is paler
at the centre and deeper at the edges, amounting to light
Carmine (21/1) in effect, with particularly good foliage;
and

'Azuma Kagami', with medium-sized hose-in-hose
flowers varying from deepish to pale Carmine Rose,
almost white at the centre. Reputed to be somewhat
tender in the early stages, it seems at least fairly hardy
when established in a planting of mutually protective
evergreen shrubs, This variety is often wrongly listed as
'Apple Blossom', a wishy washy single pink.

I boil all evergreen azaleas, for safety; though they
frequently last well in water without.

Rhododendron vaseyi

T   In a good form this can be a very lovely thing indeed,
with beautifully shaped, rather waxy, soft pink flowers
and brilliant autumn leaf colour. One needs to select
one's plant in flower to avoid possible disappointment.

Rhododendron 'Racil'

E/D   *Rhododendron* 'Racil' is a charming, early-flowering
dwarf variety of commendable toughness ('A'), whose
flowers are blush with a deeper pink edge, with buds of
a still deeper hue.

Rhododendron williamsianum

E/D   *Rhododendron williamsianum* ('B') is a really choice
dwarf with rather large flowers of the pendent bell shape
in a lovely tender pink. The colour charts at the lightest
tint of Phlox Pink (625/3) in the fully open flower, with
more richly coloured buds. It makes a ground-hugging
mound, slowly spreading to a width of four or five feet.

The foliage is finely rounded and not the least of its quiet charm lies in the coppery tinge of the young leaf growth. When I tested a sample of the latter for its lasting qualities as cut material I was happy to find that after boiling it remained fresh for a long time in water, but this dwarf rhododendron is slow-growing and is a plant for the patient gardener.

Rhododendron caucasicum 'Pictum'

E/M   *Rhododendron caucasicum* 'Pictum' ('A') is a very much more robust character. It is extremely hardy, revelling in a position in full exposure, where it will make a dense, rather low-growing, floriferous bush, with flowers of a cheerful, clean light pink spotted with red. Though the colour is in the same Phlox Pink range as *R. williamsianum* the effect is much richer in the open truss because of the dark red spotting on the upper lobe of the flower. This is a splendid plant for the flower arranger and is doubly welcome as being one of the first of the hardy, large-flowered types to bloom.

Boil, for safety.

27

Pink Flowers
(b) Late Spring

Evergreen Azaleas

E/D   The evergreen azaleas which follow are, as a rule, rather later in flower in my garden than those already described. All are comparatively large-flowered types and, with the possible exception of 'Gerda' (of which I am not very fond), there is little to choose between them for beauty.

> 'Psyche': Rhodamine Pink (527/1), one of the best;
> 'Kathleen': becoming, after a year or two, one of the most effective vivid pinks (light Tyrian Rose, 24/1–2);
> 'Betty' and 'Jeanette': both light Rose Madder (23/2);
> 'Gerda': deep magenta-pink (light Solferino Purple, 26/2);
> 'Willy': clean Phlox Pink (625/1);
> 'Vuyk's Rosy Red': China Rose (024/1)—a good colour, but of questionable hardiness; and
> 'Marie': with most effective cerise-pink hose-in-hose flowers (Rose Madder, 23/1), which has so far turned out tougher than its reputation.

Last, chronologically, in the succession of spring-flowering varieties comes 'Naomi', whose flowering coincides with that of the orange-pink evergreen azaleas 'Leo' and 'Louise'. The overall effect of this variety is light Porcelain Rose (620/1–2). It is a particularly good one for cutting.

Boil all these, for safety.

Ghent Azalea 'Fanny'

M   I have only two pink azaleas of the deciduous types, the Ghent variety, 'Fanny', which usually flowers in late spring and the *occidentalis* hybrid, 'Irene Koster', which will be found in the Midsummer Section.

'Fanny' is not of my own choosing, being one of those left to the nurseryman to select in the early days, and she isn't one of my favourites. However, I admit that she has much to commend her as an effective garden shrub, including good autumn leaf colour. To my mind there is an unfortunate hint of magenta in the vivid pink of the unfolding truss, but the touch of orange in the fully-open flower redeems this, giving an effect of Carmine Rose (621/1). 'Fanny' helps to make a pleasing colour group with the vivid lime-green foliage of *Acer japonicum* 'Aureum', the deep powder-blue of *Ceanothus impressus* and the rather unattractive light crimson of *Rhododendron* 'Cynthia'.

Boil, for safety.

Deutzia 'Rosealind'

L-T/M   Though I have one on order I am as yet unfamiliar with the recently introduced *Deutzia* 'Rosealind', but I have the assurance of a renowned plantsman that to leave this out would be unforgiveable and I take his word for its outstanding merit with confidence. So look out for this May-flowering variety, which is said to have the graceful habit of *D.* × *elegantissima*, but in a deep carmine-rose hue quite new to this genus.

Hardy Hybrid Rhododendrons

'Pink Pearl'

E/T   *Rhododendron* 'Pink Pearl' (Fuchsine Pink, 627 to 627/3) is one of the most ubiquitous of hardy hybrids and although its hardiness ('B') is sometimes disputed I have found it above reproach in this respect. I might not perhaps have bought this one, but an offer of some free layers appealed to the Scot in me and I do indeed feel some admiration for 'Pink Pearl' and much prefer it to 'Betty Wormald', which I think over-large and loud.

'Mrs. William Watson'

E/T   'Mrs. William Watson' ('A') is an old variety not often to be found in modern catalogues. The charming, chintzy, blush-white flowers heavily spotted with crimson can usually be relied upon to partner the scarlet 'Britannia', which also flowers in May, and a very fresh and cheerful combination it is.

'Sir John Ramsden'

E/T   *Rhododendron* 'Sir John Ramsden' ('B') has so far proved slow-growing and slow to produce its first crop of flowers. These are exceptionally fine and of a rather striped orange-pink. The colour ranges from the darkest to the lightest Neyron Rose (623) made warmer by a brownish flare.

Cornus florida rubra (Form of Dogwood)

Tree   *Cornus florida rubra* provides generous branches of enchanting pink butterflies for the flower arranger whenever the preceding summer has been warm enough to form the next season's flower-buds. My own tree rarely disappoints me now that it has grown to flowering size and at least as cutting material I feel that some of its airy, fly-away grace would be lost if the cloud of pink wings were too closely crowded on the branch as in its native America. It is a fast grower of attractive habit and the lowest of the sweeping branches will readily layer themselves. I would say that the officially charted Empire Rose (0621) is fairly representative and its autumn foliage brings a smoky, pinkish-plum colour only occasionally shot with flame to vary the ubiquitous scarlet, orange, yellow and bronze of the dying year. When this is grown successfully I rate it an altogether first-class plant. The branches break rather easily, usually splitting at a fork (both as a result of summer storms and winter snows) but if these are promptly and firmly bound into position and supported they knit together again as a rule.

Boil.

Vaccinium corymbosum (Form of Blueberry)

M   A visit to the gardens of Sheffield Park in May first suggested to me the possible virtues of *Vaccinium corymbosum* as a shrub for flower arrangement. The flowers are not showy, but the little pitcher-shaped pale creamy-pink bells seemed to me to promise most attractive sprays for cutting. These are followed by the blue berries, from which it gets its common name, accompanied by a brilliant show of autumn foliage. If good flower colour is wanted, it is best to plant in a sunny position.

Ornamental Cherries

Prunus 'Amanogawa' (Maypole Cherry)

L-T/ Tree   For those with very limited space who would still like to find room for a pink cherry, nothing could fit the bill better than the fastigiate *Prunus* 'Amanogawa', which shoots straight upwards like an exclamation mark, with pretty, semi-double, fragrant pale pink flowers.

Prunus 'Pink Perfection'

L-T/ Tree   For a tree of more normal, spreading habit the double-flowered *P.* 'Pink Perfection' is one of the most decorative and the vivid pink pompons are pretty for cutting.

Prunus 'Kanzan' (or 'Sekiyama')

L-T/ Tree   I wish that the inevitable *P.* 'Kanzan' might somehow have eluded me at the start. This is one of the oldest and biggest trees in the garden today and should by now be a source of real delight—instead of which I am sick of the sight of 'Kanzan'.

As a gardener I think this cherry an unmitigated bore and yet, in spite of the unkind things I have said about it I must admit that the large, rather magenta-pink, double blossoms (Rhodamine Pink, 527/1) are particularly decorative indoors if great branches can be cut for a large arrangement.

For general comments on cherries, see page 61.

Paeonia suffruticosa Hybrids (Tree Peonies)

Apart from the problems arising from the mis-labelling of imported plants (see page 72), it is none too easy to sort out the pinks from the lilacs among the tree peonies, especially as the pinks are often streaked with purple, etc. However, the following seem to me to belong in this section.

'Ayagoromo'

L-T/M   'Ayagoromo', one of my favourites, is a semi-single with two rows of frilled petals, Rose Pink (427), paler at the edges and with a purple tinge in the centre of the flower.

'Souvenir de la Reine Élizabête'

L-T/M   This cumbersome name, not surprisingly shortened, very often, to plain 'Elizabeth', belongs to a flower of equally cumbersome form but magnificent colour. Too fully double for my taste, the petals do not, however, entirely obscure the centre, which, in the more single varieties, is one of their most ornamental features. The colour includes the whole range of Carmine Rose (621 to 621/3), with a touch of purple just visible in the heart of the bloom.

'Momo-yama'

L-T/M   'Momo-yama' is, I believe, rather a scarce variety. The beautiful, cupped bloom has three rows of fringed petals of Carmine Rose (621/2–3) lightly streaked with purple from the base, with a central cluster of prominent yellow stamens.

'Tama-fuyo', 'Yuki-doro' and 'Yachiyo Tsubaki'

L-T/M   These are all exquisite pinks, 'Yachiyo Tsubaki' being, I think, one of the best of all *suffruticosa* hybrids.

For general comments on tree peonies, see pages 73–4.

Cut all tree peonies in half-open bud and boil.

Clematis montana Varieties (O)

L-T/   The now somewhat outdated *C. montana rubens* and the
Climber   newer 'Tetrarose' are on the border line for colour, both being just about as pink as a Japanese anemone, which to me is quite as much mauve as pink. *C. montana* 'Tetrarose' is larger-flowered than any other of this species; 'Elizabeth' is pinker, scented and comparatively large-flowered; and 'Picton's Variety' is pinker still. All are fast and vigorous climbers which must be carefully trained in the early stages if grown against a wall or trellis. They need some tying in several times during the growing season to prevent them from becoming an uncontrollable tangle, but in return for these few attentions they will reward you with a solid curtain of bloom in late spring. The chief drawback of the *montanas* is that the flowers are so soon over, leaving a large, flowerless expanse behind them for the rest of the year. I get over this by growing the later-flowering *Clematis × durandii* right up into the other and this semi-herbaceous variety has an exceptionally long flowering season.

For general comments on clematis, see pages 71–2 and 210–11.

Dipelta floribunda

L-T/T   The abundant, sweetly scented, weigela-like flowers of *Dipelta floribunda* are pink, flushed yellow at the throat and are followed by curious, papery-looking fruit-

PHILADELPHUS coronarius 'Aureus'

A shrub border in the author's garden in early summer

bracts which start pale green attractively flushed with pink and buff and later turn brown. Both in flower and in fruit this is regarded as something devoutly to be wished for indoor decoration, but since flower arrangers have become aware of it, it has become increasingly scarce and at the moment it is almost unobtainable. If you want it, it is up to you to keep on asking for it and the nurserymen will, we hope, sooner or later do their part in adjusting the unpredictable see-saw of supply and demand.

Some old wood and crowded shoots should be removed after flowering.

Weigela florida 'Variegata' (or *Diervilla florida* 'Variegata') and others

L-T/M   A relation of the foregoing, *Weigela florida* 'Variegata' is more valuable to me for its attractive foliage than for its flowers. In other gardens I have seen this weigela wreathed with blooms of apple-blossom pink, which combine charmingly with the cream and green leaves, but with me the flowers are sparse and are usually browned at the edges by rough weather and/or drought. Both in the garden and as cutting material *W. florida* 'Variegata' more than pays its passage from late spring to autumn.

There are of course a number of plain-leaved, pink-flowered weigelas, among the most popular of which are 'Abel Carrière', 'Conquête', 'Le Printemps' and 'Vanhouttei'.

Even though you may cut at these shrubs pretty greedily it will still be advisable to remove flowered wood after blooming.

(See also Foliage Section, page 235.)

28

Pink Flowers
(c) Midsummer

Kalmia latifolia

E/M   *Kalmia latifolia* would be one of the most desirable of evergreen shrubs for indoor decoration if only there were not so many ifs and buts about it. It needs an acid soil and some forms are shy-flowering; and even if it flowers freely the colour may turn out to be a miserably pallid pink unless you have also taken care of this by personal selection. If you have a good form, acid soil, and a sunny site, you will be the envy of less fortunate flower arrangers as well as of many gardeners. I can think of no other flower quite so cunningly constructed, looking like an icing sugar decoration fresh from the piping nozzle when in bud, and like a delicately ribbed pink parasol when fully open. These intricate little works of art come in clusters.

Hardy Hybrid Rhododendrons

Rhododendron 'Lady Clementine Mitford'

E/M to T *Rhododendron* 'Lady Clementine Mitford' ('A') is a thoroughly good garden decorator, making a neat shrub with pretty peach-pink flowers tinged yellow in the centre which are complemented by particularly good, rather silvery-green foliage.

Boil, for safety.

162

Rhododendron 'Lord Fairhaven'

E/M   *Rhododendron* 'Lord Fairhaven' ('A') has flowers of a
slightly yellower pink, amounting to Neyron Rose (623
to 623/2) in effect, the yellow markings in both cases
resulting in a less blue-pink than is common among the
pink-flowered hardy hybrids. The 'lord' makes a considerably smaller plant than the 'lady', but though it is
described by the Sunningdale Nurseries as a 'neat and
small-growing plant' my own specimen is of a loose,
sprawling habit, largely, I think, because too heavily
shaded.

Boil, for safety.

Rhododendron occidentale 'Irene Koster'

T   The fragrant flowers of the *occidentalis* azalea hybrid
'Irene Koster' are an attractive mixture of pale and
deeper pink with some yellow and the foliage colours
particularly well in the autumn.

Boil, for safety.

Evergreen Azaleas

'Satsuki'

E/D   'Satsuki' is immensely valuable in the garden because it
remains in flower over such a very long period. It has
fairly large flowers of a vivid deep pink charting at light
Crimson (22/2 or deeper) which decorate the front of
the shrub borders for many weeks of the summer.

'Vida Brown'

E/D   'Vida Brown' is another very low-growing evergreen
azalea, with unusually large hose-in-hose flowers of
much the same colour as 'Satsuki' (Rose Madder, 23/1).
The flowers are, however, less freely borne and the
flowering period less prolonged.

163

'Rosebud'

E/D The double-flowered 'Rosebud' is a pure pink counterpart of the salmon-pink 'Balsaminaeflorum' described
on page 136.

Hydrangea serrata 'Preziosa'

L-T/D This seems to me to be one of the most valuable
hydrangea introductions of recent times. The only one
of its species in mophead form, it's compact, early and
long-flowering, in a delicious tint of light, warm pink,
starting almost entirely cream and becoming pro-
gressively pinker as it opens to the full, but without a
hint of the unlovely magenta common to so many
hydrangeas—and this charming colour gradation evidently remains constant no matter what the pH rating
of the soil.
Boil and soak.

Escallonia 'Donard Seedling' and others

L-T/E/T *Escallonia* 'Donard Seedling' has prettily striped apple-
blossom-pink and white flowers carried on long, arching
wands. I find this light and airy pink much prettier for
cutting than the more richly coloured varieties which
make far better garden decorators. This must indeed be
a tough variety, for mine have survived unscathed in the
frostiest position at my disposal. No doubt if I had
realized at the time of planting that escallonias generally
are considered far from hardy I would never have risked
them in such a position. Other good pinks are the unusually hardy *E.* × *edinensis*, a bright rose-pink; 'Apple
Blossom', with small, white-eyed florets; and 'Slieve
Donard', resembling a larger, pinker 'Donard Seedling'.
For general comments on escallonias, see page 91.

Kolkwitzia amabilis (American Beauty Bush)

L-T/M I am much in love with *Kolkwitzia amabilis* as material
for flower arrangement. Every delicate flower-spray is

gracefully arched on a slender stem, carrying all along its length a profusion of tiny foxglove shapes, lilac-pink on the outside, with a pale orange throat. It really is a 'Beauty Bush', forming a dainty, soft pink cloud of blossom. Furthermore, the leaves turn to bronze in the autumn among the sprays of furry little brown seed-vessels which I also find useful indoors.

It quickly makes quite a large bush, which would no doubt become straggly and untidy in time if it were not trimmed fairly regularly. Quite a young plant will provide large quantities of cut material if it gets enough sunshine.

It is essential to condition the cut branches carefully before use or they will be a dismal flop. Strip some of the leaves; split, scrape and boil the stem-ends and then give them a long, cold drink.

Robinia pseudoacacia 'Decaisneana'

L-T/
Tree

Robinia pseudoacacia 'Decaisneana' is a rather brittle, fast-growing tree with drooping racemes of acacia-like, pale pink flowers and attractive feathery foliage. If it can be given some shelter from the wind it makes a highly ornamental tree for the back of the border where it will provide shade for such plants as require it without robbing them of nourishment.

Boil.

Deutzia × *elegantissima*

L-T/M

Though this may never prove to be one of my favourite garden shrubs the slender, arching sprays of starry little purplish-pink flowers seem almost specially designed for flower arrangement. They make remarkably graceful cutting material which lasts well in water if boiled.

We are instructed to remove the old wood after flowering.

Roses

Leaving the vast miscellany of pink H.T.s and Floribundas to the reader's choice, we start with the Garnettes.

Garnettes

L-T/
D to M One of the best known is 'Carol', possibly even more as a long-lasting florist's rose than for the garden. It includes all tones of Phlox Pink (625). The soft, light pink of 'Pink Frills' is in my opinion prettier than the rather bluer pink of 'Carol' or 'Pink Garnette'. Perhaps inappropriately, 'Pink Chiffon' is sometimes listed as a Garnette, being of much looser construction and that much less durable in consequence. It is in fact one of the most fairylike of roses and most aptly named, with a smallish bloom irresistibly shaded from the palest of pinks at the edges to a deeper shell pink at the heart, embodying all tints of French Pink (520). I've seen it described as vigorous, but it doesn't do well in the conditions I have to offer, especially in wet weather, though it would be unfair to condemn it on the performance of a single sample in such circumstances. The true Garnettes also include a more salmon pink, so named, a 'Peach Garnette' and a bright pink called 'Garnette Jingles', none of them known to me.

Climbers

L-T Messrs. Newberry list a climbing form of 'Carol', which would no doubt much reduce the number of tiresome deadheading forays by ladder required to keep less long-lasting blooms tidy. Her rather blued sugar pink would harmonize pleasantly enough with white or pale colour-washed walls or with most stonework, but not with red brick. The silvery pink repeat-flowering 'New Dawn' bears a wealth of smallish, clustered blooms which are moderately weatherproof for so delicate a hue. The popular recurrent-flowering 'Aloha' may serve as a pillar rose or even as a large shrub, or as a climber of only moderate height. It has clusters of large, warm pink flowers. Climbing 'Cécile Brunner' can hardly be said to contribute much to a garden spectacle, but the exquisitely formed, thimble-sized H.T. blooms are enchanting for small arrangements. She's an almost exact miniature replica of 'Ophelia', viewed through the wrong end of a telescope. 'Ophelia' herself, with perhaps a slightly warmer tinge of flesh pink at the heart, is a perfectly formed rose for those who appreciate so delicate a complexion, but one single burst of bloom rarely satisfies the rosarian with a choice of repeaters today.

Hybrid Musks

L-T/M 'Felicia' is a pleasing mixture of the clean, silvery pinks charted as Camellia Rose (622/1–3), fading paler. Though far from loud in colour it makes a surprisingly vivid clump when viewed from a distance. The clusters are borne in great profusion but here, in our frequently sunless autumns, I don't often get the repeat regarded as one of the features of the Hybrid Musks. 'Penelope' isn't much better in this respect, no doubt for the same reason. She's literally smothered with clusters of palest pink flowers with a more saffron-tinted centre over a long period in summer and (in other people's gardens) again in autumn. Both yield charming small buds for picking, but are too loosely constructed to be very useful indoors when past the bud stage.

Shrub Roses

L-T/T Raised by Sunningdale Nurseries, the outstanding modern shrub rose 'Constance Spry' is one that Mrs. Spry would, I feel sure, have thought a worthy namesake. It resembles the Bourbon type and is strongly scented, with generous, fully rounded great blooms of a warm, clean pink on a long-wanded bush. Alongside her I have one of the old, true Bourbons, 'Mme Ernst Calvat', which is not unlike the 'Spry' rose, with similar huge, rounded, fragrant flowers of a paler pink shading to a rich China Rose at the centre, sometimes bearing a second crop in the autumn. It makes a more moderate-sized bush, with agreeably copper-tinted foliage. The great, full-petalled blooms may seem to some a trifle blowsy, but to me they bring a heart-warming hint of 'sweet disorder' as a change from the impeccable sophistication of the ubiquitous modern Hybrid Tea. The same can be said of the old-world Common Moss, in light Phlox Pink with a mossy green casing, which is even more endearing than in the white form. The Gallica, 'Rosa Mundi' ('Versicolor'), which has been with us for more than four centuries, is vividly striped in crimson, white and bright candy pink. Though only semi-double the flowers are valued for floral decoration and in the garden it has great charm as well as curiosity value, though not to be confused, as it sometimes is, with the rose of York and Lancaster. Finally, 'Pink Grootendorst' is far too rewarding to be so rarely planted, though this may be due to its typically ferocious Rugosa prickliness. But if one has the courage, or a pair of thorn-strippers, with which to grapple with this bristling pincushion of a plant one's reward is a constant supply of clustered little fringed sugar-pink rosettes. Mr. Graham Thomas, in his *Manual of Shrub Roses*, likens them to small carnations and this exactly describes them. The colour is a light Rose Madder (23/1–2) and the flower-clusters succeed one another lickety spit, like no other rose I know of, almost non-stop throughout the summer, especially if spent clusters are regularly removed. (For further details see 'F. J. Grootendorst', pages 184–5.)

For general comments on roses see pages 79 and 82.

Daboecia cantabrica 'Bicolor' (Form of Irish Heath)

Daboecia cantabrica 'Bicolor' is an attractive blush-pink version of the large-belled Irish heath oddly intermingled with plain purple and with white flower-shoots.

For general comments see page 88.

29

Pink Flowers
(d) Late Summer and Autumn

At first sight the ration of pink for late summer and autumn may look a little thin, but most of the roses listed in the Midsummer Section will bloom far into the autumn.

Polyantha Pompon Rose 'Cameo'

L-T/D   One additional pink rose, which comes into flower later than most, is the Polyantha Pompon, 'Cameo'. I recently put in one of these, along with several others hitherto unidentified, in order to sort out the confusion in my own mind regarding the colours of some of these little roses. 'Cameo' is not altogether what I expected but its cheerful Rose Opal (022) makes a change from the numerous orange-pinks already dealt with.

For general comments on roses, see pages 79 and 82.

Hydrangea × macrophylla Varieties:

'Niedersachsen'

L-T/M   As far as my experience of hydrangeas goes I consider that 'Niedersachsen' produces the most attractive clean light pink of any, charting at Rhodamine Pink (527–527/1), and it will do so in only slightly limy soil conditions, though in a strongly acid soil it will, of course, bear pale blue flowers.

'Altona'

L-T/M   For a deeper, reddish pink, in a limy soil 'Altona' bears fine large heads of attractively fringed florets.

This variety is dealt with in greater detail in the Crimson Section on account of the autumn flower colour and also gets a further mention amongst the violet-hued hydrangeas (see pages 185, 212 and 223).

'Ami Pasquier'

L-T/D   'Ami Pasquier' is good where a dwarfer plant of similar colouring but with smaller flower-heads is required.

For pruning of the *Hydrangea* × *macrophylla* varieties, see page 91, and for conditioning, see page 76.

Fuchsia magellanica 'Alba'

L-T/M   There are quite a number of splendid fuchsias which will add colour to the garden in late summer, but *Fuchsia magellanica* 'Alba' is not one of them. As a garden plant I find it insipid, but whatever one's opinion of it as a garden ornament the wands of little blush-white flowers assume an airy grace when brought into the house and used, for instance, in association with such soft-toned roses as 'Gletscher', 'Magenta', 'Lilac Time', 'Felicia' and a host of others.

For general comments on fuchsias, see pages 145–6.

The stems should be split, scraped and boiled and the ends removed under water.

Erica vagans 'Mrs. D. F. Maxwell' and 'St. Keverne' (Forms of Cornish Heath)

E/D   Only the larger types of summer-flowering heath offer much for cutting and of these the fine deep pink 'Mrs. D. F. Maxwell' (light Rose Bengal, 25/2) is probably still the best. 'St. Keverne' ('Kevernensis') which is a much paler Neyron Rose (623/3) is another good one chosen from a number of somewhat similar varieties. Like the white forms of *E. vagans* previously described these make comparatively large, compact cushions bearing rather solid, upright flower spikes of quite a fair length, and these too put up with similar growing conditions. Trimming at least every other year is advisable, but is usually deferred until the spring because of the pleasing effect produced by the spent flower-plumes which turn to a russet hue and persist throughout the winter.

Abelia × grandiflora

L-T/E/M The tubular little pale pink flowers of *Abelia × grandiflora* are delightful on close inspection, but the dull copper calyxes which persist after the flowers have fallen are even more valuable for their long, arching sprays of subtle colour for autumn indoor arrangements. This abelia will only retain its leaves in a mild winter and is not a very hardy shrub.

It needs little pruning, but flowered sprays may be removed and old wood thinned from time to time.

30

Pink Flowers
(e) Winter

Viburnum tinus (Laurustinus)

L-T/E/T *Viburnum tinus* has never been a top favourite of mine though there is much to be said for this easy-going evergreen, whose pink and white flower-clusters have none of the half-starved appearance of other winter-flowering subjects of similar colouring. For limy gardens, where the choice of evergreens is limited, it is particularly useful and in warm coastal gardens it certainly becomes a very fine thing indeed.

It flowers freely and continuously provided only that it is not grown in dense shade.

Skimmia japonica 'Rubella'

L-T/E/ A yellow witch hazel in bloom alongside this skimmia
D to M is one of the delights of midwinter, smothered as 'Rubella' is with beady clusters of deep russet-pink buds, borne on darker stems, for months on end. On opening its palest pink (male) flowers in early spring it will pollinate nearby female skimmias for berrying purposes, but its own glowing winter colour has far more appeal for me than any number of scarlet berries.

Prunus subhirtella 'Autumnalis Rosea' (Pink Winter Cherry)

L-T/ Having described the white winter cherry on page 98 I
Tree need only add that this variety has flowers of a pale, rather unseasonable-looking pink, but is much coveted for cutting.

Boil.

31

Scarlet to Crimson and Maroon Flowers
(a) Early Spring

As I set about listing my early spring assortment of red-flowered subjects I find that I have only one lime-tolerator. This might, of course, be because I have no special need for them as I can grow evergreen azaleas, and these abound in scarlet and crimson colourings. There are, however, very few effective red-flowered trees or shrubs for alkaline soils until early summer.

Chaenomeles

L-T/D   The best of the red chaenomeles is, I think, 'Simonii', which is dwarf and semi-horizontal in habit, with fine, semi-double flowers of a dark, velvety Orient Red (819). Other good deep reds are 'Rubra Grandiflora', 'Atrococcinea', 'Crimson and Gold' (yellow-centred), 'Rowallane' (semi-double) and 'Nicoline' (double).

    For general comments on chaenomeles, see pages 130 and 152.

Evergreen Azaleas

'Kojo No Odorikarake'

E/D   'Kojo No Odorikarake' is, alas, now said to be the correct name of the light Blood Red (820/3) evergreen azalea with the splendid, glossy, fresh green foliage commonly sold under the label of 'Koran Yuki'. This is one of the very few scented varieties. Like other orange-reds, this one needs some shade to prevent scorching.

'Hinodegiri' and 'Hiryu'

E/D   I find it very difficult to tell 'Hinodegiri' and the less commonly seen 'Hiryu' apart. Both have smallish, vivid crimson flowers (Spiraea Red, 025) and excellent glossy leaves which take on fine reddish tints in winter.

Rhododendron amoenum 'Coccineum'

E/D to M *Rhododendron amoenum* 'Coccineum' has tiny flowers of much the same colour (Tyrian Rose, 24, to Spiraea Red, 025). It is rather taller-growing and has a most distinctive tiered habit, with unusually dark green foliage.

'Christmas Cheer'

E/D   'Christmas Cheer' is a much more compact grower, with small crimson flowers—not as good as any of the foregoing, in my opinion, but one of the earliest in bloom.

    Boil all these, for safety.

Rhododendron 'May Day'

E/M   In the milder garden climates this first-class hybrid will produce its glowing scarlet to blood-red flowers in abundance in April, though elsewhere flowering may be delayed until May. Of a compact habit to commend it for the small garden, it combines with its fine flower trusses the further attraction of a brown backing to the dark green leaves—altogether a most desirable subject for a fairly sheltered spot ('C' rating).

    Boil, for safety.

Rhododendron 'Elizabeth'

E/D to M Though *Rhododendron* 'Elizabeth' is by no means scarce you may have to pay a good deal of money for quite a small plant; but I can think of no more justifiable form of extravagance. It is a compact and comparatively dwarf variety, growing in time to about four feet, ablaze for several weeks with large flowers of a superlative,

174

glistening scarlet which charts at light Turkey Red (721/2).

This, too, appears to be gratifyingly hardy and can be grown in full exposure, though its 'B' rating is strictly supposed to require part shade. There is, of course, a danger, as with all early-flowering rhododendrons, that the flowers may be caught by spring frost.

Boil, for safety.

Camellia japonica Hybrids

The red-flowered *Camellia japonica* hybrids have such a splendid weather-resistant colour, in flowers of such fine texture and elegant shape, such a long succession of bloom and such magnificent, glossy evergreen foliage that their claim to be the finest of all garden ornaments in this colour group can hardly be disputed.

'Adolphe Audusson'

E/T My biggest specimen is 'Adolphe Audusson', now about sixteen years old and towering well above the porch beside which it grows. It revels in the north-west aspect and in the plentiful supply of rain-water which comes to it from a drain-pipe purposely smashed below ground level to feed this house-bed full of moisture-loving hydrangeas, roses, lilies and camellias. 'Adolphe Audusson' flowers so prolifically that the branches are bowed down by the weight of the large, semi-double blooms when the plant is in flower. The colour is Claret Rose (021), with a cluster of yellow stamens clearly displayed as a rule. In some years the flowers are more single and in other years more double in form.

'Mars'

E/M to T As far as the actual flowers are concerned I can hardly tell 'Mars' and 'Adolphe Audusson' apart, though in habit my comparatively young 'Mars' appears to be rather more spreading than the other. The flower colour

175

is light Carmine (21/1) and the flowers themselves slightly smaller than, though just as prolific as those of 'Adolphe Audusson'.

'Jupiter'

E/T 'Jupiter' is a particularly early-flowering variety, with elegant single blooms of light Geranium Lake (20/1) ornamented with a central boss of yellow stamens. I believe that 'Jupiter' also answers to the names of 'Juno' and 'Sylva'.

'Donckelarii'

E/T For those addicted to bicolour camellias 'Donckelarii' is one of the best, with large, semi-double red flowers marbled with white. It is a particularly hardy variety.

For general comments on camellias, see pages 57–8.

I find that camellia flowers last well in water if picked when not more than half-open, but I boil them just to make sure, for these choice blooms are still too precious to waste. A dab of gum on the back of the flower helps to prevent cut blooms from dropping.

32

Scarlet to Crimson and Maroon Flowers
(b) Late Spring

Embothrium lanceolatum 'Norquinco Valley' (Form of Chilean Firebush)

T Late spring provides some real startlers for colour and foremost among these is *Embothrium lanceolatum* 'Norquinco Valley', with close packed, narrow tubes of the most intense orange-scarlet. Like many South American importations it is not entirely hardy in most parts of this country. My present specimen, the third attempt, has quickly grown to flowering size in the more mature company of the present shrub borders, where it can get its head up into the sun while its roots remain shaded. It has recently survived some quite hard winters without damage, sometimes even retaining its semi-evergreen foliage and last year actually setting seed.

It isn't often that anyone has vast armfuls of this choice shrub to spare for flower arrangement, but I remember one occasion when I saw great branches of embothrium being used together with flame and scarlet azaleas, all sent, I was told, from Lord Rothschild's famous garden at Exbury.

Because the embothrium's natural habit is rather thin, at least in its early years, I pinch out the tips of the young shoots from time to time in an attempt to induce a bushier appearance and it seems to work. My plant looks a good deal more dense than others of the same age, which is all to the good from the point of view of withstanding winter cold.

Knap Hill Azalea 'Devon'

T   The deep, fiery red of *Azalea* 'Devon' is one of the most vivid hues to be found among the splendid Knap Hill strain but, as in the case of the embothriums, these hot colours must be so placed as to avoid fighting with near neighbours. I also feel very strongly that there should not be too many of them. A garden over-full of these assertive, fiery reds will not be a tranquil place.

Evergreen Azaleas

E/D   The same applies, to a lesser extent, to some of the spring-flowering evergreen azaleas, though when it is possible to plan a really intoxicating mix-up, with every hue in the palette, the orange-scarlets may be used with daring abandon alongside crimson-reds, purples and so on.

> 'Addy Wery': hot orange-scarlet, charting at the lightest tint of Signal Red (719/3); one of the most eye-catching.
> 'John Cairns': fine deep mahogany-red (Currant Red, 821).
> 'Eddy': rather later-flowering than the two foregoing; larger flowers of vivid scarlet with purple spots.
> All of these orange-red hues tend to scorch unattractively unless grown in part shade.
> 'Alice': vigorous, large-flowered Carmine (21) in effect. This is a fine plant when grown in part shade.
> 'Anny': light crimson-red (Rose Opal, 022 to 022/1).
> 'Mother's Day': more crimson still, vivid deep Rose Madder (23), with quite large, frilly, semi-double flowers. Though it is reputed to be somewhat tender it has now survived several hard winters here, even in a frost-pocket.
> Boil all these, for safety.

Hardy Hybrid Rhododendrons

'Britannia'

E/M   *Rhododendron* 'Britannia' ('B') is one of the best scarlets among the old hardy hybrids and is of a useful medium size for a small garden. Although the flowers fade to something nearer crimson than scarlet before they fall, in their prime they are a brave Turkey Red (721). They need a partially shaded site if they are to look their best.

Boil, for safety.

'Cynthia'

E/T   I wonder why it is that *Rhododendron* 'Cynthia' ('B') is so universally popular? The light Rose Red (724/2) soon blues to an unattractive Rose Bengal and I find it hard to believe that so many gardeners actually prefer her colouring to that of 'Britannia', for example. Mine was a nurseryman's choice and certainly would not be my own selection today from the many finer reds now available.

Boil, for safety.

Paeonia suffruticosa Hybrids (Tree Peonies)

'Hinode Sekai' and 'Hatsu Hinode'

L-T/M   It is a real pleasure to turn from *Rhododendron* 'Cynthia's' light bluish-crimson to the lovely glowing hues of such tree peonies as 'Hinode Sekai' and 'Hatsu Hinode', the one a light Cherry (722/3) and the other glistening Carmine. 'Hinode Sekai' is earlier-flowering and rather more double than 'Hatsu Hinode'.

For general comments on tree peonies, see pages 72–4.

Cut in half-open bud and boil, for safety.

Paeonia delavayi

L-T/M   This *Paeonia* species is undeniably more decorative

179

indoors than out. As a cut flower the single row of very dark maroon petals surrounding the cluster of yellow anthers has great depth of colour and beauty of form, but in the garden the wine-maroon colour is so dark as to be self-effacing and the flowers are considerably smaller than those of the *Paeonia suffruticosa* hybrids which are such spectacular garden decorators. As the plant is variable it is safer to choose your plant when in flower if possible.

For general comments on tree peonies, see pages 72–4.

Boil, for safety.

Weigela 'Ideal'

L-T/M Difficult as it is to place the weigelas definitely in one or other of the periods Late Spring or Midsummer, I can, however, safely include the comparatively early-flowering 'Ideal' here. This weigela is said to be a vivid carmine, which would roughly correspond in colour to that of *Camellia* 'Adolphe Audusson'. True Carmine, in terms of the colour chart, is a very fine colour indeed, so *W.* 'Ideal' should be worth looking out for if the description is a fair one. (For other reds see page 187.)

Boil.

33

Scarlet to Crimson and Maroon Flowers
(c) Midsummer

Roses

Scarlet roses do so much for the garden scene from midsummer onwards that I include a large number of these in the shrub borders. Most of mine are Floribundas which, generally speaking, make more suitable subjects for the shrub borders than the Hybrid Teas and, fortunately, many of the Floribundas provide excellent cut flowers.

Hybrid Teas, Floribundas and Garnettes

L-T/   The beautifully shaped, fragrant deep crimson H.T.,
D to M   'Papa Meilland', might be thought to qualify for special mention among the inordinate miscellany of H.T.s in this colour section, having been initially heralded with such a fanfarade and illustrated by such immensely seductive photographs in the coloured catalogues; but a few years' experience of it as a garden plant has proved it neither sufficiently free-flowering nor disease-proof except when grown under glass and it has now lost favour with the public. Tantau's 'Fragrant Cloud', on the other hand, has really proved itself not only as a vigorous, healthy and free-flowering garden rose (doing unusually well even on a poor soil, with the help of some foliar feeding), but it also has beautifully formed blooms of a most attractively hued smoky Geranium Lake.

     Among the even more formidable assortment of red Floribundas I propose to discuss only the curious 'New

Look', introduced from France by Messrs. Gandy, who must surely have had the flower arranger as his target in so doing. It seems to me inappropriately named and, not surprisingly, makes a poor showing in the shrub borders, being a very odd mixture of deep maroon-red and rather tarnished silver-buff which some gardeners find downright hideous and others even mistake for dead or dying blooms. They do indeed look rather as though they'd been preserved in borax, though the foliage is a lively copper-bronze. If I haven't made 'New Look' sound particularly bewitching it *is* nevertheless of interest for flower arrangement, repeatedly coming to the rescue in picking up indescribable muted reds in an ancestral portrait in a stately home or those of ancient tombs or murals in churches and cathedrals.

In the Garnette range Messrs. Newberry now stock a 'Scarlet Garnette' of the true type but of more recent vintage and brighter colour than the original dark crimson, which they also list. I would expect the scarlet variety, though I haven't seen it, to be equipped with the same pleasingly bronzed foliage as 'Garnette' itself, whose leaf colour is an additional asset, both indoors and out.

Climbers

L-T   Two red recurrent-flowering climbers of exceptionally fine colour are the very dark, velvety 'Don Juan', and 'Guinée'—possibly even a fraction darker. Both are so dark a red as to be almost black in bud and both are sweet-scented. For cutting purposes 'Guinée' perhaps has the edge on 'Don Juan', being slightly more fully petalled, with a little larger flower, though I find 'Don Juan' a little more floriferous. The vivid, double, cinnabar-scarlet 'Danse du Feu', with dark foliage, is immensely popular as a climber of moderate height or as a pillar rose, flowering with abandon throughout the summer—perpetual, that is, rather than recurrent. 'Danse du Feu' is of a border line hue between the

darkest of the salmon-orange section and the lightest
and brightest of scarlets in the present context.

Hybrid Musks

L-T/   The tall-growing 'Bonn' is a little ungainly in habit and
M to T   the large, semi-double flowers are admittedly none too
shapely. But they are borne so freely and so continuously that it's worth while growing this rose with a
decent skirting of dwarfer shrubs to hide its legginess
and it will then overtop them throughout the summer
and autumn with large splashes of the lovely colour
which charts at light Currant Red (821/3), the flowers
being followed by large round heps, provided that the
dead flowers aren't removed. 'Wilhelm' is a very dark
scarlet-crimson semi-double, perpetual flowering and
also yielding good fat red heps. Its brighter-hued sport,
'Will Scarlet', might be regarded as superior in its
scarlet colour but for the fact that the flower has a white
eye. Incidentally, I wonder if there are any flower
arrangement demonstrators who haven't been warned
of the hospital-born superstition that a combination of
red and white flowers indicates a death in the offing!
Not that I'd expect an audience to blench and melt away
at the mere sight of 'Will Scarlet's' white eye but, un-
superstitious though I am, I think this variation only
detracts from the effect of unadulterated scarlet. In
other respects, such as the shape of the flower, heps,
foliage and so on 'Wilhelm' and its sport 'Will Scarlet'
are closely similar.

Shrub Roses

L-T/T   The wild species, *Rosa moyesii*, from North West China,
becomes a tall, spreading shrub which is one of the
finest of roses for garden decoration and to my mind is
only surpassed by its variety, 'Geranium' (raised at
Wisley), which is slightly more vividly coloured than the
parent and considerably more compact in habit, though
this too makes a large, arching shrub. The flowers are

identical in their wide open, wild rose shape, with the single row of petals opening flat round the central cluster of yellow stamens, as in a heraldic rose. Their colour differs only slightly between the Rose Opal (022) officially attributed to *Rosa moyesii* and the Cardinal Red (822/1) of 'Geranium', which is a fraction more orange-scarlet than the blood-red of the other. In late summer and autumn the profusion of large, urn-shaped orange-scarlet heps all along the arching branches makes this second burst of colour even more spectacular than the flowering stage. They seed themselves freely and the only one I've grown on to flowering size has resulted in much the same blood-red petal colour, but with a small white circle surrounding the yellow boss of stamens. Here again I could well do without the white eye, but the outcome, all in all, was a lot better than the washy pink flower usually predicted for their seedlings, though I'd have preferred a true replica of either parent.

The only pruning required for these roses is to remove one or two of the oldest stems at ground level from time to time and to cut out any dead wood. They are, happily, immune from disease.

L-T/M 'Tuscany Superb' is one of the old Gallicas and is a little too thin and sprawling—at least in my rather sunless conditions—to make a really satisfactory shrub, but the colour is just about as near to black as a 'black' tulip. 'Tuscany' itself is known as the 'Old Velvet Rose', which suggests something of the richness of this sumptuous beauty, to which the epithet 'Superb' has been added with good reason. 'Tuscany Superb' starts as deepest mulberry-maroon, opens to dark Beetroot Purple (830)—a much lovelier hue than the name implies—and fades to a dense, smoky purple at the last. This is one of the delights of the flower arranger but not, I think, a great ornament to the shrub border.

L-T/M 'F. J. Grootendorst's' pink-flowered sport has already been mentioned and the parent plant, 'F. J. Grootendorst', resembles it closely in all respects except for its deep, warm crimson colour. Like the pink version, this Rugosa hybrid puts up an almost continuous display throughout summer and autumn, though more whole-hearted at certain times than at others. Both have deeply veined apple-green leaves turning yellow in autumn, making fairly compact bushes of about five feet either way. They're a special boon to gardeners on poor soils and in difficult areas where ordinary roses are unsuccessful, prospering even in sand and remaining unharmed by strong winds; they are also outstandingly hardy and are immune to black spot, mildew and other rose diseases. A hedge of either form of these wickedly prickly 'Grootendorsts' would defeat the boldest trespasser. Apart from their thorns I can't fault these roses as garden shrubs except as a favourite hideout for greenfly, which find a pretty secure lodging in the deeply wrinkled young leaves.

For general comments on roses, see pages 79 and 82.

Rhododendrons

'Thunderstorm'

E/M   'Thunderstorm' ('B') is regarded as of outstanding merit, having tall trusses of dark blood-red blooms with contrasting white stamens. I don't, however, much care for this oddly conspicuous feature, which passes for one of its chief virtues, and have now sold my own plant.

'Moser's Maroon'

E/T   The dark mahogany-red of the hardy 'Moser's Maroon' ('B') charts at Oxblood Red (00823) in effect, with a black-spotted flare—a lovely sombre hue. The beautifully coloured young foliage-shoots produced during the summer will be dealt with separately in the Foliage Section (see page 251).

'Beau Brummell'

E/T   'Beau Brummell' ('B') is a choice, late-flowering, vivid scarlet with black spots which has so far proved entirely hardy in my garden in spite of the fact that it is a woodland hybrid.

'Arthur Osborn'

E/D to M 'Arthur Osborn' is a very desirable semi-dwarf, rarely exceeding three to four feet in height with flowers of an intense Blood Red (820). This is a 'C' category rhododendron, said to be susceptible to the late spring frosts from which my garden suffers, but neither of my two plants has ever shown any frost damage.

'Redcap'

E/D 'Redcap' is another choice blood-red rhododendron of low-growing habit; indeed, if my plant is typical, it might even be described as sprawling. It has a 'D' rating but on the upper edge of my frost-pocket it has slowly increased in stature over the years and has recently begun to produce its waxy bells with the greatest of freedom. I suspect that some sparseness of flower in the earlier years was mainly due to bud-tenderness.

Rhododendron griersonianum

E/D to M *Rhododendron griersonianum* also seems too good to be true, in the conditions I have to offer. Officially rated as 'C', it has proved to be as tough as nails in the twelve years or so that it has been with me. Though the orthodox treatment is to grow this species in sheltered woodland I have grown mine in full exposure with the most gratifying results. One faces the risk that the vivid salmon-scarlet (lightest Signal Red, 719/3) flower-trusses may be badly scorched in some seasons, if they happen to be in bloom during a spell of prolonged sunshine—but prolonged sunshine is not as inevitable as one might expect in late June or early July.

Boil all these rhododendrons, for safety.

Ghent Azalea 'Dr. Charles Baumann'

T   This is yet another instance of leaving to the nurseryman
the choice that should have been mine. I see that I have
charted 'Dr. Charles Baumann' as light Vermilion (18/1),
which makes it difficult to say why I have so little love
for this variety. The colour is one of my favourites and
yet, inexplicably, the azalea is not.

      Boil, for safety.

Weigelas

L-T/M   Whereas most weigelas flower somewhere between late
spring and summer 'Eva Rathke' is a true midsummer
bloomer, of compact habit, with vivid red blooms amid
dark foliage, flowering all along the branches. The best
of the earliest summer varieties include the light wine-
red 'Bristol Ruby' and the rather brighter crimson
'Newport Red'.

      Boil.

Daboecia cantabrica 'Praegerae' (Form of Irish Heath)

E/D   This is the reddest of the Irish heaths, which are bigger
in all respects than those from Scotland. The comparatively large, vivid crimson flowers come on much longer
spikes, but this variety has a markedly leggy tendency.

      It should be clipped back each spring to induce as
much bushiness as possible.

Escallonias

L-T/
M to T   Most escallonias tend to flower right through to the
autumn, with good, glossy, dark evergreen foliage into
the bargain, so they may really be said to earn their keep
all the year round. Though not all are equally hardy
they seem to be less tender than used to be supposed—
indeed one of the less hardy ones gets by well enough
even in my cold garden. Being just about as pink as they

are red, 'Donard Brilliance' and 'Donard Radiance' are questionable on colour grounds for inclusion here, but are too good to pass over. Among the unequivocal reds is another worthy introduction from the Slieve Donard Nursery called 'Pride of Donard', of medium height, with a profusion of vivid light red flowers of exceptional size and one of the first to open. Other good reds are 'C. F. Ball', a tall scarlet-crimson of upright growth; 'Crimson Spire' and × *langleyensis*, two crimsons especially suitable for seaside hedges and screens; and 'E. G. Cheeseman' (unknown to me), which receives an enthusiastic accolade from Messrs. Hillier as a vigorous hybrid with deep, bright cherry-red flowers of a long, nodding bell shape, borne in panicles at the ends of the shoots amid sage or grey-green foliage. We should, I think, try to get a look at a mature plant of this unusual variety.

34

Scarlet to Crimson and Maroon Flowers and Fruits
(d) Late Summer and Autumn

The late summer and autumn season in the shrub garden inherits much of its colour from the roses already listed under Midsummer. Indeed many of them are at their best in August and September, after a brief pause in July. There is, therefore, a good deal of crimson and scarlet in the borders at this season even though there are not many new items to add here.

Hydrangea × macrophylla Varieties:

'Heinrich Seidel'

L-T/M   One of the truly reddest mophead hydrangeas is 'Heinrich Seidel'. In a rather limy patch at the foot of a wall the colour of mine is an astonishingly vivid crimson-red, approximately light Indian Lake (826/2). 'Heinrich Seidel' is a comparatively tall-growing hydrangea, bearing closely packed flower-heads in abundance when it reaches maturity. Unfortunately, it is not one of the hardiest and needs the protection of a wall to do well in my garden.

'Westfalen'

L-T/D   'Westfalen' is a first-class variety and rarely exceeds three feet in height. The colour is very variable in different soil conditions, ranging, in my garden, from Crimson (22) on lime to light Dahlia Purple (931/2–3) with a bluer eye on a moderately acid soil.

'Altona'

L-T/M   Although 'Altona' is deep pink rather than red in limy conditions I mention it again here because, no matter what the colour of the large, fringed flower-heads in their prime, they turn in the autumn to a uniform, rich plum-crimson. This spectacular aftermath persists until it is at length reduced by winter frosts to a sober beige.

  If the flower-heads are cut just at the right time, when they feel very slightly papery to the touch, they will keep their rich crimson colour indoors for a long time if the stems are put into an inch or two of water and left in it until all the water has evaporated, by which time the flower-heads should have become thoroughly dried.

  For pruning of the *Hydrangea* × *macrophylla* varieties, see page 91, and for conditioning of cut material, see page 76.

Fuchsia 'Marinka'

L-T/P   One of the hardiest fuchsias is the large-flowered, blood-red 'Marinka', wherever a plant of trailing habit is required.

Fuchsia 'Mme Cornelissen'

L-T/D   'Mme Cornelissen' is a more vigorous, upright-habited variety of about three feet in height, with scarlet sepals and white corolla. For a bicolour this shows up particularly well at a distance.

  For general comments and conditioning of fuchsias, see pages 145–6.

Cotoneaster × 'Cornubia' and *C. franchetii sternianus*

L-T/E/T   These apparently birdproof cotoneasters bear numerous heavy clusters of large, orange-scarlet berries during autumn and winter. 'Cornubia' makes a tall shrub and the other a very graceful one, together representing the pick of the genus.

Crataegus × *carrierei* (× *lavallei*) (Form of Thorn)

L-T/
Tree

There's nothing very special about this little tree in flower, but its fat clusters of three-quarter inch orange-scarlet fruits amid semi-evergreen leaves are spectacular and long-lasting.

Tropaeolum speciosum (Flame Flower)

L-T/
Climber

This charming little climber may be thought too floppy for cutting; but its slender streamers wreathed in tiny scarlet nasturtium-flowers last well in water, given some kind of support. However that may be, I am sure that you will be glad to grow it if you can, for it takes up no space and is happiest when allowed to clamber over some large shrub which will provide shade for its roots. In my garden the original group trails through the vivid evergreen tree heath, *Erica arborea* 'Alpina', and at Hidcote Manor it sets a dark yew hedge alight. It also usually succeeds against a north wall as well as anywhere. It will disappear in winter, but if it likes you—and it may not—it will pop up unfailingly in the spring. The metallic blue seeds which succeed the flowers are attractive in their own right and can in fact be used to good effect as cut material.

Cotinus coggygria 'Foliis Purpureis' (Form of Smoke Bush, Venetian Sumach)

L-T/T

The dusky fuzz which shrouds the purple-leaved cotinuses (or *Rhus*, as they used to be called) in early July isn't easy to pigeon-hole as regards colour. More commonly described as purple, I see it, as I also see the foliage, as mahogany or maroon, at least in the case of *Cotinus coggygria* 'Foliis Purpureis', which I grow in preference to 'Kromhout' or 'Notcutt's Variety', with more vivid beetroot-purple leaf-colour.

The inflorescences consist of airy panicles formed by clouds of minute gypsophila-like florets on threadlike stalks; but I understand that these are only borne with real freedom on a poor soil.

(See also Foliage Section, page 249.)

Boil.

Polyantha Pompon Roses

L-T/D The best of the reds are I think 'Nurse Cavell', a vivid scarlet flushed velvety crimson, and 'Ideal', a dark crimson-scarlet, if only because they are the most mildew-proof. It's unfortunate that most Polyanthas are so susceptible to mildew, because they're entirely free of black spot. However, good cultivation and regular applications of Karathane should keep any of them reasonably clean.

Rosa moyesii and *R.m.* 'Geranium'

L-T/T In later summer the great, arching wands of *Rosa moyesii* and *R.m.* 'Geranium' are wreathed with urn-shaped orange-scarlet heps. I find the muted bronze of the unripe heps, particularly those of *R. moyesii*, at least as attractive for cutting as the striking orange-vermilion of the ripened fruits. At any stage they last for a very long time in water.

(See also pages 183–4.)

Skimmia Varieties

L-T/E/ For red berries on your skimmias please refer to pages
D to M 59–60, where these plants have been dealt with in detail.

CLEMATIS × *durandii*

HEBE armstrongii

35

Lilac to Purple and Violet Flowers
(a) Early Spring

Daphne mezereum

L-T/D The sweetly scented, waxy blossoms of *Daphne mezereum* barely wait for the first signs of spring, flowering on the naked branches in February and March. The purple form makes a bushier plant than the white and I find that established specimens of three feet or so are not harmed by careful cutting.

The poisonous red berries germinate readily if the birds allow them to do so, providing seedlings which vary in intensity of colour from a pale pinkish-lilac to a deep red-purple.

Rhododendron × praecox

E/M Almost equally early-blooming by nature, *Rhododendron × praecox* ('A') can be forced into flower even earlier indoors if the sprays are cut when just showing chinks of colour in the bud. The softer, paler colour which results may suit some flower arrangers better than the natural, rather fierce magenta-purple, though this soon cools off to an attractive and more manageable Mauve (633/1). *R. × praecox* is rather a slow grower so that it's not possible to cut more than a few modest snippets from it for the first ten years or so.

One must be prepared occasionally to find the flowers reduced to a soggy brown pulp overnight by a March frost—and yet it is surprising how comparatively rarely this happens. One of my two specimens actually thrives at the foot of the slope, where the risk of frost is greatest, but both benefit from a living umbrella of leafless branches overhead, which is a great help in warding off frost damage to the small, delicate-textured blooms.

Boil, for safety.

Dwarf Alpine Rhododendron Species and Hybrids

Rhododendron scintillans

E/D   *Rhododendron scintillans* ('A') is regularly the first of my dwarf alpine types to open up, a few weeks later than *R. × praecox*, in early April, with masses of tiny flowers of a vivid blue-violet. Certain forms of this rhododendron are indeed very nearly blue enough to merit being classified in that colour section. My own plant is a good Methyl Violet (39/1), combining delightfully with the flame-hued chaenomeles and cool yellow primroses which may be expected to keep it company. In youth its habit is less neat than most, but this can be corrected by a little tying in and layering in the early stages.

Rhododendron impeditum

E/D   *Rhododendron impeditum* ('A') has very similar flowers —small, abundant and ranging in colour from about Amethyst Violet to Aster Violet in the bluest forms of this rather variable species. It is a better-looking garden plant than the preceding in that it makes a remarkably neat, dense, low mound attractive in flower and leaf alike. It is particularly ornamental in the winter scene, when the little blue-green leaves take on a subtle bronze tinge.

Rhododendron russatum (cantabile)

E/D to M *Rhododendron russatum* ('A') is much more upright and open in habit, with somewhat larger flowers of a redder purple charting round about Amethyst Violet. I find its colour invaluable by way of contrast to the pinks and flames and crimsons of the early evergreen azaleas and the bright yellows of some of the dwarf brooms, kerrias, etc., in flower at the same time. I find it less hardy than most alpine species and it prefers light shade.

Rhododendron 'Bluebird', *R.* 'Blue Diamond' and *R.* 'Blue Tit'

E/D to M The dwarf alpine hybrids, 'Bluebird', 'Blue Diamond' and 'Blue Tit' (all 'A' category) make rather bigger bushes, with larger flowers measuring about one inch across. All three are fairly similar, differing only slightly in stature and in the lovely light blue-violet colour of the flowers. 'Bluebird' is the earliest and, I think, the dwarfest of the three, with rather star-shaped corollas of light Veronica Violet (639/1), coinciding in bloom with two early pink evergreen azaleas, 'Kirin' and 'Myacino'. Conveniently, according to plan, the Aster Violet 'Blue Diamond' regularly synchronizes its flowering with that of the big creamy-yellow *R.* 'Unique'. 'Blue Tit', in my experience, seems to be slow to come into flower.

Boil all these, for safety.

Rhododendron 'Susan'

E/T Biggest and boldest of the early-flowering rhododendrons in this colour section is the *campanulatum* hybrid, 'Susan' ('B'), whose lovely great trusses of light blue-violet are the ideal complement to the orange-flame *Azalea* 'Queen Emma' and the primrose *Rhododendron* 'Goldsworth Yellow'. 'Susan' has a reputation, in my experience totally undeserved, for being shy-flowering. My mature plant regularly blooms with abandon, opening its flowers from engaging russet buds. The fine dark green leaves are tinged with brown on the underside.

Boil, for safety.

Evergreen Azaleas

'Hatsugiri' and *amoenum*

E/D The first peep of colour that I can expect to find in early

April, as I impatiently examine the shrub borders for signs that the real display is on the way is always to be found in *Azalea* 'Hatsugiri' or in *Rhododendron scintillans*. The controversial Orchid Purple (31/2) of *Azalea* 'Hatsugiri' is positively painful to some beholders and much admired by others; but personally I find both 'Hatsugiri' and the similar-coloured *amoenum* (Rhodamine Purple, 29) most exciting colours to handle in the landscape. One of the many virtues of the evergreen azaleas is that, so long as the root-ball is carefully kept intact, they can be switched around in full bloom without suffering, to try out different colour combinations, but be careful to see that the roots don't dry out if they have been transplanted in full flower. Dryness at the roots is bad for them at any time and in such circumstances would probably be fatal.

'Irohayama'

E/D   The flower of 'Irohayama' is shaded from near-white in the centre to pale lilac at the edges (palest Orchid Purple, 31/3). The effect is delightful among the candy-pinks and deep violets in the early spring border.
       Boil all these, for safety.

Erica australis (Form of Tree Heath)

E/M   The tree heath, *Erica australis*, is not, I think, a plant for limy soils, although most other early spring-flowering heaths are tolerant of alkaline conditions. Said to be somewhat tender, it withstood two consecutive winters of considerable severity here when quite young and although some of the main stems were split like matchwood by prolonged hard frost this plant is now the most densely furnished specimen I know. This is due to rigorous cutting back after flowering and some training and tying in, in its early years. Without these attentions *E. australis* develops a dreadfully gangling appearance; but my own bushy specimen, well furnished with long, closely packed spikes of light Rhodamine Purple (29/2) flowers with protruding black anthers, makes a handsome garden ornament and provides cutting material of considerable beauty.

Magnolia × soulangiana

L-T/
Tree

As cutting material *Magnolia × soulangiana* is exquisite, with its great white chalices stained purple at the base of the petals which appear in advance of the leaves. This is one of the magnolias which will succeed in limy gardens and even though the flowers are very vulnerable to frost damage the tree itself is exceptionally hardy.

36

Lilac to Purple and Violet Flowers
(b) Late Spring

Evergreen Azaleas

There are a tremendous number of comparatively large-flowered evergreen azaleas in this colour range to follow hard on the heels of the early spring group. I like their colours for cutting and the softer lilacs are useful in toning down the more aggressive hues which are so exciting when used with discretion in the garden.

'Akebono'

E/D   One of the coolest is 'Akebono', which came to me six years or so ago under the prosaic name of 'Joe Madden'. It has large flowers of palest lilac with a slightly deeper blotch and does best in part shade. Its rather loose habit provides fine sprays for cutting after a time.

'Atalanta' and 'Pippa'

E/D   'Atalanta' and 'Pippa' are very much alike, with fairly large flowers of a pleasing light Mallow Purple (630/1).

'J. S. Bach' and 'Beethoven'

E/D   'J. S. Bach' and 'Beethoven' would not be welcome in every garden, since their fiercer Orchid Purple (31/1) is none too easy to place, but they make a lively contribution to the real kaleidoscope of colour which I aim at in the spring.

'Maxwellii' and 'Purple Triumph'

E/D   The deepest of the magenta-purples are 'Maxwellii' (Tyrian Purple, 727/3) and the fine new 'Purple Triumph'. The large, rather frilly, semi-double flowers make a triumphant splash of rich Orchid Purple (31) and although it is said to be somewhat tender I have grown it safely for several years.

    Boil all, for safety.

Rhododendron augustinii

E/T   *Rhododendron augustinii* makes a tall, upright, small-leaved shrub with rather a variable flower colour. The best forms are even bluer than my two plants, which chart at a lovely light Hyacinth Blue (40/2)—more violet than true blue, that is. Mine had at first proved so shy-flowering that despite their 'B' rating I had assumed them to be bud-tender in this area of severe frosts. But yet again the trouble turned out to be over-shading and since moving them into more open positions they've completely redeemed their flowery reputation.

Large-flowered Clematis Hybrids

L-T/   As previously mentioned, many of the large-flowered
Climbers clematis hybrids are hard to place as regards flowering season, which depends to some extent on the type of pruning (or lack of it), some giving a second display in late summer and others flowering intermittently through spring and summer. The following are usually in flower by late May: 'Bee's Jubilee' (O), 'C. W. Dowman' (O) and 'Nelly Moser' (EWN), all somewhat alike, though the first is the most vividly coloured, with a darker band down the centre of its deeper purplish-mauve sepals and the second is considerably pinker than Nelly in all its parts; 'Barbara Jackman' (O) is another on the same pattern, but with a bright petunia bar on a much bluer ground. Starting with the bluest of the more uniform

hues and working through the purples towards the reddest, we have 'Lord Nevill' (O), with attractively waved sepals of intense violet with a darker centre; 'Beauty of Worcester' (SW), a deep violet with white stamens, sometimes producing double flowers on the old wood; 'Mrs. Cholmondeley' (O), one of the palest, with enormous light blue-violet flowers less shapely than average, but effective because quite remarkably floriferous; the large, double 'Vyvyan Pennell' (ESW), one of the finest of all modern hybrids, with a ring of wavy deep blue-violet sepals framing a frilled purple rosette and, rather disconcertingly, producing a number of single lavender-blue flowers on young wood in autumn; 'Barbara Dibley' (NWE), in the Pansy Violet range, richer-hued in part shade and fading in full sun—the *soignée* little silky wigs of her burnished seed-heads should be an inspiration to any hairdresser; 'Daniel Deronda' (O), with deep blue-purple, cream-centred blooms, often producing double or semi-double flowers on the old wood; 'Lincoln Star' (O), officially described as a maroon-centred, cochineal pink, paler at the edges.

For general comments see pages 71–2 and 210–11.

Singe or boil all clematis.

Paeonia suffruticosa and Hybrid Varieties

Paeonia suffruticosa

L-T/M This is the parent from which so many hybrids have been bred, though I doubt whether any of its progeny surpass the wilding in loveliness. The flower pattern is intricate: working outwards from the crimson carpels at the centre we have next an encircling cluster of yellow stamens and surrounding these a double row of silky petals stained maroon-purple at the base and shading through lilac to glistening white at the circumference.

'Kamata Fuji'

L-T/M In the hybrid 'Kamata Fuji' the flower is fairly double, but not to the point of marring its great beauty. The plant is dwarfer than most and the flower colour is Mallow Purple (630), darker at the centre.

'Suigan'

L-T/M   'Suigan', which flowers earlier than most, is more nearly single, with only two rows of petals. The colour includes all tints of Amaranth Rose (530 to 530/3), the pinkish-lilac of the background hue being streaked with purple radiating from a purple centre. In my opinion this is a specially lovely one for the flower arranger.

'Gekkeikan'

L-T/M   'Gekkeikan' lives up to its description as 'Rich lilac rose with fringed petals, the bases of the petals being light carmine. A gorgeous variety.'

For general comments on the tree peonies, see pages 72–4.

Cut tree peonies in half-open bud, and boil for safety.

Cercis siliquastrum (Judas Tree)

L-T/   Once I had a Judas Tree and I wish I had one now. I
Tree   should like to try another but can now no longer find room for this rather shrubby, spreading little tree with the bright rosy-purple little pea-flowers which crowd the naked branches in May.

Wisteria (*Wistaria*)

L-T/   The May-flowering *Wisteria sinensis*, which is the one
Climber   most commonly grown, is earlier in bloom than the
or Shrub   other popular species, *W. floribunda* (*multijuga*), and
M to T   has longer racemes of mauve pea-flowers. Often a slow starter, wisteria grows fast once it becomes established and needs regular training whether as a climber or as an open-ground shrub.

Stand in alcohol for a short time, then in deep, cool water.

37

Lilac to Purple and Violet Flowers
(c) Midsummer

Roses

Hybrid Teas and Floribundas

L-T/M   I believe that the trend towards mauve tints in Hybrid Teas began years ago with 'Grey Pearl', which still appears in Scott's list, though generally dropped as being too difficult. Weakling though it was, its ineffable hue—not quite grey, not mauve, nor brown, but with a hint of buff—made it an exquisite cut flower. 'Prelude' followed as one of the first true mauves and can still compete with those which have since been developed, year after year, largely for the flower arranger's benefit, so that these too have become a matter of personal choice between varieties such as 'Cologne Carnival', 'Heure Mauve', 'Intermezzo', 'Lilac Time', 'Blue Diamond', 'Blue Moon' and 'Sterling Silver', etc. I shall therefore give details only of my own firm favourite, 'Royal Tan', because for such a real beauty it seems surprisingly little known. From its name it might be thought to belong among the browns, but this elegantly shaped bloom is of an indisputable soft mauve merging into a faint smudge of milk-chocolate-brown only at the base of the petals. The nearest I can get to charting the overall colour is the lightest tint of Pansy Violet (033/3). One other H.T. worthy of special mention, though of a very different hue, is the sumptuous great reddish-purple cabbage-rose bloom of 'Pigalle' (Tyrian Purple, 727/1), which takes on a subtler, more faded mauve tinge with age and has a conspicuous backing of pale greyish-amber. In wet weather 'Pigalle' becomes a slimy brown sponge or a ball of powdery grey mildew—but then I don't know of so very many others to which the same criticism does not apply. In general the mauve H.T.s are much better value for cutting than the Floribundas which, with certain exceptions, are too few-petalled to last long in water. 'Gletscher' is an outstanding exception, with large, full, H.T.-type blooms of a luminous pinkish-mauve borne in huge trusses. In their prime they chart at lightest Magnolia Purple (030/3), fading to palest lilac. The warm lilac 'Ripples' looks a good one, though I haven't tried it. It's well named, with plenty of prettily crimped petals.

Climbers

L-T   I see that 'Sterling Silver' exists in climbing form and that LeGrice lists one called 'Royal Lavender', which combines this colour with grey and pink tints. I can't imagine these being very effective against walls etc., and the flower arranger would surely be defeating her own ends by growing them up and away out of reach except by ladder or long-armed pruner. There are of course several well-known Ramblers in this colour group, among which 'Bleu Magenta' and 'Violette' bear darkest crimson-purple clusters of bloom (larger and more double in the first case), 'Veilchenblau' is of a lighter, more amethyst hue, with very large flower-clusters and 'Améthyste', also with large clusters of double flowers, combines tones of rich mauve to violet.

Hybrid Musk

L-T/M   Usually listed as a modern Hybrid Musk, elsewhere as a Floribunda, the cruelly misnamed 'Magenta' is much larger and fuller-flowered than most, in a deep rosy-mauve charting at a light tint of Lilac Purple (031/2), from which any suggestion of crude magenta is entirely absent. This sturdy shrub is so free-flowering that the branches are often bowed with the weight of the blooms and it keeps up the performance with only brief pauses throughout the season. Although a modern rose it's suggestive of some of the old shrub types in its rather flat, full-petalled centre and associates harmoniously with them, both in colour and in design.

Old Shrub Roses

L-T/M 'Jenny Duval' (Gallica) is one of my favourites, despite a fair proportion of malformed flowers, which is easily forgiven in a rose which blooms so profusely over so long a period at midsummer, weather permitting. The slightly smaller-than-average flowers are very double, almost bursting out at the centre, and are charmingly shaded from the vivid hued purple heart to palest lilac at the edges (Orchid Purple, 31/1–3) with a somewhat ruffled air, making a surprisingly gay outdoor effect for

L-T/T one of the mauves. 'William Lobb' is a most vigorous tall Moss Rose of a smoky deep crimson-purple well swaddled in 'moss'. And the same colour is reproduced in the wide, flat bloom of the rather spindly old Hybrid Perpetual, 'Reine des Violettes', which has a button-eyed, quartered centre, but otherwise somewhat re-sembling a taller and more purple 'Tuscany Superb'.

L-T/M The prickly Rugosa, 'Roseraie de l'Hay', has quite startlingly vivid magenta-purple blooms with yellow stamens (Orchid Purple, 31) among light green, crinkly leaves which turn clear yellow in the autumn. The flowers are large and only semi-double, in clusters bearing such a succession of buds waiting to open up that it makes better cut material than might be supposed. If kept deadheaded it provides a non-stop display through-out the summer—indeed it will stand any amount of cutting and can be hard pruned to a really low shrub form if necessary. It's more intensely fragrant than any rose in this garden, scenting the air far around on a warm summer's day. Aphids take advantage of the deeply veined and wrinkled foliage to huddle in young shoots, but it's impervious to disease in any form.

For general comments on roses, see pages 79 and 82.

Large-flowered Clematis Hybrids

L-T/ Climbers There's so bewildering a choice in the purple and violet colour range among the large-flowered hybrid clematis that it's difficult to sort out one or two to suit one's particular fancy. I think it's important to see them in flower, no matter how accurate your catalogue descriptions may be. The fact that one has yellow stamens, one white, another brown, or that the sepals are longer and narrower in some than in others, let alone the effect of bars and stripes and suffusions of colour, all make it advisable to inspect the goods in order to assess their relative merits, especially when one has only room for one or two of them. In each of the sections on clematis I feel compelled to remind readers that one has only to compare the growers' lists to discover that the flowering season attributed to any particular variety is pretty arbitrary, one for instance describing 'Ville de Lyon' as spring-flowering, another as from June to October and yet others July to October. One is tempted to believe that most clematis flower just as the fancy takes them, depending on individual treatment, aspect and so on. Those described in the present section are, however, some of the most truly representative of the midsummer group.

It may be worth elaborating the point that the familiar Old Man's Beard is accustomed to scramble through trees and shrubs in the wild and that cultivated forms may similarly be used to great advantage in the garden, where they're more usually confined to the formality of walls, trellises and pergolas. Some garden species or hybrid will be in bloom at almost any season, so there's no difficulty in achieving a colour contrast with a suitable host in simultaneous bloom or in disguising the dullness of one not in flower, in either case accommodating two plants for the space of one. In the first instance one might combine a July-flowering violet-blue clematis with the yellow cascades of the Mount Etna broom, or an early pale lilac one with plum-coloured crab apple blossom amid dark leaves. I hesitate to suggest enlivening a mass of dark, dull rhododendron foliage by this means lest I may be thought to condemn all rhododendron foliage as dull—in fact the genus provides some of the best loved of all my leaves but certain hardy hybrid foliage in particular is sufficiently unremarkable to support a late summer-flowering clematis in any of the paler hues, including white. Winter-flowering subjects may pay their passage through the summer as hosts to clematis and, conversely, *C. balearica* (*calycina*) (preferably WS) may clothe the bare winter bones of a summer shrub with its pale yellow bells and ferny, bronzed foliage from January to March with the help of adequate shelter. Then again, clematis may serve to contrast with a variegated tree or shrub.

Starting once more with the bluest in the present period, we have 'Perle d'Azur' (O) which isn't far from the border line of true blue, charting at an overall Dauphin's Violet (039/1) on account of the faintly more purple band down the centre of the Wisteria Blue sepals. (I have two of these in flower as I write in August, whereas a third which bloomed well in late spring is now devoid of bud or bloom.) 'Lasurstern' (ESW) is a most handsome, large-flowered blue-violet with cream stamens and a wavy margin to the broad, tapering sepals. Here it adds colour to a patch of leafy summer boredom occupied by a large witch hazel through which it trails its flowers. 'Will Goodwin' (ESW) is another first-class variety with lavender-blue, beautifully waved and deeply veined blooms with yellow stamens. The large-flowered 'Beauty of Richmond' (ESW) is fairly similar in colour, but with a darker centre. 'W. E. Gladstone' (SW) has lavender flowers of exceptional size with darker purple stamens and 'Lady Northcliffe' (ESW) is a shapely, rather deeper violet, with a white central boss. 'The President' (O) is one of the best doers in my garden which, on the whole, is rather over-acid for their taste, regularly producing two generous crops of violet-purple flowers with redder-purple stamens and a decorative backing of silver.

L-T/
Semi-
Climber

Clematis × *durandii* (O) isn't strictly speaking a large-flowered hybrid, being semi-herbaceous, though sometimes listed among them. Its blooms aren't more than three or four inches across, made up of four very deeply ribbed, wavy sepals as solid as thick leather, with a central knob of cream-yellow stamens. Its slaty blue-grey-violet is just about unchartable, but of the utmost subtlety as a cut flower. It's too smoky-hued to show up well in the garden, except on close examination, charting somewhere between the lightest tint of the sombre Aconite Violet (937/3) and Dauphin's Violet (039). It remains constantly in flower from early summer through autumn, but shows some tendency to mildew if not kept adequately watered in a wall position and dusted or sprayed with Karathane if necessary, especially towards the close of its long season. It's not a twiner by nature, so needs careful training and tying in to prevent its lovely flowers dangling awkwardly upside down. When I bought it I understood that it would die down almost to the ground in winter, but it's never shown the slightest inclination to do so and I believe I ought to do the hard pruning that nature regularly leaves undone; but such pruning as it gets is incidental, though fairly severe, for the only factor to retain my greed for these enchanting flowers for indoor decoration is the thought that I shall need so many more of them and must therefore spare plenty of the budded side-shoots between June and October. (These have smaller blooms than the terminal ones.)

Clematis florida 'Sieboldii' (*bicolor*)

L-T/
Climber

Clematis florida 'Sieboldii' (S) is a small-flowered type with a miniature rosette-shaped bloom, about four inches across, of fascinating detail, consisting of a circle of cream-white sepals surrounding a domed cushion of petal-like purple stamens. There is something faintly suggestive of the passion flower about its colouring and design, which needs to be studied at close quarters to be properly appreciated. Its height is in keeping with the modest scale of its flowers, not exceeding about nine feet as a climber. The flowering period is roughly June to September. Unfortunately this choice little clematis is neither very hardy nor very easy to succeed with except in ideal circumstances of soil and climate; it proved too pernickety for me in the best conditions I had to offer.

For general comments on clematis, see pages 71–2 and 210–11.

Singe or boil all clematis.

Hardy Hybrid Rhododendrons

'Purple Splendour'

E/M

The deep, rich tone of *Rhododendron* 'Purple Splendour' ('A') cools the hotter colours in the shrub garden at midsummer. It makes only a medium-sized shrub which flowers with the greatest freedom and regularity. The well-formed flowers are Doge Purple (732) but look much darker on account of their black-purple eye. In the garden its colour is a fine ingredient for mixing with flame, pink, lilac or pale yellow flowers and with lime or silvery foliages.

'Mrs. T. H. Lowinsky'

E/T

'Mrs. T. H. Lowinsky' ('B') is sometimes listed among the whites, but the general effect of the shrub in bloom seems to me to be predominantly pale lilac. This is the

ZENOBIA pulverulenta

Hybrid Musk Rose 'Magenta'

colour of the flower-trusses in bud and they open to palest lilac-white with a bold, coppery-maroon blotch—a sumptuous flower-truss for a large arrangement and an attractive and free-flowering garden shrub.

'Fastuosum Flore Pleno'

E/T There are those who write off *Rhododendron* 'Fastuosum Flore Pleno' ('A') as 'looking too much like a common *ponticum*'; but for those who have eyes to see there is not much similarity. For one thing the flowers are double—in this case an added attraction, for there is nothing clumsy about them—and for another I doubt whether one would ever find a wild *R. ponticum* in such a lovely tint of light mauve-violet (Cobalt Violet, 634/2–3) with a slight green flare. 'Fastuosum Flore Pleno' is further criticized as being specially prone to attack by the rhododendron fly, but I have had no such trouble with mine, which is grown, as recommended, in part shade.

All these three varieties are so generous with their flowers that after only a few years one can well steal a fair number of trusses without their being missed.

Boil all these, for safety.

Abutilon vitifolium

L-T/T Unfortunately, *Abutilon vitifolium* is not a very hardy subject, and even in a warm garden a mature specimen will sometimes let one down quite suddenly and un-accountably. However, the cloud of pale Cobalt Violet (634/3) hollyhock-flowers is so delightful when the plant succeeds that it is very well worth trying in favourable conditions. Much of its rapid soft growth may be killed back in a cold winter. My plant perished before I was able to try it for cutting purposes.

38

Lilac to Purple and Violet Flowers and Fruits
(d) Late Summer and Autumn

Large-flowered Clematis Hybrids

L-T/ Despite the wide discrepancy in growers' assessments of
Climbers clematis flowering periods, mainly applying to those
liable to give one crop of bloom in late spring or early
summer and another later in summer or autumn, my
own classification of the late-flowerers concentrates on
those which flower *only* in late summer and autumn. In
particular this simplifies the pruning problem, because
all of these—and only these—should be cut *hard* back in
early spring, either to a good pair of embryo buds close
to the base of the previous year's growth (easily distin-
guishable) or, if necessary, right back to three or four
feet from the ground. Such wholesale reduction of any
of the other varieties will almost certainly be fatal, as I
have once or twice unintentionally proved to my own
cost. The clematis mentioned in this section, with their
one late-flowering crop of bloom, are sometimes still
referred to in the catalogues as belonging to the Jackmanii or Viticella groups, both of which stand drastic
pruning. But there has been so much interbreeding between the various groups of recent years that the group
system (on which pruning instructions had hitherto been
based) has now largely been dropped and pruning instructions codified in a simple form by all the specialist
growers.

No matter what the type of pruning recommended
any clematis may be allowed to ramble through trees

and shrubs with little or no pruning, where space and other conditions permit; but if the supporting plant itself needs to be cut back fairly hard each year at a certain season it would be as well to choose one of these true late-flowering types of clematis, able to take sufficiently drastic pruning to simplify that of its host, which would otherwise become virtually unprunable amid the dense tangle of some type of clematis allergic to anything more than a light trim.

'Ascotiensis' (O) is one of the most nearly blue of the late batch, with long, pointed, bright blue-violet sepals and green stamens and is one of many very free-flowering varieties. 'Étoile Violette' (ESW) shares an equally prodigal flowering habit, in deep violet with yellow stamens. 'Lady Betty Balfour' (S) is similar in colour, with flowers of an exceptional size for a late flowering sort—six to eight inches across, that is, about two inches more than the average among the late ones. She needs full sun to bring on her flowers which, though prolific, come unusually late in the season (September to October). Having never had a single bloom on my own 'Lady', planted years ago, in my ignorance, on the shady side of a large shrub with additional overhead shade, I can testify that full sun is essential to draw her out! 'Gipsy Queen' (ESW) is a velvety violet-purple with redder stamens; and, of a number of Jackmanii varieties 'Jackmanii Superba' (O) is my choice for its richness of hue and more generously shaped sepals. It's as dark a velvet purple as any I know, with a green centre. Either this or 'Gipsy Queen' is most effective when growing through a variegated tree such as *Acer negundo* 'Variegatum', the pallid green and white foliage of the maple making an excellent foil to the trails of rich, deep purple bloom, often fooling the passer-by into believing the tree to be in flower. 'Comtesse de Bouchaud' (O) is a most vigorous pinkish-lilac with cream stamens and 'Hagley Hybrid' (O) is a particularly popular variety of a rosy-mauve still pinker than that of the Countess. Its form is distinctive, with elegantly tapered sepals surrounding maroon-brown stamens. Two of almost startling colour are 'Ernest Markham' (ESW), in a vivid petunia-red to magenta, with cream stamens, and the bright, rather more carmine-red 'Ville de Lyon', deepening in colour at the edges and yellow-stamened.

For general comments on clematis see also pages 71–2.

Singe or boil.

Buddleia davidii Hybrids (Butterfly Bush)

'Royal Red' and 'Fromow's Purple'

L-T/T   As cutting material the most attractive buddleias are to be found among the whites, or best of all, perhaps, the unusual creamy-apricot 'Golden Glow'; but in the shrub borders these are not nearly so effective as the vivid purples and violets available nowadays among modern hybrid varieties such as 'Royal Red' and 'Fromow's Purple'. There is no truly red buddleia, though 'Royal Red' comes nearer to it than any. The colour is in fact an intense crimson-purple (Violet Purple, 733/1–2). 'Fromow's Purple' is just slightly bluer (Bishop's Violet, 34/1–2) and almost equally striking. Both are a great deal more spectacular than the rather pasty-faced *B. davidii* so often seen to survive as a gaunt antique in old-world gardens up and down the country. The newer colourings are especially useful in gardens where these can't be achieved with the hydrangeas; and even where purple and violet-hued hydrangeas abound one may still be grateful for the contrast in height and in the spiky form of the elongated flower-panicles. The spike-shape also provides welcome variation indoors among the predominantly circular forms of late summer in this colour range.

For pruning, see page 92.

212

Hydrangea villosa

L-T/
M to T
As far as I know, the only hydrangea which can be relied upon to produce a constant light violet flower-colour regardless of the *p*H value of the soil is the attractive wild species, *H. villosa*—or, if others share this convenient trait, at least they are not very generally available in commerce. It makes a tall, spreading, hairy-leaved shrub, with irregularly formed lacecap type inflorescences composed of a fluffy central cushion of tiny fertile flowers surrounded by a number of larger, sterile ones. The flower-head is less solid than most and is more adaptable as material for flower arrangement. It isn't an entirely hardy species, but I'm able to succeed with it in a very much sheltered position.

For conditioning, see page 76.

Hydrangea × macrophylla Varieties

The *Hydrangea × macrophylla* varieties can, of course, be grown in limy gardens, but those which follow could not qualify for inclusion in this colour section in such circumstances, since the flower-colour would then be red. Those that have purple or violet flowers in my particular soil conditions are:

'Westfalen': Dahlia Purple (931) with a bluer eye; dwarf.

'Ami Pasquier': similar, but slightly less dwarf.

'Europa', 'Maréchal Foch', 'Kluis Superba' and 'Altona': all of medium height. 'Altona's' deep velvety crimson autumn colour, which is not dependent on soil conditions, has already been dealt with on page 190. Before this stage of incipient desiccation sets in the colour, in this garden, is a fine deep violet.

For pruning of the *H. × macrophylla* varieties, see page 91; and for conditioning of cut material see page 76.

Caryopteris × *clandonensis*

L-T/D   Though I once had four or five plants of the violet-flowered *Caryopteris* × *clandonensis* (Dauphin's Violet, 039), I am now left with but a single survivor. It isn't really tough enough for local conditions and in this backward garden its flowers come almost too late to be appreciated, though any patch of violet is welcome among the predominating reds, flames and yellows of autumn.

The grey-blue-green characteristic of the foliage persists for a time in the seed-heads, which provide attractive spikes of clustered little blue-green beads for cutting. These also dry well, but the glaucous colour soon fades to buff.

One is told to prune to within two or three buds from the base of the previous year's growth annually in March or early April. I believe late April will be time enough in a cold garden.

Caryopteris 'Kew Blue'

L-T/D   One of my sisters grows a very much better-coloured variety called 'Kew Blue' in her garden not far from the south coast. The colour is a really intense and eye-catching blue-violet, but I don't know how this one compares for hardiness with *C.* × *clandonensis*. Quite possibly it might be even more tender, for those I saw were growing in a climate much more favourable than mine.

Hebe 'Autumn Glory' (Form of Shrubby Veronica)

L-T/E/D   Most of the hebes are too tender for me, but the low-growing 'Autumn Glory' is unusually tough. It bears small spikes of very dark, Campanula Violet (37) flowers late into the autumn and the neatly disposed evergreen foliage is tipped with brownish-purple. It will supply quite long, arching evergreen sprays for outline or short heads of dark-hued foliage for filling in, combining delightfully with *Rhododendron* × *praecox*, *Helleborus orientalis*, bergenias and such-like in earliest spring arrangements.

The seed-heads should be removed after flowering and some general clipping back in late spring prevents this hebe from becoming over-lanky.

Hebe 'Violet Snow' (Form of Shrubby Veronica)

L-T/E/M *Hebe* 'Violet Snow' is another unusually hardy variety. It makes a compact evergreen shrub of four feet or so, with much longer and larger flower-spikes in a mixture of white and light violet and with glossy light green leaves of elongated shape. The effect is cool and pleasing from July to October in the borders; but it makes awkward cutting material because the side-shoots are so stiffly angled. The best solution is to strip these and use only the terminal panicles.

Remove the spent flower-heads in late autumn and clip over occasionally in spring.

Fuchsias

'Riccartonii'

L-T/ As I have already suggested, there is no need to be faint-
M to T hearted about some of the more interesting fuchsias. If I could risk nothing more exciting than 'Riccartonii' I think I'd go without, for it is usually a mere shadow of its real self in cold gardens inland, though ablaze with colour in warmer seaboard areas.

'Margaret'

L-T/M Fortunately the large-flowered scarlet and purple 'Margaret' seems every bit as hardy as 'Riccartonii' and is a splendidly showy fuchsia of special value in the average to cold garden.

'Royal Purple'

L-T/D 'Royal Purple', which I have never seen listed as an outdoor variety, repeats the blood-red and purple combination in a much dwarfer plant. For those with a taste for bold colour schemes the Carmine hue of Rose 'Bonn' and the Orchid Purple of 'Roseraie de l'Hay' are well matched with the two last-named fuchsias in a supporting role. When stripped of all greenery I enjoy an occasional arrangement of this kind in a deep green Victorian glass lustre container.

'Rose of Castile Improved'

L-T/ 'Rose of Castile Improved' is a large-flowered, exotic-
D to M looking, flesh-pink and purple variety which one would hardly expect to succeed in the open. And yet my two plants come up and flower regularly year after year after dying to the ground in winter. This is more in keeping with my normal tastes as a cut flower and combines delightfully with roses of pink and mauve colouring.

For general comments on fuchsias and for conditioning, see pages 145–6.

Lavandula spica 'Hidcote' (or *L.s.* 'Nana Atropurpurea')

L-T/E/D Although the lavender known as 'Hidcote' is a true dwarf the flowers come with quite long stems for cutting. The colour is a specially rich deep violet and the habit is dense and bushy if the plants are dead-headed in autumn and then trimmed each spring. This is a first-class variety for the edge of the shrub borders.

Pernettya mucronata 'Davis's Hybrids'

E/D to M The cyclamen-hued berries of *Pernettya mucronata* appear in the autumn and persist throughout the winter. Even in a single cluster of fat berries the colouring varies widely in intensity from pale lilac on the shady side to rosy purple in full sunlight. Unfortunately, it is altogether too invasive for a really small garden. It is also intolerant of lime. These hybrids also come in other colours.

216

Callicarpa bodinieri giraldii (*C. giraldiana*)

L-T/   Only a few of the callicarpas are hardy enough for the
M to T   average climate and none, alas, for mine. Luckily the
spectacular fruiting shrub *Callicarpa bodinieri giraldii* is
among the hardier sorts, with rather upright branches
fairly plastered with small, glistening light lilac-violet
berries set off by tactfully hued autumn leaves tinted
pink and mauve. Full sun is necessary to effect this fine
spectacle, which is usually at its best only if several
specimens are planted together. The variety, 'Profusion',
is claimed as even more of an eyeful than the species.

Calluna vulgaris 'H. E. Beale' (Form of Heather)

E/D   *Calluna vulgaris* 'H. E. Beale' is possibly the most popular heather among flower arrangers. It provides charming cutting material, for the minute, double pompons of
soft rosy-mauve tight packed into long, branching
flower-spikes are delightful in their detail.

Clip heaths and heathers annually in the spring.

39

Lilac to Purple and Violet Flowers
(e) Winter

Erica carnea Varieties (Winter-Flowering Heaths)

L-T/E/D The winter-flowering heaths, unlike their summer-flowering relatives, will put up with moderately alkaline soil conditions. I would always find room for some of the *Erica carnea* varieties, which provide a carpet of welcome, if somewhat pallid, colour from December into April and make efficient, weed-smothering ground cover beneath the taller shrubs which will take over the display later on. *E. carnea* itself is a rather anaemic pale Mallow Purple (630/3), but most of its hybrids are considerably more colourful. One of the most vivid is 'King George' (light Cyclamen Purple, 30/2) and 'Vivellii' is even brighter, but in my experience this is not a very robust variety. 'Winter Beauty' and 'Ruby Glow' are of a lighter pinkish-mauve; and 'Springwood Pink' is a particularly vigorous grower of Pastel Mauve (433) colouring. My reasons have been given on page 96 for allowing the winter-flowering heaths space in the text while banishing most other ericas to Appendix II as insufficiently useful for cutting.

I clip the winter-flowering sorts over every other year after flowering, in place of the more usual annual trim.

Erica × darleyensis

L-T/E/D *Erica × darleyensis* makes a sturdy bush of about two feet high and its light Petunia Purple (32/3) harmonizes well with the deeper-hued *E. carnea* hybrids in the same colour range. The flower-spikes are of considerable length and are useful for cutting.

40

Blue Flowers
(a) Late Spring

The flowers of such plants as wisteria, caryopteris, *Abutilon vitifolium*, lavender, etc., which are so commonly described as blue are not my idea of blue at all. Nevertheless, one can only draw the line rather arbitrarily between blue and violet and I have done so, in terms of the H.C.C., round about Hyacinth Blue (40), which makes border-line cases of my own particular forms of *Rhododendron augustinii*, for example.

Ceanothus Varieties (Californian Lilac)

'Delight'

L-T/E/T The first spring-flowering ceanothus I tried in this garden was 'Delight', which, though picked out from a catalogue, turned out to have flowers of a fine rich blue. It survived for a number of years amid the nakedness of the newly planted shrub borders; but it got badly damaged in severe winters and became so gaunt and unsightly that I was at length obliged to throw it out. It might have fared better in the greater shelter of present-day conditions.

impressus and × *veitchianus*

L-T/E/T I now have several specimens of *Ceanothus impressus* and one of × *veitchianus* (alias 'Brilliant'), which seems to me as good, both in constitution and in the excellent deep blue flower colour, and these really have proved tolerably hardy in the less bleak surroundings of the open garden as it is today. Nevertheless the specimen of *C. impressus* which grows against the warmest house-wall is far and away the most vigorous of any.

In their early years these evergreen ceanothuses benefit from some periodical pinching out of the extreme tips of the shoots to induce a bushy habit from the start and should be cut back quite hard after flowering.

Abies delavayi forrestii (Form of Silver Fir)

L-T/E/
Tree

It may seem a mean trick to whet the flower arranger's appetite with a panegyric on this very rare tree, which costs a great deal of money whenever it may happen to be available. Some may console themselves with the knowledge that their garden couldn't hold so large a tree as this becomes, and there must always be some rich enough and with acres enough to accommodate it if they can get it. Messrs. Hillier's supply was exhausted after putting it on show recently and they say it will take a couple of years to replace their stock. If you're beginning to wonder why so much fuss about this fir I can only say that its cones must be seen to be believed, for their colour, in youth, is probably unique in horticulture. But to call this purple, or violet-blue, as some have done, is just chicken-hearted; for the young cones are an out-and-out, indisputable *navy* blue, slowly turning to more indigo-black as they age. They form a closely sealed, geometrically patterned, blunted ellipse-shape about three to four inches long by about two inches thick, perching upright on the horizontal branches like rows of tight-lipped Humpty-dumpties. These incredible, unplantlike confections are borne by quite young trees of less than human height. I saw some recently in use in one of our national flower arrangement exhibitions, so possibly this unique Oxford blue seed-head, which is what it really is, will also have caught the covetous eye of some of my readers.

41

Blue Flowers
(b) Midsummer

Hydrangea acuminata 'Bluebird'

D   I can record only three blue-flowered shrubs for midsummer in my garden and even these will only be blue in an acid soil, for all three are hydrangeas. The dwarf *Hydrangea acuminata* 'Bluebird' is one of the prettiest of the lacecap types, with intense china-blue flowers, consisting of an outer circle of the larger, sterile flowers surrounding a flat cluster of tiny fertile flowers of a rather deeper hue.

Hydrangea × *macrophylla* 'Mousseline' and *H.* × *m.* 'Générale Vicomtesse de Vibraye'

M   Among the solid-flowered *Hydrangea* × *macrophylla* varieties two of the earliest are 'Mousseline' and 'Générale Vicomtesse de Vibraye' (commonly abbreviated to 'Vibraye', or 'Vicomtesse de Vibraye' with good reason). Both are excellent light blues (Butterfly Blue, 645/1) in an acid soil (an uninteresting pale pink in alkaline conditions). 'Vibraye' is perhaps the better of the two. The desiccating flower-heads turn to a wonderful sea-blue-green in autumn.

Other *H.* × *macrophylla* varieties will be found in the Late Summer and Autumn Section.

For pruning of the above hydrangeas, see page 91.

For conditioning, see page 76.

42

Blue Flowers
(c) Late Summer and Autumn

Hydrangea × macrophylla Varieties

'Altona'

M   Most of the hydrangeas previously described as purple
    or violet might well be truly blue in a garden soil more
    acid than mine, so let me once more commend to you
    the splendid 'Altona' in particular, for a good deep
    violet-blue. (See also pages 170, 185 and 212.)

'Bluewave'

M   The lacecap *Hydrangea* 'Bluewave' is one of the largest-
    flowered and latest of its kind, with a flat cluster of tiny
    fertile florets enclosed by a number of showy, sterile
    flowers. In a really acid soil these will combine several
    of the lighter tints of Gentian Blue (42/1–3).

'Veitchii'

M   *H. × m.* 'Veitchii' is much prettier in acid-soiled gar-
    dens, when the central cluster will be a deep china-blue,
    offset by an outer ring of large florets of pure white.
    Unfortunately, I find this hydrangea uncommonly sus-
    ceptible to botrytis fungus, which ruins the immaculate
    appearance of the inflorescences with unsightly brown
    blotches.
        For pruning of *H. × m.* varieties, see page 91.
        For conditioning, see page 76.

Ceanothus (Californian Lilac)

The genus isn't renowned for its hardiness, though I believe one might manage the toughest of them in a shrub border, even in a garden as cold as mine, by shrouding them in fine-mesh windbreak netting in winter.

L-T/E/T Two of the hardiest evergreen forms are the soft-hued 'Autumnal Blue' and the denser, more vivid blue × *burkwoodii*. These will get by without extra winter coddling in reasonably favourable climates, but will generally do better in wall positions in average conditions.

L-T/T Some fairly hardy deciduous varieties include 'Gloire de Versailles', a true powder blue (light Flax Blue)—often most inaccurately advertized as rich blue, deep sky blue, etc.—the genuine muted light grey-blue showing to perfection against faded, mellow old brick. 'Topaz' is said to be similar but of a deeper blue, and 'Henri Desfosse' one of the most colourful, neither making as tall a plant as 'Gloire de Versailles'.

The genus is regarded as lime-tolerant, but I understand that there's a limit to the amount of lime it can digest without coming to grief.

Hibiscus syriacus 'Coelestis' and 'Blue Bird' (Forms of Bush Mallow or Tree Hollyhock)

L-T/T The main colour of the hollyhock-flowers of *Hibiscus syriacus* 'Coelestis' is an intense violet-blue, shading to wine at the heart. Whenever the weather permits a generous crop of bloom this hibiscus makes a cloud of lovely and unusual colour in late summer, but unless it can bask in warm sunshine too many of the flower-buds will turn yellow and drop off unopened. (Being narrower and more upright than most of its kind, *H.s.* 'Coelestis' requires comparatively little space and is worthy of the shelter of a warm house-wall in a cold garden. The more recent 'Blue Bird' is an improvement on 'Coelestis', with large flowers opening wider and rather earlier than the more funnel-shape of the older variety.

No pruning is necessary, but it will stand plenty of cutting at the hands of the flower arranger.

43

Green Flowers
(a) Early Spring

I cannot lay claim to any truly green-flowered shrubs or trees, though I once tried, and failed with, *Itea ilicifolia* (see Late Summer, page 228). I have included several shrubs for their greenish fruits in autumn.

Betula pendula (Silver Birch)

L-T/ Tree   The silver birch is not commonly regarded as a flowering tree although, as flower arrangers will know, its cloud of tight green catkins in early spring are in fact flowers. The fine tracery of the drooping branches hung with their tiny green 'sausages' among the tender young leaves makes wonderfully graceful outlines for pedestal arrangements for just as long as it is there for the picking.

44

Green Flowers and Fruits
(b) Midsummer

Rosa viridiflora

L-T/M   This oddly unroselike pure green jumble of what passes for petals and the rest of the 'works' appears to be a 'must' for the flower arranger, though regarded as a monstrosity or at best as a curiosity by most rosarians. (Available from LeGrice.)

Ballota pseudodictamnus

L-T/E/D   *Ballota pseudodictamnus* is variously described as a sub-shrub or as a herbaceous perennial, but to me it looks distinctly more shrubby than otherwise. The main attraction lies in the woolly whorls of tightly clustered, tiny grey-green funnels which ring the main stem at intervals rather than in the almost invisible, minute lilac flower which peeps out from the centre of each little funnel. The velvety whorls are borne on strong but slender, furry stems, which are often intriguingly curved and contorted and vary from eighteen inches to two feet in length. They provide enchanting live material for the flower arranger, when stripped of their leaves, and also dry well, retaining much of their silvery-green colouring. One must be on one's guard, when using them live in a monochromatic scheme, for example, lest undetected tiny lilac flowers open in water. They can quite easily be plucked out when still in bud by long finger-nails or eyebrow-pluckers.

(See also Foliage Section, page 248.)

45

Green Flowers and Fruits
(c) Late Summer and Autumn

Itea ilicifolia

L-T/E/M *Itea ilicifolia* is an evergreen shrub which bears drooping racemes like long, slender tassels composed of fragrant, tiny pale green flowers among the glossy, holly-like leaves from which it gets its specific name. It is generally recommended as a wall shrub in all but the warmest gardens. The elegantly tapered, catkin-like flower-sprays make lovely cutting material.

Hydrangea × *macrophylla* 'Mme Émile Mouillère', *H. cinerea* 'Sterilis' and *H.* × *m.* 'Vibraye'

L-T/M As far as I know there is no such thing as a green-flowered hydrangea, but the flowers of one or two of the *H.* × *macrophylla* varieties pass through an interesting green stage before fading to their winter buff colour.

The white-flowered 'Mme Émile Mouillère' and *H. cinerea* 'Sterilis', for instance, take on a most pleasing light apple-green tint in autumn. And the light Butterfly Blue of *H.* 'Vibraye' is transformed, in my acid soil conditions, to a luminous deep sea-green throughout late summer and autumn. At this stage of their metamorphosis the flower-heads contrast excitingly with such roses as 'Orangeade', 'Shepherd's Delight' and 'Super Star' or will effectively light up monochromatic arrangements in combination with the glaucous foliage of *Crambe maritima*, eucalyptus and rue and the match-

228

ing seed-heads of opium poppies and *Caryopteris* ×
clandonensis.

At this stage the flower-heads of these hydrangeas
last for ages in water without special conditioning.

Chaenomeles (Japonica)

L-T/
D to T
    Some of the best green fruits come from the chaenomeles
and in particular from the dwarf species *C. japonica* and
C.j. 'Dwarf Poppy Red', which bear several little ribbed
and puckered yellowish-green quinces to the sprig.

    The larger fruits of *C.* × *superba* 'Knap Hill Scarlet'
and of the *speciosa* varieties 'Simonii' and 'Moerloosii'
etc. are presented rather awkwardly on the branch for
cutting purposes, but these can be remounted on handier
stems and will last in this way for weeks without
deteriorating. These rather pointed apple-shapes range
from light yellow to dark green with paler flecks and
sometimes a russet flush.

Pyracantha atalantioides 'Aurea' (Form of Firethorn)

L-T/E/T
    Among the fruits which I find invaluable for flower
arrangement are those of *Pyracantha atalantioides*
'Aurea' before they have fully ripened to their ultimate
warm yellow hue.

    (See also pages 78 and 121.)

Enkianthus campanulatus

T
    Another favourite for cutting in the seeding stage is
Enkianthus campanulatus, with its neat little upturned
clusters of green beads, which has been more fully dealt
with on pages 132–3.

Hypericum kouytchense (Form of Shrubby St. John's Wort)

L-T/M
    Hypericum kouytchense is an undemanding plant which
will make do with any old corner out of sight. It isn't
perhaps one of the best of the hypericums, but I consider
the green and russet fruits a most welcome addition to
the assortment available for indoor decoration.

46

Green Flowers
(d) Winter

Garrya elliptica

E/T It may seem a bit of a quibble to have included the ballota and *Garrya elliptica* in a section on green flowers, the one being silver-green and the other rather more grey than green; but both fit more suitably here than elsewhere and must not be omitted.

G. elliptica is generously hung with clusters of long, elegantly tapered grey-green catkins against dark, leathery evergreen leaves throughout the leanest months, from November to February. By far the best catkins come from the male plants, mostly around six inches but sometimes as much as twelve inches long, which is more than double the size of the female catkins. It's a fast-growing shrub, but not 100 per cent hardy, so that in most gardens it needs protection from the north and east if grown in open-ground positions and is usually safer against a wall. Garryas must never be cut back during the summer.

Ribes laurifolium

L-T/E/D This uncommon ribes is far from spectacular but should be of considerable interest to flower arrangers in particular by reason of its pendent racemes of rather starry pale green flowers borne in late winter. The leathery leaves are large for the size of the plant and it seems perfectly hardy. Its dwarf habit recommended it to me as a suitable evergreen for shading the base of a clematis growing against a north-east wall. It is in any case especially appropriate for house beds and will put up with the coldest aspects.

47

Preface to the Foliage Section

Now, at last, it is time to turn to the 'lovely leaves'. Fortunately for the flower arranger many foliage plants are sufficiently ornamental in themselves, either in colour or in form, to deserve a place of honour in the shrub garden, though if you share my *penchant* for foliage arrangements you will have to resist the temptation to overload your borders with trees and shrubs grown primarily or solely for their ornamental leaves.

Because foliages, even when deciduous, are so much more permanent than flowers there is no reason to continue the seasonal sub-divisions here. Evergreen plants will, as usual, be designated by the marginal letter E; and unless stated otherwise the foliage may be assumed to persist from spring until late autumn.

48

Variegated Foliage

Though I have already sounded a warning to flower arrangers against excessive indulgence of their appetite for foliage plants generally in the small shrub garden I feel I ought to add another here in respect of variegation, which tends to be over-obtrusive in the landscape.

I mention this because variegated foliage presents a special temptation to many flower arrangers besides myself. All the same, my own belief is that with careful placing a modest collection of these may be included in one's planting with advantage.

Acer negundo 'Variegatum' (Form of Maple)

L-T/
Tree

Biggest and most conspicuous is my graceful green and white maple, *Acer negundo* 'Variegatum', which I regard as a real asset to the shrub garden. The dark, velvety purple blooms of a *Clematis* 'Jackmanii Superba' trail through the cool green and white tracery of my variegated maple in late summer with delightful effect.

This maple is one of the sluggards, but though it may take its time about coming into leaf in spring, it makes up for it later by providing generous quantities of cut foliage from early summer until well into the autumn. The branches assume good, informal lines and the delicate leaf colouring makes a most graceful framework for green and white arrangements as well as for a variety of colours.

When boiled and soaked and stem-tipped under water it has never given me any trouble whatever, even in most testing conditions under canvas in a heat-wave after a long journey by car.

Euonymus fortunei 'Variegatus' ('Gracilis')

L-T/E/ D to Climber

In *Euonymus fortunei* 'Variegatus' the colour combination is also green and white. This obligingly lime-tolerant shrub is especially valuable on account of its evergreen character, the small green leaves margined with white assuming an attractive pink tinge in winter. In the open garden it makes a dense, low mound, but if grown against a wall it will clamber slowly to a height of nine or ten feet, clinging to the surface with aerial roots, like ivy. All but the palest of clematis look well against it and on a north wall the dainty little scarlet flowers of *Tropaeolum speciosum* would make gay trails through the green and white foliage of the euonymus, though only in lime-free conditions.

Euonymus japonicus 'Albomarginatus'

L-T/E/ M to T

Euonymus japonicus 'Albomarginatus' is another good evergreen variety, especially for cutting. The glossy, rounded, oval leaves are larger and less closely packed than those of *E. fortunei* 'Variegatus' and the colour is an exceptionally light green in the centre with an edging of cream or white. It is somewhat slow-growing and of doubtful hardiness.

Cornus alba 'Elegantissima' (Form of Dogwood)

L-T/M

Cornus alba 'Elegantissima' is a form of variegated dogwood with well-shaped, tapering leaves striped green and white which have all the elegance their name suggests. Since I couldn't find room for both I chose this in preference to its green and yellow counterpart, *C. alba* 'Spaethii', particularly as material for flower arrangement. Both varieties are attractive garden shrubs, with decorative red-barked stems to provide colour in the winter when the branches are bare.

My *C. alba* 'Elegantissima' forms part of a satisfying group of shrubs planted solely for foliage effect on an awkward bank where little else had succeeded. The planting includes grey-green senecio, purplish-brown cotinus and berberis, blue-green eucalyptus, juniper and rue, silvery santolina, old-gold hebe, purple sage, a variety of lime-green subjects and the grey-green shot with plum-purple which makes up the indescribable foliage of *Rosa rubrifolia.*

Weigela florida 'Variegata' (or *Diervilla florida* 'Variegata')

L-T/M *Weigela florida* 'Variegata' carries its attractive cream-margined foliage in slender, arching sprays, with here and there a tall straight shoot of bolder leaves supplied by the newest growth; so it can hardly fail to please most flower arrangers.

The spent flower-shoots (the flowers are pale apple-blossom pink) should be removed in later summer and I also find it advisable to cut out some of the oldest wood and tangled, spindly shoots from time to time, though the foliage proves so useful for indoor decoration that my bush gets a great deal of incidental pruning.

The foliage certainly needs boiling in the earlier part of the season, though it often lasts perfectly well in late summer and autumn with no more than a good preliminary soaking.

Elaeagnus pungens 'Maculata'

L-T/E/ *Elaeagnus pungens* 'Maculata' is one of the most spectac-
M to T ularly colourful of all variegated evergreen shrubs and one of great merit in the winter landscape in particular, with its leathery, oval, dark green leaves gaily splashed and striped with vivid yellow and backed with scaly silver. Unfortunately, it takes a long time to achieve a mature specimen from which any cut material will be available. I find the leaf-shoots somewhat awkwardly disposed at unco-operative angles for anything other than a very large arrangement.

Whenever plain green leaves appear the whole shoot should be cut away immediately.

Ligustrum ovalifolium 'Aureum' (Golden Privet)

L-T/T   This old friend will certainly be familiar to you under the name of golden privet. And friend it truly is, to gardener and flower arranger alike. Very nearly evergreen, it keeps its vivid yellow-greenery throughout the winter, shedding its leaves only when we are beginning to feel that we can spare them, with the promise of spring just around the corner—and the new ones quickly follow.

The degree of yellowness in the foliage is largely dependent on exposure to sunlight—plants, or those parts of them, growing in the shade tending to lime, or greener, colouring with very little trace of variegation, instead of the more characteristic bright yellow with its slight admixture of green.

Phormium tenax 'Variegatum' (Form of New Zealand Flax)

L-T/E/   In spite of their enormously tall spikes of mahogany-
M to T   coloured flowers the chief decorative value of all phormiums lies in the dense clumps of sword-like evergreen foliage which rise to a height of six feet or so to provide a dramatically contrasting shape in the shrub beds and striking material for large indoor arrangements. In the variegated form the tall, immensely tough leaf-blades are more or less conspicuously striped with cream. It is as well to select your own plant if possible.

The phormiums are said to prefer moist situations, but the most massive specimens I know flourish at the top of an arid, sandy bank!

Yucca filamentosa 'Variegata'

L-T/E/D   *Yucca filamentosa* 'Variegata' is of similar leaf structure on a much reduced scale. I have kept one alive for fourteen years, but, in all this time it has had a single flower-spike and the cluster of green and cream-striped sword-blades has virtually stood still. The foliage is sufficiently spectacular to make me long to succeed with it. There is more deep cream than green in the striping of the leaves but, alas, they are far from numerous. I suppose I have been over-optimistic in attempting to grow this semi-tropical desert plant in the open garden, however warm and sheltered the position; it is now beginning to perk up at the foot of a south wall.

Actinidia kolomikta

L-T/ Climber *Actinidia kolomikta* is a climber of unique appearance. The young foliage is ordinary enough to start with, but by some mysterious alchemy the terminal half of most of the leaves soon breaks into a patchwork of clear pink and white, while the rest retains a regulation green colour. On paper this may sound a bit of a mess, but the visual effect is in fact delightful.

This actinidia certainly needs a warm wall and after an uncommonly slow start my own plant has reached eight feet in as many years, most of this growth having, however, been made in the last two seasons. Now that it has at last got going an isolated late spring frost has wrecked the foliage two years running, just as the pink and white zones were beginning to appear. I have, however, learnt not to be in too much of a hurry to throw any difficult plant on the rubbish heap.

Though I have never had an opportunity to try *A. kolomikta* as cut foliage I have seen it used, so I think it may be assumed to last satisfactorily in water.

Hedera canariensis 'Variegata' ('Gloire de Marengo') (Form of Ivy)

L-T/E/ Climber *Hedera canariensis* 'Variegata' is a fine ivy with large, ovate, light green leaves, strikingly bordered with deep cream. Less hardy than most, it prefers a warmer aspect than those suitable for the majority of ivies. The tough, gaily coloured evergreen foliage is useful for cutting at any time of year and is a particularly welcome winter substitute for the variegated hostas.

Lonicera japonica 'Aureoreticulata' (Form of Honeysuckle)

L-T/E/
Climber

Another climber which is perhaps suitable for inclusion here, though hardly variegated in the strictest sense, is *Lonicera japonica* 'Aureoreticulata', whose small, rounded green leaves are patterned with a close network of fine yellow veins. The trailing leaf sprays are favourite cutting material but are not sufficiently ornamental to deserve a prominent position in the garden.

The sprays need a good soaking after cutting and I prefer to remove the stem-tips under water, for safety, for I have often seen this honeysuckle foliage in a badly wilted condition.

Ruta graveolens 'Variegata' (Form of Rue)

L-T/E/D There is a charming variegated rue with blue and cream leaves which is much less common than the plain glaucous form. The lacy foliage pattern is identical but the added cream splashes intensify the frothy effect of the much divided leaves, especially around midsummer, when the new season's growth is most markedly mottled. It tends, however, to be less dense and vigorous than the type, with a suggestion of legginess in the case of my own plants, possibly due here to lack of warmth. Both root very readily from cuttings.

For general comments on *R. graveolens*, see Blue-Green Foliage Section, pages 242–3.

Arundinaria chrysantha (*Sasa chrysantha*) (Form of Bamboo)

L-T/E/
D to M

My own feeling about the variegated dwarf bamboo, *Arundinaria chrysantha*, is that it comes in for more esteem from connoisseurs than it deserves. It makes useful ground cover in rough areas and in poor soil, which will keep its rampant habit in check. In these conditions it will vary in height from one to three feet, but in a richer soil it may grow twice as tall and become tiresomely invasive.

This is the only bamboo I can make last when cut, by boiling in vinegar for a few minutes before standing it in cold water.

Vinca major 'Variegata' and *V. minor* 'Argenteo-variegata' (Forms of Periwinkle)

L-T/E/P Up to now I have had a great affection for the variegated periwinkles as a useful, easy and ornamental form of evergreen ground cover. When faced with the making of a shrub garden one is naturally grateful for the speed with which they will colonize a large area of bare earth, taking root wherever the trailing leafy shoots make contact with it. The trouble is that they are altogether *too* easy and will not be confined. As they spread their tentacles around them they clamber over and under and through all the dwarfer shrubs, half smothering them in their ruthless advance.

I have already tried to transfer *V. major* 'Variegata' from the front of one shrub bed to another part of the garden, only to find it popping up again almost as exuberantly as ever in its original surroundings. And the variegated Lesser Periwinkle, *V. minor* 'Argenteo-variegata', is every bit as obstinate.

Nevertheless, I have no intention of discarding either of them altogether. Places *can* be found for them where they may profitably be allowed to run riot without danger of swamping their neighbours, beneath tall shrubs or in dry walls and on rough banks. They are especially useful in densely shaded places.

Both these periwinkles yield graceful, drooping trails for the flower arranger, silvery-green and white in the case of the small-leaved *V. minor* 'Argenteo-variegata' and very long, more sparsely furnished sprays of bold, cream and green leaves in the case of *V. major* 'Variegata'. But the latter will be riddled with slug holes unless it is constantly protected. It is also somewhat unreliable in water, but removing the stem-tip under water cures this fault. Both varieties need a good soaking before use.

49

Blue-Green Foliage

Eucalyptus gunnii

L-T/E/
Tree

The most commonly planted and undoubtedly the toughest of its kind is *Eucalyptus gunnii*, which should be carefully selected, if possible, to obtain a form of really good colouring, for some are of a much more pronounced blue-green than others. As the tree develops it sometimes puzzles its owner by the unexpected contrast between what is in fact the juvenile and the adult foliage. The former is blue-green and almost circular, whereas in the adult stage the shape is more elongated and tapering and the colour more grey-green, lacking the characteristic glaucous bloom which coats the young growths in summertime. (The cream-coloured flowers have already been described on page 120.)

The hardiness of *Eucalyptus gunnii* is such that it can safely be planted almost anywhere in the British Isles except in the worst frost pockets, flourishing greatly on the Wirral peninsula in Cheshire and in many parts of Scotland, so long as it's in full sunlight.

Experts advise adding bone meal when planting in poor, dry or sandy soils, but stress that no fertilizers should be added to reasonably good ones, since this will encourage top-heaviness, as I found to my cost at my first attempt with *E. gunnii*. Having done it proud with rich compost and manure, as I watched my tiny tree shoot upwards my spirits soared with it. But not for long. It grew, and grew, and grew—in length but not at all in density and after it had been wind-rocked almost to extinction there began an endless struggle with all

240

ROSA rugosa 'Pink Grootendorst'

MAHONIA japonica

manner of unsightly props, stakes, guy ropes and wire hawsers. In spite of efforts to improve it I was finally forced to discard this one.

I have, in fact, two other fairly successful specimens, but I believe that these also would have been improved if I had had the courage to cut back the young growth more ruthlessly during their earlier years.

Generally speaking the foliage lasts a very long time in water without any special conditioning; but if the cut branches terminate in very tender, feathery growth boiling and soaking will be necessary to prevent wilting at the tips.

Eucalyptus perriniana

L-T/E/
M or
Tree

Eucalyptus perriniana, which is considered somewhat less reliably hardy than *E. gunnii*, is rather more curious than ornamental as a garden plant. The narrow, ovate grey-green adult foliage is not unlike that of *E. gunnii*, but the glaucous juvenile leaves are much larger and rounder, the discs encircling the stem at intervals as though threaded on a string and usually decreasing in size towards the tip. If the adult growths are cut off once the plant has reached a height of four or five feet it can be kept to a shrub of medium size with quantities of the fascinating disc-shaped leaves for cutting.

It is usually necessary to boil and soak cut sprays of *E. perriniana* because the tender young tips of the shoots quickly wilt if not properly conditioned.

Rhododendron concatenans

E/M

The foliage of *Rhododendron concatenans* ('B') is so very lovely as to justify a place in the shrub garden on this score alone. The leaves are somewhat spoon-shaped and are a fine blue-green, which is most pronounced in the young growth at midsummer.

Juniperus horizontalis, J. squamata 'Meyeri' and Chamaecyparis lawsoniana 'Allumii'

L-T/E/P,

I have a number of blue-hued conifers which introduce

Q
241

L-T/E/T useful contrasts of form as well as of colour in the shrub
and garden. Among these are the low-growing *Juniperus*
L-T/E/T *horizontalis*, whose far-reaching, prostrate, blue-green
foliage is displayed to best advantage on a sloping site;
the prickly, vividly glaucous pyramid of *J. squamata*
'Meyeri'; and a chamaecyparis of similar shape but with
neat, smooth blue foliage of typical Lawson's Cypress
pattern, which is, I believe, *Chamaecyparis lawsoniana*
'Allumii'.

Cedrus atlantica 'Glauca' (Blue Cedar)

L-T/E/ But the most telling of my blue conifers is without a
Tree doubt *Cedrus atlantica* 'Glauca', which has grown surprisingly fast into a large and graceful tree. After eleven
years it was already tall and broad enough to be really
majestic, with long, sweeping branches closely tufted
with the beautifully coloured blue-green needles. The
choice is unwise for a small garden and if I had known
of *E. gunnii* at the time of ordering I would have left it
to the eucalyptus to provide the glaucous colouring with
much greater economy of space.

It is possible to cut splendid curving branches of all
sizes and at all seasons from the spreading lower limbs
of *Cedrus atlantica* 'Glauca', which can well do with
some fairly hard cutting back. The cut foliage lasts a
very long time in water—and quite a long time out of
it—with only the routine splitting of the woody stem-
ends.

Ruta graveolens 'Jackman's Blue' (Rue)

L-T/E/D *Ruta graveolens* 'Jackman's Blue' is a particularly good
form of rue, with strikingly vivid glaucous evergreen
foliage of an attractive lacy design. To achieve a compact, bushy plant one should remove the flower-spikes
as soon as they can be detected, but it is useful to grow
on a few of the undistinguished little yellow flower-
clusters because these are followed by seed-heads which
are of value for dried arrangements. One is also advised

to cut rue back in April, but specimens grown for indoor decoration are hardly likely to need extra pruning.

Not only is this obliging plant ridiculously easy to propagate but it is also extremely well behaved as cut material.

Hebe pinguifolia 'Pagei' (Form of Shrubby Veronica)

L-T/E/P *Hebe* 'Pagei' is a delightful little evergreen, carpeting, shrubby veronica. The tiny, fleshy, oval leaves are only slightly more grey-blue than silver-grey, with a faint reddish outline. It looks best when grown in full exposure, when it will form a dense, compact carpet; but I find it expedient to grow a plant or two in part shade, in a rich leaf mould, in which conditions it will snake about with a lot more abandon. The result is much less dense and tidy, but it produces longer and more sinuous leaf-sprays for cutting. The neat, but rather insignificant, white flower-spikes appear in April and should be removed when dead.

It will last interminably in water without any conditioning and will often grow roots in water only.

Rosa rubrifolia

L-T/ The foliage of *Rosa rubrifolia* is such a subtle blend of
M to T bluish-greyish-green overlaid with a plum-coloured bloom that I am at a loss to know whether to treat it as blue-green, grey or purple. The leaves are borne on long, arching, almost thorn-free wands whose red-brown bark adds still further to the beauty of the whole. The more this plant is cut, the finer the quality of the foliage.

Though the small, single, rather blue-pink blooms seem to me insignificant and lacking in charm, I appreciate the globular, dark mahogany-red heps as cutting material; but it is above all in the dusky foliage of this shrub rose that its great beauty lies.

Both boiling and soaking are required to produce long-lasting results in water.

50

Grey and Silver Foliage

Senecio greyi

L-T/E/
D to M

Foremost among grey-foliaged shrubs is the indispensable *Senecio greyi* (often confused with *S. laxifolius*) which, although reputedly somewhat tender, yet survives the severest winters in this north-east-facing garden without very much damage. It is, of course, a useful stand-by for cutting at all seasons, but I am even more grateful for its dense, mounded grey-green form year in and year out in the shrub borders.

If you plant just one you can soon, if you wish, have many more, for I know of no shrub which layers itself more freely round its perimeter, particularly in a decaying leaf mulch. Grow it in a sunny position if you want a compact, well-rounded plant. I cut my bushes back without special reference to the calendar, during spring or summer, in a rather haphazard fashion, but I believe ideally April is the time for hard pruning.

I often remove the clusters of bright yellow daisies, which do little to embellish the shrub when they appear at midsummer, though in the closed silvery bud stage they make graceful cut sprays. It should not set seed.

Senecio leucostachys

L-T/E/D

Senecio leucostachys is a much more fragile-looking member of the family and in this garden it hasn't proved to be any hardier than its appearance suggests. Its silver tracery is, however, so delightful for flower arrangement that I am determined to keep a supply of the delicately drawn, artemisia-like foliage to cut from even if it means renewing my stock annually in the spring.

Unlike some silver foliages, *S. leucostachys* lasts for ages when cut if singed and stood in warm water.

Senecio cineraria (*Cineraria maritima*)

L-T/E/D Having twice tried, and failed, to grow *Senecio cineraria* I have now abandoned the attempt, and yet I don't doubt that it is as likely to succeed as *S. leucostachys*. In gardens less arctic than mine I have seen tantalizingly hearty clumps of its handsome, much-lobed, silvery-grey foliage, which is something like a large and more heavily scalloped oak-leaf in design. Two of the best varieties are 'Ramparts' and 'White Diamond', the latter being, I think, the whitest of all senecios. Rather surprisingly, both are tougher than the species itself.

Mrs. Underwood advises singeing, then placing in hot water. Eschew water-retaining products for all kinds of downy silver foliage.

Santolina chamaecyparissus (*incana*) (Cotton Lavender)

L-T/E/D *Santolina chamaecyparissus* is a much more useful dwarf evergreen for the open garden. It is reasonably hardy in a sunny position, making a lovely dense silvery splodge to light up the front of the border provided it is cut hard back each spring. Left to itself it makes a lot of straggly old wood and flops apart.

As a garden plant it is not only much hardier but also much more effective than the loose-limbed *S. leucostachys* which is so much lovelier for cutting. I rarely make much use of its closely packed sprigs of feathery foliage but the mature shoots seem to last better in water than the young growth, which is inclined to wilt at the tips. It will be more dependable if stood in hot water after cutting.

Chamaecyparis pisifera 'Plumosa'

L-T/E/M The conifer *Chamaecyparis pisifera* 'Plumosa' is the prettiest of greyish-greens mixed with a hint of blue and cream and is delightfully curled and feathered. The plant increases in stature very slowly, making a broad-based cone-shape which rarely exceeds six feet.

Populus alba (White Poplar)

L-T/
Tree

Populus alba is not perhaps a tree of great distinction and is one which might never have found its way into my garden if I had known of *Eucalyptus gunnii* twenty years ago. It is, however, almost equally fast-growing. The leaves are a matt silver-white on the underside and dark grey-green above, so that the tree seems to shimmer as the foliage is set fluttering by the lightest breeze.

It has a tiresome habit of throwing up far-flung suckers and the widely-questing roots will threaten the foundations and the drains of any building within a surprising distance from the main trunk.

As material for flower decoration it is at its best in early spring, when the leaves are just beginning to emerge from the white bud, but at any time, until leaf-fall, splendid curves and arabesques may be found among the leafy branches for cutting purposes. Throughout the summer these will need a very careful looking-over before use, to make sure that they are not disfigured by caterpillar holes.

Boil.

Elaeagnus macrophylla

L-T/E/T I first began to covet *Elaeagnus macrophylla* when I saw its long, arching foliage sprays used with such fine effect by Mrs. Thoyts in her pedestal arrangements. (A shady position is necessary to induce this habit, growth being much more compact in full light.) The tough, spoon-shaped, wavy-margined leaves are silver-white on the underside and grey-green above and are loosely disposed on immensely graceful, sinuous, yellow-barked branches. The rather similar *E.* × *ebbingei* may be a more handsome garden shrub but it lacks some of the grace of the other for flower arrangement.

Unfortunately, *E. macrophylla* is not one of the hardiest, but so far my young plant has got away to a faster start than is usual among its kind. If any plain green leaf-shoots should appear these should at once be cut out.

Ballota pseudodictamnus

L-T/E/D Though the woolly silver-green whorls enclosing the flowers of *Ballota pseudodictamnus* are what commend it most to flower arrangers it is almost equally desirable as a foliage plant, when grown in a warm position in full sun. The heart-shaped, velvety leaves are about the size of a twopenny piece and of the same soft silver-green colour as the rest of the plant.

(See also page 227.)

Boil and then stand in warm water.

Helichrysum petiolatum

L-T/E/D *Helichrysum petiolatum* makes a low, loose, spreading evergreen shrub whose foliage is remarkably similar to that of the ballota in colour, size and shape, but the helichrysum is undoubtedly much the more tender of the two.

Boil and stand in warm water.

51

Bronze, Copper and Purple-Brown Foliage

Some careful thought must be given to the siting of the darker-foliaged trees and shrubs within this colour range if they are not to stick out like a sore thumb among the prevailing greens of the garden landscape. One of the most satisfying solutions is to use them as part of a deliberate planting of widely contrasted foliage colours and shapes such as that described on page 235.

Cotinus coggygria 'Foliis Purpureis'; *C.c.* 'Notcutt's Variety' and *C.c.* 'Kromhout' (Forms of Smokebush)

L-T/T The most useful and effective dual-purpose shrubs in this colour category are the forms of *Cotinus coggygria* (*Rhus cotinus*). The deeper the colour of the foliage the better the plant is commonly thought to be, for which reason 'Kromhout' and 'Notcutt's Variety' are usually the most highly esteemed. My own preference is, however, for *C.c.* 'Foliis Purpureis', whose mahogany-purple foliage has less of the dark beetroot in its make-up.

In all three the whorls of rounded leaves, varying in diameter up to almost three inches, appear rather late in the spring and are borne on gracefully curving branches.

Except in the case of thoroughly mature foliage in late summer, it is essential to boil and soak cut branches to prevent rapid wilting in water.

(See also pages 191–2.)

Acer palmatum 'Atropurpureum' (Form of Japanese Maple)

Tree The Japanese maples cannot truly be described as lime-tolerators, although they may survive in slightly alkaline soils. For those who can offer it suitable soil conditions and some shelter from the wind, particularly in its early years, *Acer palmatum* 'Atropurpureum' makes a fairly fast-growing, graceful, small tree with deeply lobed foliage of a lighter copper colour than that of the cotinuses.

It is disappointing that foliage of such grace and refinement should not be entirely dependable as cut material. I use it often enough in my own home, after boiling; but even the most conscientious conditioning will not guarantee its good behaviour for any length of time in any but ideal circumstances.

Berberis thunbergii 'Atropurpurea' (Form of Barberry)

L T/   *Berberis thunbergii* 'Atropurpurea' cannot be said to be
M to T in the top rank of choice garden shrubs, but the colour is so good of its kind (except in dense shade) and the arching wands of foliage so graceful that I am happy to spare a place for it in a group of coloured foliages on a dry bank where more exacting plants have failed.

A fairly sunny position is necessary to obtain the attractive copper colour in the leaves, which become a nondescript dirty purplish-green when too heavily shaded. It has many virtues—and not the least of these is adaptability. It is equally good with dark reds, purples, blues, pale yellow, apricot or flame; and is suitable in size for any type of arrangement, from pedestal to near-miniature. Unless one takes the trouble to boil it and to give it a really long soaking it will last only a brief hour or so.

Phormium tenax 'Purpureum' (Form of New Zealand Flax)

L-T/E/M Of the three varieties of phormium in my possession *P. tenax* 'Purpureum' is, I suppose, the least effective garden decorator. Apart from the fact that its colour is a rather sombre bronzy mixture of grey-green shot with reddish-purple, it is less lusty than the other two, demanding greater warmth; and in one of my two purple forms the sword-blades are designed on a much smaller, narrower scale. Both make fascinating cutting material. For general comments on phormiums, see page 236.

Rhododendron fulvum

E/T   I grow *Rhododendron fulvum* ('B') entirely on account of the vivid ginger-brown indumentum on the underside of the dark green leaves. Though this is a fairly recent acquisition I was able to get hold of a fair-sized specimen so densely furnished that I was soon able to cut quite a number of small foliage shoots for indoor decoration and it has since rapidly grown to a large size in a fairly densely shaded position.

Rhododendron 'Moser's Maroon'

E/T   *Rhododendron* 'Moser's Maroon' ('B') may at first seem out of place in this environment, since the mature foliage is a quite unremarkable green. In early summer, however, the colour of the young leaf-shoots is a splendid burnished copper, adding yet further glamour to a plant already highly prized for cutting on account of the rich, dark maroon colour of its flowers. This rhododendron does, however, make a somewhat scraggy, thin-habited shrub.

The young leaf-shoots should be boiled and soaked (see page 185).

Magnolia grandiflora 'Exmouth', 'Ferruginea' and 'Goliath'

L-T/E/   All the evergreen magnolias are noble foliage plants, but
Tree   if foliage is your special interest you should, I think, choose *M. grandiflora* 'Exmouth' or 'Ferruginea', whose large, thick, glossy light green leaves are all the finer for being coated with rusty-brown on the underside. The flowers of 'Goliath' are bigger but the leaves lack most of the attractive rusty indumentum of the other two.

For general comments see page 90.

Thuja occidentalis 'Rheingold'

L-T/E/   *Thuja occidentalis* 'Rheingold' is a dwarf variety which
D to M   has seemed to mark time for a good many years but
recently it has begun to make up for lost time and is now
a dense, broad-based evergreen pyramid about six feet
high, from which I can cut occasional titbits of warm
yellow, feathery foliage tinged bronze at the tips of the
shoots. In winter the bronze flush spreads over the
undertone of yellow and becomes intensified.

Weigela florida 'Foliis Purpureis'

L-T/D   This rather unusual, compact-habited weigela is a fairly
dull-looking plant in infancy; but although reputedly
slow-growing mine has taken only three years to make
a strong clump of maroon-barked shoots with rather
small, muted bronze-brown leaves with light green vein-
ing. The plant looks unlikely to exceed three feet in
height but the diagonally angled growth is of quite a
reasonable length. I regret rather than welcome its
muddy pink flowers.

Leucothoe fontanesiana and *L.f.* 'Rainbow' ('Multicolor')

E/D to M The chief virtue of *Leucothoe fontanesiana* (until recently named *L. catesbaei*) lies in the pinkish-copper of
the young shoots and in the purplish-plum and crimson
foliage hues which succeed the orthodox green of midsummer. The narrow evergreen leaves grow on arching
shoots which vary in height from two to four feet or
more according to conditions.

It is one of the most long-lasting of all cut foliages,
remaining in good condition for weeks, or even months,
in water.

The more recent, variegated 'Rainbow' is even finer,
being mainly copper-toned, with maroon, yellow and
white streaks.

Vitis vinifera 'Purpurea' (Claret Vine)

L-T/
Climber

The reddish-purple leaf colour of *Vitis vinifera* 'Purpurea' can hardly fail to appeal to flower arrangers. My own little plant only arrived a few weeks ago, so I can claim no personal experience of its habits or requirements. If only it will yield me some bunches of its little blue-black fruits for cutting I shall be well content, for to me all outdoor fruiting vines are irresistible for flower arrangement from the moment the bunches are sufficiently formed to be recognizable as embryonic grapes.

This is reputed to be a slow grower. I understand that once it has covered its allotted space it should be spurred back fairly hard in early winter.

Boil and soak.

Parthenocissus quinquefolia (Virginia Creeper)

L-T/
Climber

Of the various names under which the Virginia Creeper is listed I believe *Parthenocissus quinquefolia* to be currently in favour, superseding *Ampelopsis* and *Vitis*.

Autumn leaf colour in the garden is an extra bonus provided by many flowering trees and shrubs, but among purely foliage plants the Virginia creeper is one of the few which are grown almost entirely for the vivid orange-scarlet of their autumn leaves. I hardly feel that it deserves the precious wall-space which it usually occupies. It is, however, possible to get a delightful (and economical) autumn effect by training it up into a silver birch.

Remove stem-tips under water and immerse.

52

Lime-Green and Yellow Foliage

Acer japonicum 'Aureum' (Form of Japanese Maple)

Small
Tree

If only it would grow a little faster *Acer japonicum* 'Aureum' would be unbeatable among the foliage plants of lime-green colouring. My own is already ten years old and though my fingers itch to cut the foliage I dare not do so yet awhile. As a rule the plant will be pathetically tiny on arrival, but a small plant often suffers less of a setback from transplanting than a large one. There really is nothing for it but patience.

At least it will not be so long before this little tree becomes an effective garden ornament, making a brave splash of vivid yellow-green in spring, which later passes to a sunlit yellow. I find it most enchanting in spring-time, when the tightly pleated little chartreuse fans burst out of the shrimp-pink sheaths encasing the leaf-buds.

This is another of the maples which will not do well on lime.

Unlike *A. palmatum* 'Atropurpureum', it lasts well when cut so long as it has been previously boiled and soaked.

Physocarpus opulifolius 'Luteus'

L-T/T

I believe that *Physocarpus opulifolius* 'Luteus' is the more correct name for what I have hitherto known as *Spiraea opulifolia* 'Lutea'. Its foliage is worth more to me for flower arrangement than many grander plants. And even as a garden ornament I think it has considerable beauty, though connoisseurs may dismiss it as 'coarse'.

The leaves are shaped rather like those of the flowering currant, only smaller, and are borne both on immensely tall straight shoots and on shorter curving sprays, providing useful alternatives for cutting. The small clusters of little white flowers in June have only a nuisance value. Like most lime-yellow foliage plants, it is at its best in spring, when the leaf-colour is most vivid. Again in autumn it is particularly attractive for cutting, when the tips of the leaf-shoots become tinged with bronze.

The shrub is tall and upright and is apt to present a somewhat gangling appearance if left unpruned. Indeed it benefits from quite ruthless cutting back, also removing a few of the oldest stems at ground level each year.

As cut material it needs boiling and a long drink, but not actual immersion. If it is left soaking for more than the briefest period the leaves become spotted with brown and quite unusable.

Philadelphus coronarius 'Aureus' (Form of 'Syringa' or Mock Orange)

L-T/M No foliage is of a more vivid lime-yellow than that of *Philadelphus coronarius* 'Aureus' in spring and early summer. From what I have seen of plants grown in full sun these are usually more yellow than lime. The foliage is not only better coloured but more luscious in part shade. Although planted purely for cutting purposes, it provides quite as much colour as a flowering shrub, in the early part of the season, adding its quota to a group which includes the blue-mauve *Rhododendron* 'Fastuosum Flore Pleno', a flame-coloured azalea and the blue-green *Cedrus atlantica* 'Glauca'. The smallish white flowers are also rather charming and are very sweetly scented. Pruning as for other kinds of philadelphus is necessary for good foliage.

Boiling and soaking is particularly necessary in the case of the young foliage.

Hebe armstrongii (Form of Shrubby Veronica)

L-T/E/D *Hebe armstrongii*, a dwarf shrubby veronica of highly uncharacteristic, conifer-like appearance, is one of my favourites of all foliage plants for cutting and this, from a foliage addict such as I, is praise indeed. Its colour is a unique and subtle old-gold which harmonizes with almost any other colouring; its curious whipcord structure is at once solid and yet feathery; it lasts indefinitely in water; and the burnished olive-khaki of the low-growing evergreen hummock is particularly interesting in winter, when the colour seems to have an added intensity. A position in full sun is necessary to achieve the richest colour and will also make for sturdier growth. The tiny white flower stars are insignificant and if it has a fault it is that it is just the least bit tender.

It doesn't seem to sprout very readily from any point at which it is cut, so any bit required for indoor use must be judiciously selected with an eye to what your plants can spare; but some light clipping over from time to time is essential to prevent ultimate scragginess.

Cassinia fulvida (syn. *Diplopappus chrysophyllus*)

L-T/E/M Speaking as a flower arranger I find *Cassinia fulvida* very nearly as fascinating and indispensable as *Hebe armstrongii*. The tiny, heath-like foliage is dark olive-green on the upper surface and backed with an intense acid yellow to match the slender stems on which it is borne. Light, delicate-looking trails can be found for use where the hebe might be a little too stiff or solid, but the two are admirable mixers and somewhat alike in colour. As a garden shrub *Cassinia fulvida* is altogether more raggle-taggle in habit, requiring a good deal of clipping into shape.

It is particularly long-lasting in water.

Cupressus macrocarpa 'Lutea' and *Chamaecyparis pisifera* 'Filifera Aurea'

L-T/E/T   I have only a small assortment of conifers and the
and   yellow-foliaged varieties I grow are both a mixture of
L-T/E/M   green and light yellow; *Cupressus macrocarpa* 'Lutea'
being tall and pyramidal, while *Chamaecyparis pisifera* 'Filifera Aurea' has wispy, thread-like foliage of weeping habit, and is usually broader than it is tall.

Skimmias

L-T/E/   Though one tends to think of skimmia foliage as plain
D to M   green, when grown in full sunlight the leaves are a distinctly limy-yellow fading almost to silver at the margin. The leathery, oval, evergreen foliage is somewhat laurel-like, only smaller and less glossy, and is borne in neatly disposed clusters at the tips of the shoots, which makes this shapely and long-lasting greenery convenient for flower arrangement.

For general comments on skimmias, see pages 59–60 and 192.

Calluna vulgaris 'Aurea' and *C.v.* 'Searlei Aurea' (Forms of Heather)

E/D   Two heathers in particular provide finely coloured low-growing evergreen mounds of lime-yellow for the front of the shrub borders, soil conditions permitting. *Calluna* 'Aurea' is a vivid greenish-yellow in spring and summer, becoming tinged with red in winter; and *Calluna* 'Searlei Aurea' forms a bolder and more solid mass made up of dense spikes of bright lime-yellow foliage.

Both benefit from a light clipping over in the spring.

Seed-heads of *CLEMATIS* 'Barbara Dibley'

EUCALYPTUS perriniana

53

Green Foliage of Striking Form

Apart from the wealth of handsome evergreen foliage to be found among the camellias, rhododendrons, evergreen azaleas, certain magnolias and other trees and shrubs esteemed primarily for the splendour of their flowers, there are, of course, a number of plants, grown chiefly or solely for their foliage, in which the interest lies mainly in the leaf shape.

Fatsia japonica (Aralia sieboldii) (*not* Castor Oil Plant)

L-T/E/ Foremost among these is *Fatsia japonica*. My own
M to T young plant, growing well in a house-bed at the foot of a north wall, is now about four feet high and has not as yet shown any signs of flowering. So long as it will thrive sufficiently to keep me supplied with its huge, glossy, rich green leaves, midway between an ivy and a fig-leaf in design, I shall consider that it fully earns its keep. The leaves last interminably in water (I have some-times lent mine out and had them returned to carry on for weeks), fading to a fine, clear yellow with age, if one keeps them long enough. They can also be preserved in a glycerine solution if the stalks are supported at the leaf junction in the process.

For further comments, see page 95.
Soak.

Phormium tenax (New Zealand Flax)

L-T/E/ There could hardly be a more striking contrast of shape
M to T than that of the stiffly erect greyish-green sword-leaves of *Phormium tenax*, which rise in dense evergreen

clusters from ground level to a height of six feet or more, topped by even taller flower-spikes in late summer. It is the most vigorous of the three varieties I grow.

For general comments on phormiums, see page 236.

Mahonia japonica

L-T/E/
M to T

I, for one, would grow this stately evergreen shrub for its foliage alone. The immensely tough, shiny, holly-like, pinnate leaves are borne in huge whorls, radiating from the hub like the spokes of a wheel. Although the predominating colour is dark green the young growth is copper-tinted and the older leaves finally take on a variety of crimson, flame and purplish hues.

M. japonica is generally considered to be only moderately hardy, but it grows very strongly with me without any harm to date.

The leaves are just about indestructible in water. I once used a whole whorl in a large foliage arrangement which proved so everlasting that when, after many weeks, I finally tired of it and threw it away the mahonia leaves were still as good as new. The leaf-surfaces do, however, collect grime from the outdoor atmosphere and should therefore be sponged with warm, soapy water before being used in an arrangement. Some people like to wipe over the leaves of this mahonia with a little thin oil on a swab. A little unobtrusive oil may be excusable, but surely varnish is not?

M. japonica foliage is a good subject for glycerine treatment, turning to a fine dark sepia and lasting almost for ever.

(For general comments, see also page 125, and the first paragraph in particular.)

Mahonia aquifolium (Holly-Leaved Barberry)

L-T/E/
D to M

Commonly regarded as something of a poor relation to the foregoing, the much dwarfer and less spectacular *Mahonia aquifolium* is nevertheless trebly useful to the flower arranger and an exceptionally accommodating garden plant. Apart from the yellow flowers in earliest spring and the dark blue fruits in summer the evergreen foliage is by no means to be despised. It may lack the noble architectural quality of *M. japonica*, but the leaf-form and colour phases are similar, and it shares the long-lasting properties of the other as cut material.

(See also page 101.)

Erica arborea 'Alpina' (Form of Tree Heath)

L-T/E/ Given some judicious clipping back in late spring or
M to T early summer, the feathery evergreen plumes of *Erica arborea* 'Alpina' will form a compact mass of spectacularly vivid green which lights up the garden landscape and provides fine material for foliage arrangements. It will tolerate only a slight degree of liminess.

(See also page 61.)

Cotoneaster horizontalis (Fishbone Cotoneaster)

L-T/M *Cotoneaster horizontalis* is equally willing to make do with all kinds of awkward and inhospitable situations, as for instance the steep, densely shaded, north-facing, dry-walled bank which it clothes in my own garden. Growing out of the wall itself, a number of *C. horizontalis* positively hold the whole thing together, reaching outward in neat herringbones, broad fans and long, arching sprays of tiny leaves from which I can take my pick for cutting. I resent the little pink flowers in spring, and later the small scarlet berries which only clutter up the fine design of leaf and branch. The foliage turns a fine colour in the autumn and even in winter there is a special fascination in the pattern of the stripped skeleton.

The foliage sprays make splendid dried material when preserved in glycerine in late summer, which turns the leaves to a rich, dark mahogany-brown.

× *Fatshedera lizei*

L-T/E/ I can't imagine why so few gardeners grow this ridicu-
M to T lously easy yet handsome evergreen. In appearance it's

exactly what one would expect as a result of crossing a fatsia with an ivy (or hedera), which is how this plant came about—the leaves being larger than all but the largest of ivies, but smaller, less deeply indented and fewer-fingered than fatsia, in a glossy, rather light, fresh green. As with the fatsia, fading leaves often turn to a soft yellow before they fall. It looks almost too elegant a shrub to be so undemanding, yet it will make do with any soil and aspect (especially good for shade), is hardy and fast-growing and any cutting pushed unceremoniously into the soil of a shady border will almost unfailingly strike. If allowed to grow very tall a little support will probably be necessary. The fact that it is so little grown out of doors may be due to its also being sold as a house plant, perhaps giving a false impression that it isn't hardy. It's remarkably long-lasting in water.

Hebe hectorii (Form of Shrubby Veronica)

L-T/E/D *Hebe hectorii* bears a fairly close resemblance to *H. armstrongii*, including the dwarf conifer-like appearance. It makes a low, evergreen hummock of much the same size and shape, but the curious, scaly leaf-shoots are thicker-fingered and less feathery and the colour is appreciably greener, corresponding to one of the lighter tints of Fern Green (0862/2), which, without the authority of the Chart, I would have described as dark olive-green.

If I had room for only one of these hebes, *H. armstrongii* would be the one for me, particularly as I have found *H. hectorii* rather more tender than the other.

This looks like a lot of leaves, I know. Compared with the meagre ration of winter-flowering trees and shrubs in particular the foliage plants may seem to have usurped more than their fair share of garden room—and, perhaps, of my affections. I may be guilty on the second count but not, I think, on the first. Most of my foliage plants are not only decorative, and often colourful, garden ornaments from early spring until leaf-fall, but many are evergreens which never take time off. If, as a gardener, I use contrasting evergreen foliages in preference to winter flowers, at least the shrub borders will be almost as fully, though more soberly, clothed from November until March as they are from April till October.

As for flower arrangement, I am well content to exploit the fascination of leaves at any time of year, with or without the complement of flowers and fruits. And in winter the evergreens provide all the variety I could wish in colour and shape and texture. If by mid-winter foliage arrangements begin to seem too sombre there is always the sparkle and frivolity of Christmas decorations to jazz things up for a week or two. And then with what a sense of relief one packs them all away and returns to the restful charm of the evergreen leaves once more, until the first breath of spring sets the multicoloured kaleidoscope to work in the shrub borders all over again.

List of Non-Shrubby Subjects included in the Shrub Borders

(A) EARLY SPRING

Anemone appenina	Light blue-violet, many-petalled. Ground-covering.
Hepatica nobilis triloba (*Anemone hepatica*)	Similar to above, but with fewer and larger petals.
— — — 'Ballardii'	Inch-wide powder-blue saucers on 6-in. stalks.
Bergenia (various)	Sturdy short-stemmed purplish-pink clusters. (See also Foliages, page 269.)
Crocus tomasinianus	Slim, silvery-lavender goblets.
Euphorbia characias	Tall, nodding, columnar umbels of green, maroon-eyed florets.
Euphorbia veneta (*E. wulfenii*)	As above but yellower and lacking maroon eye.
Fritillaria meleagris	Sombre purple to deep maroon bells, 9 in.
— — 'Aphrodite'	White bells, tinged green, 9 in.
— *verticillata thunbergii*	Creamish bells veined green, 1 ft.
Galanthus (various)	Snowdrop.
Helleborus lividus subsp. *corsicus*	Clusters of pale green saucers each about the size of a tenpenny piece; sculptural, leathery grey-green leaves, 2 ft. (Formerly *H. corsicus*.)
— *foetidus*	Large clusters light apple-green cups edged maroon, fine seed-heads and handsome dark green, many-fingered leaves, 2 ft.

Helleborus orientalis	Blush-white to dark Erythrite Red (0027) saucers, often tinged green, 18 in.
Iris reticulata	Dark violet strap-petals, marked orange-yellow; dwarf.
—— *krelagei*	Redder-purple version of above.
Narcissus bulbocodium	Miniature Hoop Petticoat daffodil.
— *cyclamineus*	Miniature daffodil with reflexing perianth.
Primula denticulata	Deep lilac, spherical heads, 1 ft.
— *vulgaris*	Common primrose.
Scilla bifolia	Neat, starry panicles of vivid Flax Blue (642); dwarf.
— *sibirica*	Later, larger and looser-flowered than above; Spectrum Blue (45).

(B) LATE SPRING

Convallaria majalis	Lily-of-the-Valley.
Endymion hispanicus vars.	White, lilac-pink, or porcelain-blue Spanish Bluebell. Decorative seed-heads.
Epimedium × *rubrum*	Small crimson and light yellow aquilegia-like flowers on 9-in. sprays. (See also Foliages, page 268.)
— *versicolor* 'Sulphureum'	Pale yellow version of above. (See also Foliages, page 268.)
Euphorbia cyparissias	Frothy miniature lime-green umbels; invasive.
— *robbiae*	Similar to but very much bolder than our native spurge. Dark green foliage rosettes make good ground cover even in dense shade.
Ipheion uniflorum	Palest milky-blue stars, barred darker blue; dwarf. (Formerly *Brodiaea, Milla* or *Tritelia*.)

263

Ornithogalum nutans	Starry, wide - open - bluebell - type inflorescence, silver-grey, banded green and white.
— *umbellatum*	Green and white starred clusters, 1–1½ ft.
Paeonia mlokosewitschii	Pale lemon cupped species; grey-green leaves, 2 ft.
Polygonatum multiflorum	Solomon's Seal. Pendent little green and white tubes on tall, arching, leafy stems.
Tellima grandiflora and *T.g.* 'Purpurea'	Slender 2-ft. spikes of tiny green-ish-cream bells. (See also Foliages, pages 268–9.)
Tiarella cordifolia	Creamy-white 'Foam Flowers' on 9-in. stems; carpeting vine-shaped foliage.
Trillium grandiflorum	Glistening white triangles with green collar, calcifuge.

(C) MIDSUMMER

Alchemilla mollis	Chartreuse-green froth on 18-in. stems; ground-covering clumps of circular, pleated, silky, grey-green leaves.
Astrantia major	Tall, starry clusters of greenish-greyish-white, tinged pink, above ground-covering dark green, divided leaves.
Dierama 'Hermia'	Coppery bells on dwarfer wands than those of *D. pulcherrimum* vars.
Digitalis ambigua	Pale yellow perennial foxglove, 2 ft.
— 'Sutton's Apricot'	Exquisite apricot-hued biennial foxglove, 5 ft.
Euphorbia myrsinites	Flat, lime-yellow inflorescence, prostrate. (See also Foliages, page 268.)

Euphorbia griffithii	Brilliant flame-coloured bracts on 2-ft. stems.
— *sikkimensis*	Flat heads of lime-yellow; vivid red shoots in spring; 3 ft.
Lilium 'Citronella' Strain	Light sulphur, chocolate spots, reflexed petals.
— *hansonii*	Tangerine Orange (9), fleshy Turk's Cap.
— *martagon*	Small, sombre purple Turk's Caps. Decorative seed-heads.
— — 'Album'	White version of above.
— Mid-Century Hybrids	Large spikes of up-facing, wide-open flowers; 'Croesus': deep yellow, dark spots; 'Destiny': pale lemon-yellow, dark spots; 'Enchantment': heavily flowered, brilliant Nasturtium Red (14).
— *pyrenaicum*	Pale sulphur-yellow Turk's Cap, marred by too thick a stem.
— *regale*	Large yellow and white trumpets, barred pink reverse.
× *testaceum*	Nankeen Lily. Pale apricot, scarlet anthers.
umbellatum 'Golden Fleece'	Deep yellow, up-facing trumpets.
— — 'Orange Triumph'	Apricot-orange, maroon spotted, up-facing.

(D) LATE SUMMER AND AUTUMN

Agapanthus umbellatus mooreanus (or *campanulatus*)	Tall-stemmed, starry umbels, Lobelia Blue (41/1); hardy. Good spidery seed-heads.
Colchicum autumnale minor	Rosy-lilac Meadow Saffron. (See also Foliages, page 269.)
Crinum × *powellii* 'Album'	Long, lily-like white trumpets; 3 ft.

Cyclamen neapolitanum	Pale pink dwarf; marbled grey-green leaves in winter.
Cyclamen n. 'Album'	White form of above.
Dierama pulcherrimum	Tall arching wands of white, pink or purple bells. Charming seed-heads like tear-drops.
Eucomis comosa (*punctata*)	Close-packed columns of starry pale green florets tinged purple. Hardy against a warm wall, 18 in.
Hosta (*Funkia*) (various)	Elegant spikes of tiny lilac trumpets, decorative seed-heads, 1½–2 ft. (See also Foliages, pages 268–9.)
Lilium auratum	Japanese Golden Ray Lily. Huge, waxy white funnels heavily barred yellow and spotted crimson.
— *henryi*	Light Orpiment Orange (10/1–2) banded green; reflexed petals.
— *pardalinum*	Vivid scarlet and yellow, spotted maroon.
— *speciosum rubrum*	Waxy pink and white, spotted crimson; reflexed petals.
— *tigrinum* 'Splendens'	Large Turk's Caps in pinkish-copper, spotted chocolate.
Nerine bowdenii	Large umbels of spidery, sugar pink flowers, 1½ ft.

(E) WINTER

Helleborus niger	Christmas Rose. Waxy white saucers, sometimes tinged pink, 1 ft.

FOLIAGES

Variegated

Arum italicum (*pictum*)	Conspicuous white veining on dark

	green arrowheads, 1 ft., throughout winter and spring.
Hosta decorata ('Thomas Hogg')	Deep green, margined white, 1 ft.
Hosta fortunei 'Albopicta'	Yellow splashed vivid lime-green in spring; more uniform green later, 2 ft.
— *undulata*	Small-leaved and much waved at edges; light green with central white band, 1 ft. or less.
Iris pseudacorus 'Variegatus'	Cream stripes on tall, light green blades chiefly conspicuous in spring and early summer.
Sedum albo-roseum 'Variegatum'	Fleshy Glaucous leaves heavily splashed creamy-yellow, 1½ ft.

Blue-Green

Euphorbia myrsinites	Curious prostrate rolls of fleshy scales.
Hosta sieboldiana	Large, heart-shaped and deeply veined, 2 ft.

Bronze, Copper and Purple-Brown

Epimedium × *rubrum* and *E. versicolor* 'Sulphureum'	Heart-shaped leaves on wiry, branching stems, copper-tinted spring and autumn, 1 ft.
Epimedium × *youngianum* 'Roseum'	Dwarfer than above, but a more brilliant coral hue in spring.
Sedum maximum 'Atropurpureum'	Fleshy, dark mahogany, 1½–2 ft.
Tellima grandiflora	Circular, deeply veined and 'waffled' leaves, beautifully mottled brown on green. Forms ground-covering clumps.

— — 'Purpurea'	More purple in leaf, but flimsier than above.

Lime-Green and Yellow

Hosta fortunei 'Aurea'	Uniform light butter-yellow, but rather flimsy for cutting, 1 ft.

Green

Aspidistra elatior	Broadly lanceolate arching deep green blades, 2 ft.; will sometimes succeed out of doors.
Bergenia cordifolia (Megasea)	Large, leathery, circular Elephant's Ear Saxifrage; dull green, turning purplish in autumn and winter. Excellent ground cover.
— *crassifolia*	Similar to above, but spoon-shaped and clearer green.
Colchicum autumnale minor	Low clumps of vivid green blades in spring.
Galax aphylla	Tough, circular, glossy evergreen leaves often margined brownish-crimson, 9 in. Delightful ground cover for acid soils only.
Hosta fortunei	Large, heart-shaped and deeply veined, 2 ft.
— *lancifolia*	Smaller and narrower than above. Dark, glossy green, conspicuously veined, 1–1½ ft.

APPENDIX II

Trees, Shrubs and Carpeting Plants of Little Value for Flower Arrangement, but Desirable for Continuity of Bloom, Verge Plantings etc. in the Shrub Garden

WHITE

Early Spring

E/D   *Rhododendron microleucum* (alpine variety)

Late Spring

L-T/Tree   *Malus sargentii* (ornamental crab apple)

Midsummer

L-T/E   *Cistus* (Rock Rose):
D   *C. obtusifolius, C. palhinhae* (plain whites)
M   *C.* 'Elma', *C. laurifolius* (hardiest), (plain whites)
D   *C.* × *lusitanicus* 'Decumbens' (central dark blotch)
M   *C.* × *aguilarii* 'Maculatus', *C.* × *cyprius* (central dark blotch)
L-T/E/D   × *Halimiocistus sahucii* (plain white), × *H. wintonensis* (centred maroon and yellow)
L-T/E/P   *Helianthemum*: 'The Bride', 'Snowball' (Sun Roses)

Late Summer and Autumn

E/D   *Erica cinerea* 'Alba Major', 'Domino', 'Hookstone White' (Heaths)

CREAM TO YELLOW

Early Spring

L-T/D   *Cytisus* × *beanii, C.* × *kewensis, C. purgans* (dwarf Brooms)

Late Spring

L-T/D   *Genista hispanica* (Spanish Gorse)
L-T/E/D   *Halimium libanotis*

Midsummer

L-T/D   *Genista lydia* (*spathulata*)
L-T/E/D   *Halimium lasianthum, H. ocymoides* (*Helianthemum algarvense*) (both with central chocolate blotch)
L-T/E/P   *Helianthemum*: 'Ben Attow', 'Ben Fhada', 'Glaucum', 'Jubilee' (double), 'Wisley Primrose' (Sun Roses)
L-T/D and M   *Potentilla* 'Elizabeth' (*arbuscula*), *P. fruticosa* 'Purdomii' (Shrubby Cinquefoils)

Late Summer and Autumn

L-T/D to M   *Cytisus nigricans* (Broom)
L-T/Tree   *Genista aethnensis* (Mt. Etna Broom)
L-T/P   *Genista tinctoria* 'Plena' (creeping double Broom)
L-T/Tree   *Koelreuteria paniculata* (Golden Rain Tree)
L-T/M   *Spartium junceum* (Spanish Broom)

APRICOT TO SALMON-ORANGE

Early Spring

L-T/E/M   *Berberis × stenophylla* 'Coccinea' (× *irwinii* 'Coccinea')

Midsummer

L-T/D   *Helianthemum*: 'Apricot', 'Ben Affleck', 'Ben Dearg', 'Ben Venue', 'Magnificence' ('Magnificum'), 'Miss Mould', 'Mrs. Clay', 'Peach'

L-T/D   *Potentilla fruticosa* 'Day Dawn', *P.f.* 'Tangerine' (Shrubby Cinquefoils)

PINK

Midsummer

L-T/E/D   *Cistus: creticus* (*villosus*), *parviflorus*, × *pulverulentus*, 'Silver Pink', × *skanbergii*, 'Sunset' (Rock Roses)

Late Summer and Autumn

E/D   *Erica cinerea*: 'Old Rose', 'Rosea', 'Startler' (Heaths)

SCARLET TO CRIMSON AND MAROON

Late Spring

L-T/E/P   *Helianthemum* 'Supreme' (Sun Rose)

Midsummer

E/D   *Erica cinerea* 'Coccinea', 'Stephen Davis' (Heaths)

L-T/E/P   *Helianthemum*: 'Ben Hope', 'Ben Ledi', 'Ben Macdhui', 'Fire Dragon' (Sun Roses)

Late Summer and Autumn

E/D   *Erica cinerea*: 'Atrorubens', 'Atrosanguinea', 'C. D. Eason' (Heaths)

LILAC TO PURPLE AND VIOLET

Late Summer and Autumn

E/D   *Erica cinerea*: 'Grandiflora', 'P. S. Patrick', 'Purple Beauty' (Heaths)

BLUE

Late Spring

E/P   *Lithospermum diffusum* 'Grace Ward', *L.d.* 'Heavenly Blue' (Gromwells)

Late Summer and Autumn

L-T/D   *Ceratostigma plumbaginoides, C. willmottianum* (Plumbagos)

FOLIAGE

L-T/E/T   *Arundinaria japonica* (*Pseudosasa japonica*), *A. murieliae* (*Sinarundinaria murieliae*) (Bamboos)

E/D
Calluna vulgaris, some good foliage varieties, mostly yellow during summer and red-bronze in winter: 'Blazeaway', 'Cuprea', 'Golden Feather', 'Gold Haze', 'Joy Vanstone', 'Orange Queen', 'Robert Chapman', 'Spitfire', 'Sunset', 'Tricolorifolia'

E/D
Erica cinerea 'Golden Drop' (copper, turning rusty red in winter), *E.c.* 'Golden Hue' (yellow)

Pruning Calendar for Regular Annual Operations

SPRING

Ballota pseudodictamnus (April)
Berberis, coloured foliage vars.
Buddleia davidii and × *weyerana* vars. (April)
Callicarpa bodinieri giraldii (early spring)
Caryopteris (April)
Cassinia fulvida (or periodically)
Ceanothus, late-flg. vars. (April)
Ceratostigma (dead wood)
Chaenomeles
Cytisus battandieri
Daboecia
Erica carnea vars. and other winter-flg. heaths (after flg.)
Eucalyptus (March–April)
Forsythia (after flg.)
Fuchsia, hardy vars. (dead wood)
Heaths and heathers, summer-flg.
Hebe, late-flg. vars.
Hydrangea cinerea 'Sterilis' and *H.* × *macrophylla* vars. (dead wood, and thin out new basal shoots)
Hydrangea paniculata vars. and *H. villosa* (dead-head)
Hypericum
Jasminum primulinum (after flg.)
Lavandula 'Hidcote'
Phygelius capensis (dead wood)
Pieris, early-flg. (as *floribunda, japonica*) (dead-head)
Potentilla (dead-head, and thin if necessary)

Rhododendrons, early-flg. (dead-head)
Ribes sanguineum vars. (after flg.)
Romneya (April)
Roses, bush types
Ruta graveolens vars.
Santolina (late March)
Senecio greyi (late March)
Sorbaria arborea
Spiraea, early-flg. (after flg.)
Spiraea, late summer-flg.
Symphoricarpos rivularis vars.
Zauschneria (dead wood)

SUMMER

Azaleas, deciduous (dead-head)
Buddleia globosa (after flg.)
Ceanothus, all (pinch out periodically)
Ceanothus, spring-flg. vars. (after flg.)
Chaenomeles (pinch out periodically)
Cistus (pinch out periodically)
Cytisus, early-flg. vars. (after flg., clip several times annually in
    youth)
Deutzia (after flg.)
Dipelta floribunda (after flg.)
Erica arborea 'Alpina' and other Tree Heaths (after flg.)
Genista, spring-flg. vars. (after flg., clip several times annually
    in youth)
× Halimiocistus (pinch out periodically)
Halimium (pinch out periodically)
Hebe armstrongii (clip lightly periodically)
Hebe 'Pagei' (dead-head)
Helianthemum (lightly, after flg.)
Iberis sempervirens (after flg.)
Kalmia latifolia (dead-head)
Kerria japonica (after flg.)
Kolkwitzia amabilis (after flg.)
Lithospermum diffusum vars. (after flg.)

Paeonia suffruticosa vars. and other Tree Peonies (dead-head)
Philadelphus (after flg.)
Physocarpus opulifolius 'Luteus' (or in winter)
Pieris formosa vars. (dead-head)
Pyracantha (lightly)
Rhododendrons (dead-head)
Rosa rubrifolia
Senecio cineraria vars. (mid-May)
Senecio greyi (pinch out periodically)
Senecio leucostachys (pinch out periodically)
Syringa (after flg.)
Weigela (after flg.)
Zenobia pulverulenta (after flg.)

AUTUMN

Cytisus nigricans (after flg.)
Escallonia (after flg.)
Genista, summer-flg. vars. (after flg.)
Hebe, late-flg. vars. (dead-head)
Lavandula 'Hidcote' (dead-head only—see also SPRING)
Pyracantha (again, lightly)
Roses, Rambler
Spartium junceum (after flg.)

WINTER

Abelia × *grandiflora* (dead-head and old wood)
Campsis (early winter)
*Clematis, Viticella and Jackmanii types (hard prune February
    to March)
Hydrangea × *macrophylla* vars. (one or two old stems)
Jasminium nudiflorum (cut hard for indoors, or after flg.)
Lonicera, climbing vars.
Ornamental vines, including *Vitis vinifera* 'Purpurea' (not after
    late December)
Wisteria (hard prune late winter)

* For pruning of other types of clematis see instructions included in all specialist growers' catalogues.

Index

(Figures in bold type indicate main references)